新基点（New Benchmark）全国高职高专院校商务英语系列规划教材

国际商务函电

（第二版）

主　编　李宏亮　廖雄英　陈锦阳
副主编　方军霞　王志娟　吴建晓　杨　慧
参　编　康春晓　邱嘉瑛　唐　婧　吕丹丹
　　　　顾国栋　董玉好　胡建成

对外经济贸易大学出版社
中国·北京

图书在版编目（CIP）数据

国际商务函电 / 李宏亮，廖雄英主编. —2 版. —北京：对外经济贸易大学出版社，2014（2023. 2 重印）

新基点（New Benchmark）全国高职高专院校商务英语系列规划教材

ISBN 978-7-5663-1076-7

Ⅰ. ①国… Ⅱ. ①李… ②廖… Ⅲ. ①国际商务-英语-电报信函-写作-高等职业教育-教材 Ⅳ. ①H315

中国版本图书馆 CIP 数据核字（2014）第 136048 号

国际商务函电（第二版）

李宏亮 廖雄英 陈锦阳 **主编**

责任编辑：李 丽

对 外 经 济 贸 易 大 学 出 版 社

北京市朝阳区惠新东街 10 号 邮政编码：100029

邮购电话：010-64492338 发行部电话：010-64492342

网址：http://www.uibep.com E-mail：uibep@ 126.com

三河市少明印务有限公司印装 新华书店经销

成品尺寸：185mm×260mm 17. 25 印张 398 千字

2014 年 8 月北京第 2 版 2023 年 2 月第 6 次印刷

ISBN 978-7-5663-1076-7

印数：7 801-8 800 册 定价：35. 00 元

出版说明

“新基点（New Benchmark）全国高职高专院校商务英语系列规划教材”是对外经济贸易大学出版社联合全国重点职业学院的骨干教师推出的一套全新的商务英语系列教材。本套教材适用于全国高职高专院校英语专业商务/应用/外贸英语方向以及财经类专业的学生。

目前高职教育提出了“工学结合、项目为中心、案例驱动教学、边讲边练”为核心的理念。本套教材就是贯彻这个理念，着眼于提高学生实际操作能力和就业能力的目的，采取了模块化、多案例、互动式、重实训的编写方式，让学生在理论够用的基础上，在实训环节上有所突破。

我国高职高专教育的培养目标是以能力培养和技术应用为本位, 其基础理论教学以应用为目的、够用为尺度、就业为导向；教材强调应用性和适用性，符合高职高专教育的特点，既能满足学科教育又能满足职业资格教育的“双证书”（毕业证和技术等级证）教学的需要。本套教材编写始终贯彻商务英语教学的基本思路：将英语听说读写译技能与商务知识有机融合，使学生在提高英语语言技能的同时了解有关商务知识，造就学生“两条腿走路”的本领，培养以商务知识为底蕴、语言技能为依托的新时代复合型、实用型人才。

本套教材包括《商务英语综合教程》（1～4 册）、《商务英语听说》（1～2 册）、《商务英语口语》（1～2 册）、《国际商务报刊选读》、《商务英语写作》、《商务英语翻译》、《国际商务函电》、《国际商务谈判》、《国际商务制单》、《国际商务英语模拟实训教程》、《商务礼仪》、《英语应用文》、《跨文化交际》、《英美概况》、《旅游英语》、《酒店英语》、《物流英语》、《财经英语》、《文秘英语》、《会计英语》、《餐饮与服务英语》、《劳动与社会保障英语》等。本套教材不是封闭的，而是随着教学模式、课程设置和课时的变化，不断推陈出新。

本套教材的作者不仅具有丰富的商务英语教学经验，而且具有本专业中级以上职称、企业第一线工作经历、主持或参与过多项应用技术研究。这是本套教材编写质量的重要保证。

此外，本套教材配有教师用书或课件等立体化教学资源，供教师教学参考。

对外经济贸易大学出版社

2014 年 1 月

再版前言

随着世界经济的飞速发展，国际交流的广泛化和多样化的步伐不断加快，为了适应新形势的发展和用人单位对从业人员的要求，本课程要打破传统的外语教学理念，大胆改革以语言知识点为主要教学内容的教学目标为以培养具有较强的英语实用能力+扎实涉外专业知识的外语人才为主要目标，以适应我国加入 WTO 后对涉外人才的需求，使学生不仅懂得外贸英文函电的基本知识，并能熟练地加以运用。

本书的编写正是在上述前提下应运而生。它是对外经济贸易大学出版社《新基点商务英语高职高专系列教材》之一。本书是受对外经贸大学出版社委托，浙江经济职业技术学院联合广东交通职业技术学院、浙江横店影视职业学院、衢州中专等院校与杭州福牛贸易有限公司、好利威实业有限公司、浙江温州时步贸易有限公司、海赢中国贸易有限公司等进出口经营企业进行的一部探索“校企合作、中高职衔接”、外贸专业岗位能力本位的教材；是浙江省高校访问工程师项目“基于浙江省外向型区域经济特色的商务英语专业人才职业核心能力研究（FW2013139）”和浙江省教学改革项目“外贸电子商务人才培养模式的创新研究—以专业群建设为依托（JG2013395）”的成果之一。

编写中按照教育部《关于加强高职高专教育教材建设的若干意见》的要求，本着理论知识“必须、够用”为度、以“加强实践教学环节、注重学生职业能力培养”等宗旨，和“细化教学目标为应知、应会目标”的原则进行编写。

编写内容与结构：本书参照外贸业务实际结合教学规律共分为 5 大模块 15 个单元，内容编排按照外贸业务操作步骤、由浅入深：模块一（M1）：商务函电知识；模块二（M2）：外贸洽谈业务；模块三（M3）：外贸合同执行；模块四（M4）：综合技能实训；模块五（M5）：**Skills training**（单元技能训练）。模块二（M2）与模块三（M3）每个单元编写又具体分为 10 个环节：即 **Study Aims**（应知、应会目标），**Lead in**（业务知识导入），**Writing Skills**（写作技巧），**Key Sentences Patterns**（核心句式），**Case Study**（案例学习），**Notes**（注解分析），**New Words and Expressions**（生词表达），**Task Practice**（实训任务），**Business Link**（商务链接），**More to Practice**（课后实践）。

编写特色：（1）校、企、行合作，中高职学校联合编写（2）案例教学与任务实训结合（3）融英语语言能力运用与外贸业务知识和相关单证内容（4）图文并茂，内容仿真性。本书集知识性，实践性，真实性于一体。编写重点突出，内容新颖，简明扼要，科学有趣，易学易练。

值得一提的是本书的 Business Link 部分不但是正文的相关补充，而且增加了外贸订单、合同、信用证、信用证修改通知书等样例，非常实用，还有很多有趣的、前沿的知识，使本书的可读性较强。

授课建议：1. 把握每单元的学习目标（应知和应会），力争转化为学生的应会实践能力体现；2. 每单元可安排 4～6 课时；3. M2 和 M3 的每单元含 4 封样信，其中 2 封为案例学习，2 封为实训任务，教师可根据授课对象，灵活安排教学内容。

编写任务：本书由李宏亮、廖雄英、陈锦阳任主编并负责全书的策划和统稿。方军霞、王志娟、吴建晓、杨慧任副主编。具体分工如下：李宏亮负责第 8、9、10 单元，廖雄英负责第 6、7 单元及附录 II、III，陈锦阳负责第 2 单元，王志娟负责第 1 单元，方军霞负责第 15 单元以及附录 I，吴建晓 5、13 单元、杨慧、康春晓负责第 3、4 单元，唐婧负责第 11、12 单元，邱嘉瑛负责第 14 单元，吕丹丹负责附录 IV、V 并参与本书部分单元的商务链接的编写。单元技能训练部分李宏亮负责第 1～5 单元，廖雄英负责第 6～10 单元，唐婧负责第 11～13 单元，邱嘉瑛负责第 14 单元，方军霞负责第 15 单元。另外来自国际商贸企业一线的人员也参与了本书的素材提供、资料汇编：顾国栋、董玉好、胡建成等。

本书从收集材料到正式出版，其过程历经艰苦，在此向如下人员深表谢意：

感谢英语教育界的教授、感谢外贸企业界的从业人员和专家，感谢银行界的专业人士！

感谢对外经济贸易大学出版社的宋海玲、李丽、沈德军等出版界的朋友们！

本书的编写过程中，参考了大量的相关书籍和资料，在此也一并表示感谢！

由于本书编者水平有限，书中难免有缺点和错漏之处，恳请专家和读者，尤其是高职一线的教师和外贸行业专家人士批评指正。

编　者

2014 年 1 月

Contents

Unit 1

Basic Knowledge of Business Communication

Study Aims

应知目标

1. To understand writing principles and language characteristics.
2. To be familiar with parts of business letters.
3. To be familiar with structures of business letters.
4. To learn three writing formats of business letters.
5. To learn how to write an envelope.

应会目标

1. To be able to recognize parts of business letters.
2. To be able to recognize three writing formats of business letters.
3. To be able to write a business letter in proper structure.
4. To be able to write an envelope.

Lead in

- There are a lot of means of business communication. Besides face-to-face communication with your customers, you also need some written forms of communication to contact with the outside world and conclude a deal. Written communication in business plays an important role in an age of electronic communication. Its advantages are as follows:

1) To keep a record of all important facts for ready reference;
2) To decrease the cost of negotiations;
3) To rush the long-distance communication conveniently;
4) To be much clearer compared with oral expression;
5) To solve daily problems efficiently, etc.

- Nowadays millions of business letters are being sent by fax or email to carry out business rountine, such as E-commerce involving offering, ordering, enquiring, payment and complaints. All these are on the basis of writing skills in business letters.

Good writing can lead you to gain more opportunities. It is also the stepstone to success. Otherwise bad writing may cause misunderstanding, conflicts, even miserable business war. So when you write business letters, you should be careful enough to express your meaning in correct words and expressions. This unit is intended to develop skills in writing such good business letters.

Parts of Business Letters

一封完整商务信函由若干部分构成，目前众说纷纭，没有形成统一的定论。不过根据其重要性来划分，一封完整的商务信函可以分为七个主要部分和七个次要部分。

I. Seven Principal Parts（七个主要部分）

主要部分，顾名思义是必不可少的部分。因此，一封商务信函至少应该由以下七个部分构成。

1. Letterhead（信头）

信头是写信人的地址和姓名。它主要包括写信人的公司名称、街道名称、城市名称、国家名称、邮政编码等，还包括写信人的电话号码、传真号码以及电子邮件地址等信息。值得注意的是，英文地址的书写顺序由小往大，示例如下：

Jameson & Sons Ltd.
34 Madison Square
Melbourne E.C.2.
Australia
Tel: +61-2-70525345
Fax: +61-2-70525345

2. Date（日期）

每封信都必须标明日期，包括日、月、年。日和年可用阿拉伯数字书写。日期一般有两种写法。如果日期是 2008 年 8 月 9 日，可以写成：August 9, 2008，日和年之间最好用逗号隔开；还可写为：9 August, 2008。值得注意的是月必须用英文书写，不要出现以下的形式：8，9，2008；或 9/8/2008，以免混淆。

3. Inside Name and Address（信内地址和姓名）

信内地址和姓名是指收信人的地址和姓名。收信人的地址和姓名相当重要，它包括收信人的姓名、收信人的职位或头衔、公司名称、街道名称、城市名称、国家名称、邮政编码等，书写顺序也是由小往大，但是最好要在姓名前加上头衔或称呼，如：

Mr. Goe Smith
Jameson & Sons Ltd.
34 Madison Square
Melbourne E.C.2.
Australia

4. Salutation（称谓）

称谓一般位于信内地址下面空一行处。如知道收信人的姓名或性别，如男性可称 Dear Mr. Goe Smith，如女性，无论对方婚否，都可称之 Dear Ms. Mary White。如不明确收信人的姓名或性别或人数，可称 Dear Sirs, Dear Ladies and Gentlemen，如只知收信人为某一人，可称 Dear Sir or Madam。

5. Body（正文）

内容部分可书写在称谓或主题下面，可包括开头语、正文及结尾等，正文是信函的主体，是写信人给收信人提供详尽的信息，表达写信人意愿的部分，通常一个段落表达一个意思。

6. Complementary Close（结束语）

结束语是内容之后的客气话，类似于中文信函的“此致，敬礼”部分。常见的结束语有：Sincerely, Sincerely yours, Yours truly, Yours faithfully, Yours, Best regards 等。必须注意的是只有第一字母必须大写。结束语一般位于内容下面空一行处。

7. Signature（签名）

常用签名包括四部分，即公司名称、写信人的手写签名、写信人的打印签名、写信人的职务或头衔。如：

ABC Co., Ltd.

John Smith

John Smith

General Manager

II. Seven Optional Parts（七个次要部分）

次要部分，又称为可选择部分或辅助性部分。因此，写信人可根据自身的需要，有针对性地选择若干个次要部分添加在信函中，目的是使该商务信函更加具体、清晰。这七个次要部分如下：

1. The Reference Number（编号）

编号一般可位于信头下面空一行处。形式可如下：

Our ref. 123

Your ref. 45

目的是使写信人和收信人都快速地联想起前几次相关函电。

2. The Attention Line（注意项）

注意项是提醒该信函应提交给某特定的人或该公司某部门。形式可如下：

For the attention of Mr. Joe Brown

Attention: Mr. Joe Brown

<u>Attention: Mr. Joe Brown</u>

3. Subject（主题）

主题的意义就在于使收信人一目了然明白信件的内容，可以使主题字母全部大写或加下划线，也可用以下几个词，如：

Subject: ORDER NO12

Re: ORDER NO12

4. Enclosure（附件）

附件指随信附寄了文件或物品，可写为：

Enclosed is my resume.

Enclosure: A Resume.

Enc.: A Resume.

如附寄多个文件，则须加上编码,

如 Enclosure 3; Enc. 3; Encl. 3

1. A Resume
2. A Picture
3. A Letter of Reference

5. Initial Indentation（首字母缩写）

如果信函的签名人和打印人不是同一人，有必要在信函中标明的，通常在签名下方直接写上签名人和打印人的姓名的首字母缩写。

如：经理 Joe Brown 为签名人，秘书 Alice Green 为打印人，可缩写成 J. B. (sales manager)/A.G. (typist)

6. The Copy Line（抄送）

抄送栏的主要目的是使收信人明白还有其他人收到相同的文件或信函。其形式如下：

C : for copy

Cc: for carton copy

7. Postscript（附言）

如在核查信件的正文部分时发现有遗忘而希望表达的语句，可以在签名之后加注附言。但是，为了避免混乱，现代函电当中一般不提倡使用附言。其形式如下：

P.S.: The sample will be sent to you on May 11.

Layouts of Business Letters

There are three main layouts of business letters:

一般说来，英文中有三种信函书写格式。即：缩进式、齐头式和综合式。

1. Indented Style（缩进式）

Indented style is the traditional British practice with the heading usually in the middle and the date on the right–hand side. The complimentary close and signature may be in the center or commence at the center point. The first line of each paragraph should be indented.

缩进式即是一种传统的英式写信格式，它就是信头居中，日期居右，结束语和签名可居于中右，每个自然段落首行缩进 4～6 个字母。

格式如下：

(1) Letter head

(2) Date

(3) Inside name and address

(4) Salutation

(5) Body

****

****

(6) **Complementary close**

(7) Signature

Example 1

ABC Trading Co.
188 Newton Palace
New York

Tel:
Fax:

May 9, 2013

M.J. Marks, manager
30 Arlington
Cambridge

Dear Ms. Mark,

Thank you for your enquiry in your letter of Apr 25 for our T-shirts.

We are now sending our quotation sheet for your selection. We also enclose a sample and are sure that you will be satisfied with their fine quality.

Hope to serve you soon.

Yours sincerely,
John Smith

2. Block Style（齐头式）

Block style is now the most popular practice of displaying business communication.The letterhead is usually in the middle. Its remarkable feature is that all typing lines, including those for date, inside name and address, salution, subject, each paragraph and complimentary close, begin at the left-hand margin.

齐头式是一种现代最时尚的写信格式。它最明显的特征就是打印格式，即除了信头居中外，所有部分如日期、信内姓名和地址、称谓、主题、每个段落及结束语等都从左顶格书写。

格式如下：

(1) Letter head

(2) Date

(3) Inside name and address

(4) Salutation

(5) Body

****

****

(6) Complementary close

(7) Signature

Example 2

ABC Trading Co.
188 Newton Palace
New York
Tel:
Fax:

May 9, 2013

M.J. Marks, manager
30 Arlington
Cambridge

Dear Ms. Mark,
Thank you for your enquiry in your letter of Apr 25 for our T-shirts.
We are now sending our quotation sheet for your selection. We also enclose a sample and are sure that you will be satisfied with their fine quality.
Hope to serve you soon.
Yours sincerely,
John Smith

3. Modified Style（综合式）

Modified style is the mixture of the above two styles. The letterhead is usually in the middle. The first line of a paragraph is lined up with the left margin, but date, closing and signature are indented.

综合式是以上两种写作格式的混合体。也即是信头居中，每个自然段落的首行都从左顶格书写，但日期，结束语和签名等都要求缩进书写。

(1) Letter head

(2) Date

(3) Inside name and address

(4) Salutation

(5) Body

****

****

(6) Complementary close

(7) Signature

Example 3

ABC Trading Co.
188 Newton Palace
New York
Tel:
Fax:

May 9, 2013

M.J. Marks, manager
30 Arlington
Cambridge

Dear Ms. Mark,

Thank you for your enquiry in your letter of Apr 25 for our T-shirts.

We are now sending our quotation sheet for your selection. We also enclose a sample and are sure that you will be satisfied with their fine quality.

Hope to serve you soon.

Yours sincerely,
John Smith

Writing Principles of Business Letters

◆ Completeness（完整）

A bussiness letter is successful and effective only when it contains all the necessary information to the readers and answers all the questions and requirements put forward by the readers.

所谓完整就是要在商务信函中尽可能包含收信人需要的所有信息以及回答发信人提出的各种问题，这样才算有效而成功的信件。

◆ Concreteness（具体）

A business letter should be specific, definite instead of being vague, general and abstract.

一封商务信函应该具体、明确，而不要模棱两可、泛泛而谈或者很抽象。

e.g. a) we wish to confirm our fax sent yesterday.

b) We confirm our fax of Sep 10, 2006.

分析：b) 句比 a) 句要具体得多。

◆ Clarity（清楚）

It is wise for a writer to make himself understood well by using clear expressions and simple words.

写信人使用清晰的表达和简单易懂的词汇是使他人明白自己意思的明智做法。

e.g.

A	B
metropolitan	big city
render	give
finalize	finish
demonstrate	show

分析：B 组用词比 A 组用词要清楚易懂得多。

◆ Conciseness（简洁）

A concise letter can save time and costs for both writers and readers.

简洁的信函为写信人和收信人节约了时间和成本。

e.g.

A	B
At this time	now
Come to a decision	decide
For the purpose	for
For the reason	since, because
In most cases	usually
At an early date	soon

分析：B 组表达比 A 组表达要简洁得多。

◆ Courtesy（客气）

Courtesy here refers to polite expressions and sentences in letter writing.

客气是指在写信中使用礼貌婉转的表达和句式。

e.g.

a) We cannot deliver the goods all at one time.

b) I'm afraid we cannot deliver the goods all at one time.

c) You ought to have accepted the offer.

d) It seems to us that you ought to have accepted the offer.

分析：b)和 d)句比 a) 和 c)句表达要客气和礼貌得多。

◆ Consideration（体谅）

An effective business letter is written on the basis of putting yourself into your readers' shoes. You'll be better understood if you consider readers' attitude and feeling much more than yours.

一封高效的商务函电是基于从收信者的角度出发写作而成的。如果多考虑对方的态度和感觉，那么别人就会更好地理解你。

A	B
"We" attitude	"You" attitude
We allow a 5% discount....	You earn a 5% discount when....
We are pleased to announce that....	You will be pleased to know that....

分析：B 组表达比 A 组表达显得更加体谅对方。

◆ Correctness（正确）

The reader gets meaning out of what is said and how it is said in the letter. So the writer has to make his letter correct and proper including its grammar, structure, and even spelling.

读信人从信中读取内容及了解内容是如何陈述的。因此，写信人必须保证书写内容正确、语言得体，包括语法结构以及拼写等方面。

e.g.

a) This product is absolutely the best on the market.

b) This product is the best one we can offer.

分析：b)句表达比 a)句表达要得体得多。

Envelope Addressing (信封的写法)

There are two basic requirements of envelope addressing: accuracy and clearness.

Layout:

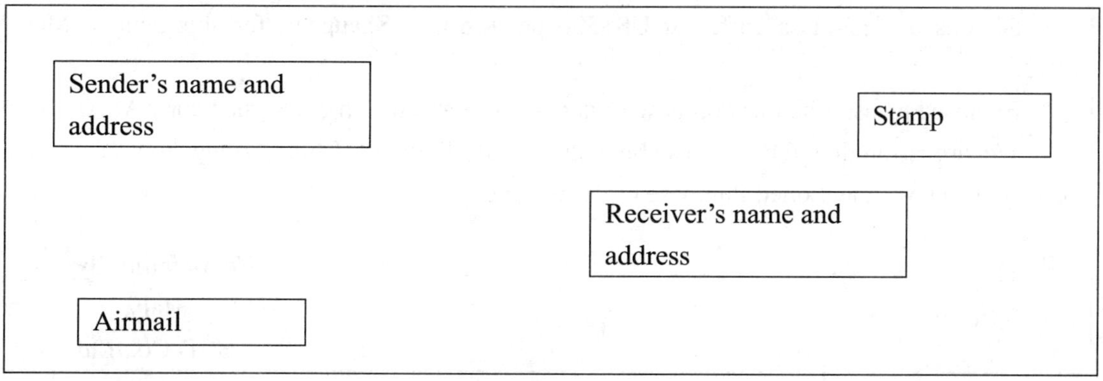

e.g.

China National Chemicals Imp. and Exp. Corp. 318 Qingchun Road, Qingchun Mansion Hangzhou, Zhejiang China	Stamp
	President John Gates ABC Co., Ltd. 156 Madison Street London U.K.
Airmail	

Email Addressing (电子邮件的格式)

e.g.

Email 1

From: prettygirl@yahoo.com (BCD Co., Ltd.)
To: coolboy@hotmail.com (ABC Co., Ltd.)
Date: Jan 8, 2013
Subject: order
Attachment: Purchase order

Dear Sir or Madam:

Thank you for your email of Jan, 8.

We appreciate your cooperation and are pleased to confirm the order as follows:

50 tons of first-class coffee at US$500 per ton CIF Shanghai, for shipment in May, 2013.

Enclosed please find our Purchase Order NO.123 and return one signed copy ASAP.

We are arranging the L/C establishment with Bank of China, Hangzhou when we receive the above mentioned Purchase Order in time.

Yours faithfully,

Mary

BCD Co., Ltd.

Email 2

From: goodboy@yahoo.com (BCD Co., Ltd.)
To: coolsir@hotmail.com (ABC Co., Ltd.)
Date: June 8, 2013
Subject: initial order
Attachment:
Dear Sir or Madam: We'd like to place an initial order with you on the terms and conditions as follows: Articles: Haier Brand Air Conditioner Specifications: HRAP 35 GW Quantity: 2,000 sets Unit price: US$300 /set CIF OSAKA, JAPAN Total Amt.: US$600,000 Payment: by irrevocable confirmed L/C Shipment: to be shipped within 15 days after receipt of L/C Insurance: by seller Look forward to receiving your confirmation ASAP. Yours faithfully, Mike BCD Co., Ltd.

Business Link

◆ **国际贸易**

一国货物及服务与另一国货物及服务进行交换，这就是国际贸易。这种贸易除了有形的（即商品的进出口）外，还有无形的（即国际间服务交流）。希腊、挪威这类国家拥有大量的商船船队，可以提供交通运输服务，这就是一种无形贸易。对某些国家来说，无形贸易与其他一些国家的原材料出口或商品贸易一样重要。在这种情况下，每个国家都可以赚取外汇以购进本国的必需品。

◆ **世界贸易组织 WTO**

WTO 是世界贸易组织（The World Trade Organization）的缩写，成立于 1995 年 1 月 1 日，其前身为关贸总协定（GATT）。

WTO 的宗旨是：在提高生活水平和保证充分就业的前提下，扩大货物和服务的生产与贸易，按照可持续发展的原则实现全球资源的最佳配置；努力确保发展中国家，尤其是最不发达国家在国际贸易增长中的份额与其经济需要相称；保护和维护环境。

WTO 的目标是：建立一个完整的、更具活力和永久性的多边贸易体制，以巩固原来的关贸总协定为贸易自由化所作的努力和乌拉圭回合多边贸易谈判的所有成果。为实现这些目标，各成员应通过互惠互利的安排，切实降低关税和其他贸易壁垒，在国际贸易中消除歧视性待遇。概括起来，就是实现贸易自由化。根本目标：在全球范围内，实现物流、人流、资金流（投资自由化）、技术流（知识产权）四大流动。

WTO 实现宗旨与目标的途径是：WTO 规定各成员应通过达成的互惠互利的安排，大幅度削减关税和贸易壁垒，消除歧视性待遇，坚持非歧视贸易原则，对发展中国家给予特殊和差别待遇，扩大市场准入程序，提高贸易政策和法规的透明度，实施审议制度和争端解决机制，从而协调各成员间的贸易政策，共同管理全球贸易。

WTO 的基本原则是在继承 GATT（General Agreement on Tariffs and Trade：关税与贸易总协定）基本原则的基础上，进行必要的补充和修改而来的。最主要的几项原则如下：

1. 最惠国待遇原则
2. 国民待遇原则
3. 无歧视待遇原则
4. 互惠原则
5. 关税减让原则
6. 取消数量限制原则
7. 透明度原则

◆ **中华人民共和国商务部，中国国际贸易学会**

中华人民共和国商务部组建于 2003 年，隶属于国务院，是主管国内外贸易和国际经济合作的专门机构。其下设多个司、商会和学会。对其中的中国国际贸易学会做一简介：

中国国际贸易学会于 1981 年 7 月在北京成立，是我国改革开放后成立的第一个具有社团法人地位的全国性国际贸易学术团体，也是在中华人民共和国商务部的直接领导下，由政、学、企各界人士组成的专门从事外经贸研究与交流的权威学术组织。其宗旨是团结和组织我国从事国际经贸问题研究的专家、学者和企业家以及从事我国对外经贸政策、理论研究的专家和实际工作者，在党的基本路线指引下，以邓小平同志建设有中国特色的社会主义理论为基础，坚持改革开放政策和科学发展观，贯彻“百花齐放、百家争鸣”和学术民主的方针，发扬理论联系实际和实事求是的学风，对社会主义市场经济体制下我国对外经济贸易发展与改革的理论与实践问题进行研究和探索，为促进我国对外贸易又好又快发展和加快社会主义现代化建设服务。

中国国际贸易学会的会员分为团体会员、个人会员和通讯会员。学会章程规定，凡承认本会章程并交纳会费的学术团体、研究机构、院校、各类企业、新闻出版单位及个人均可申请入会，经会长办公会议通过后，即可成为学会的会员，并享受学会提供的各项服务。

◆ **中国国际贸易促进委员会**

中国国际贸易促进委员会是由中国经济贸易界有代表性的人士、企业和团体组成的全国民间对外经贸组织，成立于 1952 年 5 月。

中国国际贸易促进委员会简称中国贸促会；英文名称为：China Council for the Promotion of International Trade，英文缩写为 CCPIT。

中国贸促会的宗旨是：遵循中华人民共和国的法律和政府的政策，开展促进对外贸易、利用外资、引进外国先进技术及各种形式的中外经济技术合作等活动，促进中国同世界各国、各地区之间的贸易和经济关系的发展，增进中国同世界各国人民以及经贸界之间的了解与友谊。

经中国政府批准，中国贸促会 1988 年 6 月组建了中国国际商会（China Chamber of International Commerce，英文缩写为 CCOIC）。

Exercises and Practice

I. Please write a business letter in one of three mentioned layouts according to the following message.

1. Sender's information:
   BCD CO., LTD.
   Add: NOVEMRE, 21012 CASSANO ITALY
   Tel:+91-02-6699585 Fax: +91-02-6699585
2. Recipient's information:
   ABC CO., LTD.
   Add: NO.58 YANAN ROAD HANGZHOU, ZHEJIANG, CHINA
   Tel:+86-571-28877556 Fax: +86-571-28877556
3. Date: Mar. 8, 2008
4. Subject: Water pumps
5. The message:
   Thank you very much for your initial order with us.
   Enclosed please find our S/C no.168 and let us know if everything is acceptable to you.
   If everything is OK, please sign them and return one copy to us.
6. Signature: Clark

II. Address an airmail envelope to the above letter.

III. Send a reply to BCD CO., LTD. on behalf of ABC CO., LTD. by Email.

Unit 2

Establishment of Business Relations

Study Aims

应知目标

1. To know the writing steps of a letter of establishing business relations.
2. To know the writing steps of a reply to a letter of establishing business relations.
3. To know the knowledge of "Lead in" Part.
4. To know the knowledge of "Business Link" Part.

应会目标

1. To be able to translate a letter of establishing business relations properly.
2. To be able to write a letter of establishing business relations properly.
3. To be able to translate a reply to business relations establishment letter.
4. To be able to reply a letter of establishing business relations properly.

Lead in

- It is fairly true to say no customer, no business. To establish business relations with prospective dealers is one of the vitally important measures either for a newly established firm or an old one that wishes to enlarge its business scope and turnover.
- If a new firm wishes to open up a market to sell something to or buy something from firms in foreign countries, the person in charge must acquire information about the target market. Usually, such information is obtainable through the following channels:

1) Business correspondence
2) Attendance at the export commodities fairs
3) Attendance at exhibitions held at home and abroad
4) Mutual visits by trade delegations and groups

Of all the above channels, the first one is widely used in business activities.

Writing Skills

Step 1: To state the source of customer's information

Step 2: To introduce briefly one's own company
Step 3: To express the purpose of writing the letter
Step 4: To express the wish of business relations establishment and an early reply

Key Sentence Patterns

1. From the email sent back by our New York Office, we have learned that you are interested in our product.
2. From your email of June 6, we're glad to know that you wish to enter into business relations with us in the line of various papers.
3. We have got your name and address from Trade Fairs in Shanghai last month, which informed us that you are in the market for printers.
4. We are one of the largest printer manufacturers in our country and have been in the line for over 20 years.
5. We write to introduce ourselves as a leading exporter of fresh water pearls in China.
6. We take the opportunity to introduce ourselves as one of the largest importers of seafood in our area.
7. We express our desire to establish business relations with your company.
8. Specializing in the export in electronic products, we wish to trade with you in the line.
9. We are specialized in import and export business of foodstuff and wish to enter into trade relations with you.
10. We are looking forward to your early reply.
11. We look forward to receiving your reply ASAP.
12. Your early reply will be highly appreciated.
13. We look forward to your favorable reply.
14. We are looking forward to hearing from you soon.

Case Study

Case 1
Business background

Sender's information:

Name:	Clark
Company:	Hangzhou Fornew Trade Co., Ltd.
Add:	198 Wenhui Rd Hangzhou, Zhejiang, P.R.China 310000
Tel:	0086-571-88886666
Fax:	0086-571-88886667
Website:	www.hzfnw.com.cn
Email:	coolboy@hotmail.com
Business scope:	textiles, suits, waists, silk products, pearls
Overseas markets:	Europe, America, Asia, South Africa

Recipient's information:

Name:	Alice
Company:	Southafrican Sunflower Trade Co., Ltd.
Add:	227 Long St Cape town, South Africa
Tel:	27-21-3456666
Fax:	27-21-3456667
Website:	www.afslt.com.sa
Email:	prettygirl@gmail.com
Business scope:	textiles, garments, foodstuff
Overseas markets:	Europe, America, Asia, Africa

Task description

Clark, on behalf of Hangzhou Fornew Trade Co., Ltd. (herein called A Co., Ltd.) met Alice of Southafrican Sunflower Trade Co., Ltd. (herein called B Co., Ltd.) in South African Textile Garment and Shoes Exhibition in Cape town last November. He will send an email to Alice for establishing business relations between two companies.

Hints

- mention meeting at the fair in South Africa
- give a brief introduction of one's own company
- express desire of business relationship establishment
- enclose one's latest catalogue
- wish to get an early reply

Specimen letter 1

From: coolboy@hotmail.com (A Co., Ltd.)

To: prettygirl@gmail.com (B Co., Ltd.)

Date: Dec 8, 2013

Subject: business relations establishment

Attachment: our catalogue

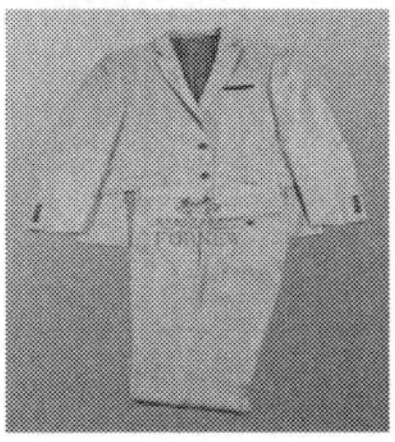

Dear Alice:

We have got your name and address from Trade Fair in South Africa last month, which informed us that you are in the market for suits.

We take the opportunity to introduce ourselves as one of the largest exporters of men's garments in our area. And we have been in this line for over 20 years and enjoyed a good reputation.

We express our desire to establish business relations with your company.

To give you a general idea of our product, we enclose our latest catalogue covering the main items available at present.

We look forward to receiving your reply ASAP.

Yours sincerely,
Clark
Sales manager
A Co., Ltd.

Case 2
Business background

Sender's information:

Name:	Mike
Company:	Wenzhou Timestep International Trade Co., Ltd.
Add:	298 Shidai Rd Wenzhou, Zhejiang, P.R.China 318000
Tel:	0086-577-68886666
Fax:	0086-577-68886667
Website:	www.wztsit.com.cn
Email:	coolboy@hotmail.com
Business scope:	shoe products, socks
Overseas markets:	Japan, Korea, South Africa

Recipient's information:

Name:	Steven
Company:	Japan Sun Trade Co., Ltd.
Add:	228 Lucky St Tokyo, Japan,
Tel:	+81-3-3456666
Fax:	+81-3-3456667
Website:	www.jst.com.cn
Email:	coolsir@hotmail.com
Business scope:	shoes, garments
Overseas markets:	America, Europe, Asia

Task description

Mike, on behalf of Wenzhou Timestep International Trade Co., Ltd. (herein called C Co., Ltd.) got name and email address information of Japan Sun Trade Co., Ltd. (herein called D Co., Ltd.) from the Commercial Counselor's Office of Embassy in Shanghai, China last month. He will send an email to Steven for establishing business relations between two companies.

Hints

- mention the way of getting the customer's information
- give a brief introduction of one's own company
- express desire of business relationship establishment
- enclose latest catalogue
- wish to get an early reply

Specimen letter 2

From: coolboy@hotmail.com (C Co., Ltd.)

To: coolsir@hotmail.com (D Co., Ltd.)

Date: June 8, 2013

Subject: business relations establishment

Attachment:

Dear Steven:

We have obtained your name and address from the Commercial Counselor's Office of Embassy in Shanghai.

We are one of the largest shoes manufacturers in our city and have been in the line for over 10 years. We can assure you of our products fine quality at competitive prices.

We express our desire to establish business relations with your company.

Look forward to receiving your favorable reply ASAP.

Yours sincerely,

Mike

C Co., Ltd.

Task Practice

Task 1

Description

ABC Co., Ltd. is one of the largest exporters of water pearls products and has been in this line for 20 years with a good reputation.

Simon, a foreign salesperson of ABC Co., Ltd. has got the information of BCD Co., Ltd. at the website of alibaba. He will send an email to BCD Co., Ltd. for establishing business relations between two companies.

Requirements

You are required to send an email to BCD Co., Ltd. as the role of Simon, according to the following tips.

Tips

- mention the way of getting the customer's information
- give a brief introduction of one's own company
- express desire of business relationship establishment
- enclose latest catalogue
- wish to get an early reply

From: ______________________________

To: ______________________________

Date: ______________________________

Subject: ______________________________

____

____

____

____

____

____

____

____

Specimen letter 3

Suggested answer for Task 1

From: coolboy@hotmail.com (ABC Co., Ltd.)
To: prettygirl@yahoo.com (BCD Co., Ltd.)
Date: Jan 8, 2013
Subject: business relations establishment
Attachment: latest catalogue
Dear Sir or Madam: We have learnt your name and address from the Internet, and we are writing to you in the hope of establishing business relations with you. We are one of the largest exporters of fresh water pearls in China and have enjoyed a good reputation through 20 years' business experience. We hope you will be satisfied with the fine quality and excellent workmanship of our pearls products. To give you a general idea of our product, we enclose our catalogue covering the main items suppliable now for your reference. We look forward to receiving your early reply. Yours faithfully, Simon ABC Co., Ltd.

Task 2

Description

B Co., Ltd. is a new set-up firm of garments.

Mary, a foreign salesperson of B Co., Ltd. has got the email from Clark of A Co., Ltd. She will send an email to Clark for establishing business relations between two companies as a reply.

Requirements

You are required to write an email to Clark as the role of Mary, according to the following tips.

Tips

- thank for email and mention the trade fair
- give a brief introduction of one's company
- express desire of business relationship establishment
- show interest of products on catalogue
- wish to get an early reply

From: ______________________________

To: ______________________________

Date: ______________________________

Subject: ______________________________

____

____

____

____

____

____

____

____

____

____

Specimen letter 4

Suggested answer for Task 2—A Reply

From: prettygirl@yahoo.com (B Co., Ltd.)
To: coolboy@hotmail.com (A Co., Ltd.)
Date: Dec 9, 2013
Subject: reply to business relations establishment
Attachment:
Dear Clark: Thank you for your email of Dec, 8. I'm so glad to meet you at the fair. We are a new set-up firm of garments in our city and glad to establish business relations with

your company.
At present we are interested in Art. No. 168 and No. 178 in your catalogue sent us.
We look forward to receiving your best quotation ASAP.
Yours sincerely,
Mary
B Co., Ltd.

Notes

1. From…, sb. learn / know that… 某人从哪里获悉……
   From your email of yesterday, we learn that you are interested in our typewriter No. 2188.
   从贵方昨日的电邮中，获悉贵方对我方 No. 2188 的打字机有兴趣。
   类似的表达还有：be glad/pleased to learn/know that… 欣悉……
2. Sb. be in the market for sth. 某人打算购买某物
3. Sb. be in the line of sth. 某人经营某一行业
4. establish business relations with sb. 与某人建立业务关系
5. look forward to + N./ V-ing 期待某物，期望或做某事
6. ASAP 是“as soon as possible”的固定缩写，商务中较常用。
7. assure sb. of sth. 向某人保证某物或某事
8. We are writing to you in the hope of V-ing 向贵方特致此函希望做某事
9. to give you a general idea of sth. 给贵方关于某事的一个大概了解
10. We enclose our catalogue covering sth. 我方随函附上一个关于什么的产品目录。

New Words and Expressions

1. establish *v.* 建立，创建
2. business relations 业务关系
3. inform *v.* 通知
4. enclose *v.* 附上
5. catalogue *n.* 产品目录
6. obtainable *a.* 可以获得的
7. Commercial Counselor's Office 商务参赞处
8. embassy *n.* 大使馆
9. fresh water pearls 淡水珍珠
10. reputation *n.* 声誉，名声

Business Link

◆ 大使馆

大使馆是一国在建交国首都派驻的常设外交代表机构。

大使馆的首要职责是代表派遣国促进两国的政治关系，其次是促进经济、文化、教育、科技等方面的关系。

大使馆的职责范围遍及所驻国的各个地区，而领事馆只负责所辖地区。大使馆通常受政府和外交部门的直接领导，而领事馆则通常接受外交部门和所驻国大使馆的双重领导。

◆ 广交会

中国进出口商品交易会，简称广交会，原名中国出口商品交易会，创办于 1957 年春季，每年春秋两季在广州举办，迄今已有五十多年的历史，是中国目前历史最长、层次最高、规模最大、商品种类最全、到会客商最多、成交效果最好的综合性国际贸易盛会。广交会贸易方式灵活多样，除传统的看样成交外，还举办网上交易会。广交会以出口贸易为主，也做进口生意，还可以开展多种形式的经济技术合作与交流，以及商检、保险、运输、广告、咨询等业务活动。

成千上万的外国客商从世界各地汇集到广州参会。他们被参展的各种各样的商品所吸引。广交会本身就是反映中国经济的一面镜子。中国的主要产品，如丝绸、茶叶、煤等在国际市场上很畅销。轻纺产品包括服装和机械产品在许多国家很受欢迎。

在广交会上，许多外国客商与中国出口商进行洽谈磋商，签订了大量合同。外国客商称中国出口的商品质量上乘、价格合理。

◆ 阿里巴巴网站

阿里巴巴（Alibaba.com）是全球企业间（B2B）电子商务的著名品牌,是目前全球最大的网上交易市场和商务交流社区，被商人们评为“最受欢迎的 B2B 网站”。

阿里巴巴曾入选哈佛大学商学 MBA 案例，在美国学术界掀起研究热潮；两次被美国权威财经杂志《福布斯》选为全球最佳 B2B 站点之一；多次被相关机构评为全球最受欢迎的 B2B 网站、中国商务类优秀网站、中国百家优秀网站、中国最佳贸易网。

阿里巴巴创始人、首席执行官马云被著名的“世界经济论坛”选为“未来领袖”、被美国亚洲商业协会选为“商业领袖”，是 50 年来第一位成为《福布斯》封面人物的中国企业家，并曾多次应邀为全球著名高等学府麻省理工学院、沃顿商学院、哈佛大学讲学。阿里巴巴成立至今，全球十几种语言 400 多家著名新闻传媒对阿里巴巴的追踪报道从未间断，被传媒界誉为“真正的世界级品牌”。

◆ 淡水珍珠

珍珠，是象征美好、富有魅力的灵物，是自然界最美妙的生命结晶，也是人类最早的宝石朋友之一。中国是世界最大的珍珠生产国，在世界珍珠行业中有着举足轻重的地位。尤其是淡水珍珠，自从 60 年代在中国试养成功后，其养殖势头得到快速发展，2006 年中国淡水珍珠产量达到 1 200 吨，占到了世界珍珠总产量的 95%左右。

养殖珍珠又分为淡水养殖珠和海水养殖珠两种。

淡水养殖珠无核，是在湖泊、池塘等水深不超过 4 米的环境中人工养殖的；海水养殖珠产于热带或亚热带的浅海水域中，均采用有核培植法；天然珍珠多呈圆粒状，核极小，通常肉眼看不到。

中国淡水珍珠主要分布在长江中下游、五大淡水湖区域，特别是以浙江为最。同时淡水珍珠作为中国传统的民族产业，有着悠久的发展历史。

More to Practice

I. Translate the following business terms or expressions into English.

1. 有限公司
2. 信誉
3. 建立业务关系
4. 产品目录
5. 在……行业
6. 经营
7. 商务参赞处
8. 品质优良
9. 有竞争力的价格
10. 一流的工艺

II. Translate the following sentences into Chinese.

1. We, therefore, take pleasure in informing you that we are an enterprise manufacturing shoes.
2. The products manufactured here have been proved by a scrupulous test to be sound.
3. The designs have been clearly explained in our illustrated catalogue we enclosed.
4. We write to you today in the hope of establishing business relations with you.
5. We enclose here a copy of our illustrated catalogue about the main items available at present.
6. We are looking forward to receiving your early reply.
7. You have been introduced to us by Mr. Lee as a prospective buyer.
8. We would like to establish direct business relations with you on the basis of equality and mutual benefit.
9. We specialize in the export business of light industrial products for more than 30 years.
10. If you are interested in any item listed in our catalogue, please let us know ASAP.

III. Translate the following sentences into English.

1. 很高兴告知贵方我们是一家衬衣制造商。
2. 我们向贵方保证我们的产品质优价廉。
3. 我们经营这一行已经 20 多年了，并在当地享有一定的声誉。
4. 从贵方 5 月 5 日的来函中获悉贵方打算购买我方的丝绸产品。
5. 从贵国驻我国大使馆的商务参赞处得知贵方对我方产品有兴趣。
6. 本公司愿意与贵公司建立业务关系。
7. 良好的业务关系不但能促进双方的贸易而且能增进之间的友谊。
8. 从阿里巴巴网站上获悉贵方有意购买中国绿茶，我公司经营茶叶已十余年，很愿意与贵方建立业务关系。

9. 本公司是本地一家中等规模的玩具出口商，在欧美市场享有一定的知名度。

10. 期待早日收到贵方的答复。

IV. Writing practice.

Please write a letter of establishing business relations according to the following given information.

Sender's information:
Name: Louis
Company: Sunshine Farm Produces Co., Ltd.
Email: greenidea@hotmail.com
Business scope: export of fresh fruits and vegetables

Recipient's information:
Name: unknown
Company: Green Products Imp and Exp Co., Ltd.
Email: sunnygirl@gmail.com
Subject: business relations establishment
Date: Jan 8, 2013

Unit 3

Enquiry

Study Aims

应知目标

1. To know the writing steps of a letter of an enquiry.
2. To know the writing steps of a reply to an enquiry.
3. To know the knowledge of "Lead in" Part.
4. To know the knowledge of "Business Link" Part.

应会目标

1. To be able to translate an enquiry properly.
2. To be able to make an enquiry properly.
3. To be able to translate a reply to an enquiry properly.
4. To be able to reply to an enquiry properly.

Lead in

- As a start of international trade, enquiry is very important. It refers to the process that the buyer asks the seller questions about the goods he is interested in or going to purchase and other information such as catalogue, shipment, delivery etc. Generally speaking, it is made by the buyer, also by the seller. It can be divided into general enquiry and specific enquiry. The former is about asking for quotations, catalogues and samples, etc., while the latter includes many details in terms of transaction.
- The purpose of enquiry is to obtain information. An enquiry letter may contain different contents, but if you want to get a friendly reply, the following principles should be pursued:

1) Preciseness in enquiring information
2) Reasonableness in necessary explanations
3) Courtesy in choosing expressions
4) Appreciation in proper way

Since enquiry has become the general practice in international business correspondence, let's learn how to write it.

Writing Skills

Step 1: To state the source of the seller's information

Step 2: To express what information or service you need

Step 3: To give references about the buyer's company

Step 4: To show the wish of further business and an early reply

Key Sentence Patterns

1. Your firm has been recommended to us by ABC Co., with whom we have done business for many years.
2. We have a considerable demand here for your goods.
3. We would like you to send us some samples/patterns.
4. We should be obliged if you would kindly send us some samples for our inspection.
5. Please quote your price gross/net/FOB.
6. Will you please give us detailed information of FOB prices and discounts?
7. Full information as to prices, quality, quantity available and other relative particulars would be appreciated.
8. We should appreciate further details/information about your product.
9. Please include information about packing and shipping.
10. Please let us know on what term you can give us some discount.
11. For information about our company please refer to/contact ABC Co.
12. In order to make us familiarized with your products, we shall appreciate your giving us the technical details of them.
13. If the goods come up to our expectations, we would expect to place regular order.
14. If your prices are competitive and your goods up to standard, we shall order on a regular basis.
15. We trust that you will send us your reply as soon as possible.

Case Study

Case 1

Business background

Sender's information:

Name:	Jack
Company:	American Coconut Trade Co., Ltd.
Add:	18 Down Street, Dahlonega, Georgia, USA 30533
Tel:	001-706-545-888
Fax:	001-706-545-887
Website:	www.coconuttrade.com
Email:	magnificient@yahoo.com
Business scope:	textiles, garments
Overseas markets:	Europe, Asia, Africa

Recipient's information:

Name:	Ben
Company:	Quzhou Kingdom Trade Co., Ltd.
Add:	220 Laodong Rd Quzhou, Zhejiang, P.R.China 324000
Tel:	0086-570-8886666
Fax:	0086-570-8886667
Website:	www.abctrade.com.cn
Email:	kingdom@hotmail.com
Business scope:	textiles, table cloth, carpets, cleaning mops
Overseas markets:	America, Europe, Asia, South Africa

Task description

Jack, on behalf of American Coconut Trade Co., Ltd. (herein called ACT Co., Ltd.) got the information of Ben of Quzhou Kingdom Trade Co., Ltd. (herein called QKT Co., Ltd.) through Brother Company which is a long-term cooperation company of both. He will send an email to Ben for making an enquiry to establish business relations between two companies.

Hints

- mention the source of the seller's information
- give a brief introduction of one's own company
- state information or service one needs
- show the desire for further business relationship
- wish to get an early reply

Specimen letter 1

<table>
<tr><td>From: magnificent@yahoo.com (ACT Co., Ltd.)</td><td rowspan="5">Table Cloth
</td></tr>
<tr><td>To: kingdom@hotmail.com (QKT Co., Ltd.)</td></tr>
<tr><td>Date: Mar 15, 2013</td></tr>
<tr><td>Subject: an enquiry</td></tr>
<tr><td>Attachment:</td></tr>
</table>

Dear Ben,

We learn from Brother Co. that you are a leading exporter of table cloth.

Would you please send us details of your various ranges, including sizes, colors, prices, and samples of the different qualities of material used? We are a large dealer in textiles and believe there is a promising market between us. If your prices are competitive and your goods up to standard, we shall order on a regular basis.

When quoting, could you give the following details:

1. Terms of payment
2. Discount
3. Delivery time when we purchase 5,000 pieces of table cloth

We look forward to hearing from you soon.

Yours sincerely,
Jack
ACT Co., Ltd.

Case 2
Business background

Sender's information:

Name:	Howard
Company:	American Lemon Tree International Trade Co., Ltd.
Add:	298 Conepinetree Rd, New York, USA
Tel:	001-212-222-2222
Fax:	001-212-222-2221
Website:	www.amebingo.com
Email:	lemontreehd@hotmail.com
Business scope:	arts, crafts, household ware
Overseas markets:	China, Japan, Korea, South Africa

Recipient's information:

Name:	Amy
Company:	Jinwen Art & Craft Trade Co., Ltd.
Add:	228 Wenhui Rd, Hangzhou, Zhejiang, China 310000
Tel:	0086-571-77776666
Fax:	0086-571-77776667
Website:	www.hzjinwen.com.cn
Email:	artcraftamy@yahoo.com
Business scope:	arts, crafts, silk products
Overseas markets:	America, Europe, Asia

Task description

Howard, on behalf of Lemon Tree International Trade Co., Ltd. (herein called LIT Co., Ltd.) got the information about the introduction and products of JinWen Art & Craft Trade Co., Ltd. (herein called JACT Co., Ltd.) at the website of alibaba on the Internet last week. He will send an email to Amy for an enquiry to establish business relations.

Hints

◆ mention the source of the seller's information
◆ give a brief introduction of one's own company
◆ state information or service one needs
◆ show the desire for further business relationship
◆ wish to get an early reply

Specimen letter 2

From: lemontreehd@hotmail.com (LIT Co., Ltd.)	 
To: artcraftamy@yahoo.com (JACT Co., Ltd.)	
Date: July 8, 2013	
Subject: an enquiry	
Attachment:	

Dear Amy,

We have seen the introduction of your products at the website of alibaba.
We are one of the leading importers of Chinese arts and crafts and have enjoyed a good reputation from our customers.
At present we are quite interested in your products. Please let us know what quantities you are able to deliver at regular intervals, quoting your best terms CIF New York.
Should your price be found competitive and delivery date acceptable, we intend to place a large order with you.

We look forward to receiving your early reply.

Yours sincerely,
Howard
LIT Co., Ltd.

Task Practice

Task 1

Description

Conepine Tree International Trade Co., Ltd. is one of the largest importers of Christmas products and has been in this line for years with a good reputation.

Howard, a manager of Conepine Tree International Trade Co., Ltd. has got the information of Happy Gifts International Trade Co., Ltd. at the website of alibaba. He will send an email to Happy Gifts International Trade Co., Ltd. for an enquiry.

Requirements

You are required to send an email to Happy Gifts International Trade Co., Ltd. as the role of Howard, according to the following tips.

Tips

- mention the way of getting the customer's information
- give a brief introduction of one's own company
- state information or service one needs
- show the desire for further business relationship
- wish to get an early reply

From: ____________________

To: ____________________

Date: ____________________

Subject: ____________________

____

____

Specimen letter 3

Suggested answer for Task 1

From: howardtree@hotmail.com (CTIT Co., Ltd.)
To: happymay@yahoo.com (HGIT Co., Ltd.)
Date: Jan 8, 2013
Subject: enquiry
Attachment:

Dear sir or madam,

We have learnt your name and address at the website of alibaba. As a growing exporter on gifts, you are looking forward to entering into American market. This happens to coincide with our desire.

We are very interested in importing your goods at present. Would you please let us know the detailed information on CIF San Francisco basis? It would be appreciated if you could tell us discounts and terms of payment; and let us have illustrated catalogues or even samples if possible.

We hope this will be a good start for long and profitable business relations.

Wish to have your early reply.

Yours faithfully,
Howard
CTIT Co., Ltd.

Task 2

Description

Happy Gifts International Trade Co., Ltd. is a well-known firm of arts and crafts.

May, a foreign salesperson of Happy Gifts International Trade Co., Ltd. has got the email from Howard of Conepine Tree International Trade Co., Ltd. She will send an email to Howard to reply the enquiry.

Requirements

You are required to reply an email to Howard as the role of May, according to the following tips.

Tips

- thank for the buyer's interest and email
- state clearly of all the information asked for
- show the desire for further business relationship
- wish to get the early order

From: ______________________________

To: ______________________________

Date: ______________________________

Subject: ______________________________

____

____

____

____

____

____

____

____

____

____

Specimen letter 4

Suggested answer for Task 2—A Reply

From: happymay@yahoo.com (HGIT Co., Ltd.)
To: howardtree@hotmail.com (CTIT Co., Ltd.)
Date: Jan 12, 2013
Subject: reply to enquiry
Attachment: latest catalogue
Dear Howard, Thank you for your enquiry of Jan 8 and your interest in our commodities. Enclosed please find some copies of our illustrated catalogues and a price list. Also under separate cover, we are sending you some samples which will show you clearly the quality and specifications. We trust that when you see them you will agree that our products would appeal to the most selective buyers. Should your order be large, we would offer you attractive prices. As to the terms of payment, we usually require Letter of Credit payable by sight draft. We are looking forward to your order and you may be assured that it will receive our prompt and careful attention. Yours truly, May HHIT Co., Ltd.

Notes

1. on behalf of 代表……
   He spoke on behalf of all the members of the faculty and staff.
   他代表全体教职员工讲了话。
2. for business relations between two companies 在两家公司之间建立业务关系
3. There is a promising market between us. 在我们之间存在广泛的合作市场。
4. You are able to deliver at regular intervals. 你可以定期交货。
5. This happens to coincide with our desire. 这刚好与我们的愿望不谋而合。
6. our products appeal to the most selective buyers 我方产品能够满足最挑剔的买方
7. Enclosed please find some copies of our illustrated catalogues and a price list.
   随函附上一些配有图片的产品目录和一份价目单请查收。

8. As to the terms of payment, we usually require Letter of Credit payable by sight draft.
我方要求用信用证即期汇票付款。

New Words and Expressions

1. enquiry　　*n.* 询盘
2. competitive　　*a.* 竞争的
3. textiles　　*n.* 纺织品
4. quote　　*v.* 报价
5. illustrated　　*a.* 有插图的
6. separately　　*ad.* 分别地
7. irrevocable　　*a.* 不可撤销的
8. arts and crafts　　工艺品
9. at regular intervals　　每隔一定时间，定期
10. be assured　　保证，请放心

Business Link

◆ **外贸询盘回复技巧**

供应商给买家回复电子邮件时，要尽量遵循以下五大要决：

全面：要全面彻底地回答买家查询的方方面面，包括买家所有的问题和感兴趣的点点滴滴。

准确：要将回复信写得很清楚，首先要正确理解买家来函的准确意思；其次，供应商要多使用有说服力，准确的数据，切忌使用模棱两可或含糊的词语和内容。

清楚：电子邮件也应像传统的商业书信一样，不论是排版还是语句都应整洁明了，少使用难懂的词语或表达法。

具体：给买家回复的信息无疑越具体，越能方便买家做出决策。

礼貌：要多使用正式的表达，少用口语语气，尊重对方的风土人格、禁忌和宗教信仰。

◆ **询价文件涉及的主要内容**

一、询价项目的“品名”与“料号”

二、询价项目的“数量”

三、询价项目的“规格书”

四、询价项目的“品质”要求

A. 品牌（Brand or Trade Names）

B. 或同级品（“Or Equal”）

C. 商业标准（Commercial Standard）

D. 材料与制造方法规格（Material or Method-of-Manufacture Specification）

E. 性能或功能规格（Performance or Function Specification）

F. 工程图面（Engineering Drawing）

G. 市场等级（Market Grade）

H. 样品（Sample）

I. 工作说明书（Statement of Work, SOW）

◆ **询价函件内容框架如下：**

(1) 怎样得知对方公司名称和地址的？

如：We have obtained your name and address form the Internet.

Our market survey showed that you are the largest importer of cases and bags in Canada.

(2) 表明建立业务关系的愿望

如：We wish to establish friendly business relations with you so that both of us could benefit from it.

We are willing to have business relations with your firm on the basis of equality and mutual benefit.

(3) 提供本公司简介

如：We are a leading company with 30 years experience in making chemical laboratory equipment.

A credible sales network has been set up and our company has regular clients from over 100 countries and regions worldwide.

(4) 提供销售的商品及有关条件

如：Art No. JD102 is a newly launched product with excellent quality, fashionable design and competitive price.

To give you a general idea of our products, we attached the catalogue for your reference.

(5) 介绍市场状况

如：The present price fluctuation in the world market has necessitated the adjustment of the price.

Owing to the heavy demand, we can accept orders only for shipment during April/May.

(6) 告知对方应从何处了解写信人的信用情况

如：As to our credit standing, please refer to the following bank: The Bank of Tokyo, Osaka Branch (address).

For our business and financial standing, we may refer you to Bank of China Hong Kong Branch.

(7) 结尾写上期待对方回应的话

如：We believe that your initial order will be disposed of without delay.

We are looking forward to your specific enquiries.

Your comments on our products or any information on your market demand will be appreciated.

注意：对客户来函来电，要认真及时答复，以树立良好的贸易形象。

More to Practice

I. Translate the following business terms or expressions into English.

1. 享有良好声誉
2. 询盘
3. 从……获悉
4. 插图目录
5. 广阔的市场
6. 定期交货数量
7. 进口领跑企业
8. 收到有关信用证后
9. 公道的价格
10. 盼复

II. Translate the following sentences into Chinese.

1. Please send us your brochure and wholesale price list with terms of payment.
2. What is your best price for five machine tools?
3. Please send us a sample of each of the items listed above.
4. Would you please let us know if these goods are still available?
5. We are interested in purchasing computers but we need to have further details of the costs before making a final decision.
6. We are in the market for the men's ties illustrated in your catalogue No. 8.
7. We would like to know if you can supply porcelain to our design. If so, please let us have full details.
8. If your products and terms compare favorably with those of other suppliers, we shall send you an order.
9. Please quote us your lowest price with the best discount and the date of delivery.
10. We are glad to send you samples of our products with their quotations.

III. Translate the following sentences into English.

1. 我方一客户对意大利皮鞋感兴趣，请寄样品及报价单。
2. 请报最低价及最早交货期。
3. 请报洛杉矶成本加运费价，包括 5%的佣金。
4. 我方对你方太阳镜感兴趣，请报最低价和最优折扣。
5. 请寄可提供花色的样品。
6. 如订购数量超过 1 000 台，我们将给予 30%的折扣。
7. 请告知最大的定期交货数量。
8. 为使贵方对我们的产品有所了解，现附寄了我们的产品目录供你方参考。
9. 请告知我方成本加保险加运费价、折扣以及付款条件的详情。
10. 我们在这个领域合作具有广阔的前景。

IV. Writing practice.

Please write a letter of enquiry according to the following given information:

Sender's information:
Name: Daniel
Company:Qiantangfeng Longevity Imp and Exp Co., Ltd.
Email: greenqiantang@hotmail.com
Business scope: import and export of healthy food and fruits

Recipient's information:
Name: unknown
Company: Great Sam Imp and Exp Co., Ltd.
Email: sunnysam@gmail.com
Subject: enquiry
Date: Jan 8, 2013

Unit 4

Offer

Study Aims

应知目标

1. To know the writing steps of a firm offer.
2. To know the writing steps of a non-firm offer.
3. To know the difference between a firm offer and a non-firm one.
4. To know the knowledge of "Lead in" Part.
5. To know the knowledge of "Business Link" Part.

应会目标

1. To be able to translate a firm offer properly.
2. To be able to make a letter of firm offer properly.
3. To be able to translate a non-firm offer correctly.
4. To be able to make a non-firm offer properly.

Lead in

- Since the potential buyer has made an enquiry, it is the seller that offers him the information he needs. An offer is a promise made by the seller to supply goods on terms stated.
- There are two types of offers: firm offer and non-firm offer. A firm offer is an irrevocable offer with engagement while a non-firm offer is the revocable offer without engagement. Generally speaking, most offers are non-firm offers with reservation words such as "The offer is subject to…", "The offer holds goods until…"
- A firm offer should satisfy the following conditions:

1) There should be no ambiguous words such as "about", "reference price";

2) The terms should be clearly and completely stated, which include the quality, the quantity, packing, price, shipment, payment, validity, etc.

3) There should be no reservation words such as "subject to our final confirmation", "subject to goods being unsold".

Writing Skills

Step 1: To express thanks to the reader for the enquiry

Step 2: To explain the details of price, discount, and delivery etc.

Step 3: To show validity of the offer

Step 4: To express the wish that the offer can be accepted

Key Sentence Patterns

1. Thank you for your letter of May 9.
2. In reply to your letter of November 12, we have pleasure in enclosing a detailed quotation for our table cloth.
3. It's a pleasure for us to offer you the goods as follows.
4. Referring to your email dated July 10 in which you enquired for leather bag, we have pleasure in giving you an offer as follows.
5. We regret being unable to quote on FOB basis, as it is our general practice to do business with all our clients on CIF terms.
6. We can offer you a quotation based upon the international market.
7. Our offer is RMB300 per set of tea pot, FOB Shanghai.
8. My offer was based on reasonable profit, not on wild speculations.
9. This offer is based on an expanding market and is competitive.
10. Our offers are for 3 days.
11. The offer holds good until 4 o'clock p.m. 3rd of June, Beijing time.
12. This offer is subject to the goods being unsold.
13. The offer is given without engagement.
14. We are looking forward to your early reply.
15. We are waiting for your order.

Case Study

Case 1

Business background

Sender's information:

Name:	Jim
Company:	Henan Happy House Trade Co., Ltd.
Add:	58 Zhongshan Rd Zhengzhou, Henan, P.R.China 450000
Tel:	0086-371-88886666
Fax:	0086-371-88886667
Website:	www.hhthn.com.cn
Email:	happyjim@hotmail.com
Business scope:	teapots, cups, handmade pots, hand-painted china
Overseas markets:	Europe, America, Canada, South Africa

Recipient's information:

Name:	Elizabeth
Company:	Canada Houschold Goods Trade Co., Ltd.
Add:	8288 11th Avenue, Burnaby, Toronto, Canada
Tcl:	001-647-985-6666
Fax:	001-647-985-6667
Website:	www.beautifulhouse.com
Email:	beautyeli@gmail.com
Business scope:	teapots, household products
Overseas markets:	Europe, America, Asia

Task description

Jim, on behalf of Henan Happy House Trade Co., Ltd. (herein called HHHT Co., Ltd.) got the enquiry from Elizabeth of Canada Household Goods Trade Co., Ltd. (herein called CHGT Co., Ltd.) on December 3rd. He will send an email to Elizabeth to explain the details of prices, terms of payments and so on.

Hints

- make an expression of thanks for the enquiry
- offer the name of commodities, quality, quantity
- offer the details of prices, terms of payment or discount
- offer the packing and date of delivery, the validity of the offer
- express the wish to accept the offer

Specimen letter 1

From: happyjim@hotmail.com (HHHT Co., Ltd.)

To: beautyeli@gmail.com (CHGT Co., Ltd.)

Date: Dec 8, 2013

Subject: an offer

Attachment: our catalogue

Dear Elizabeth,

In reply to your enquiry letter of December 3rd, we have pleasure in making an offer for teapots.

Besides those advertised in *the Economist*, our illustrated catalogue enclosed shows various types of teapots. Most types can be supplied from stock. 45-60 days should be allowed for delivery of those marked with an asterisk.

We can allow 2% discount on all orders of US$10,000 in value and over, and 3% on orders exceeding US$25,000.

The offer holds good until 4 o'clock p.m. 18th of December, Beijing time. Please take all the necessary steps you can do without delay.

Looking forward to receiving your order soon.

Yours sincerely,

Jim

Sales Manager

HHHT Co., Ltd.

Case 2
Business background

Sender's information:

Name:	Liang Yixun
Company:	Jinhua Moonsun International Trade Co., Ltd.
Add:	88 Shidai Square, Jinhua, Zhejiang, P.R.China 321000
Tel:	0086-579-82566666
Fax:	0086-579-82566668
Website:	www.jhmoonsun.com.cn
Email:	liangyixun28@hotmail.com
Business scope:	electronic calculators, electronic products
Overseas markets:	South Africa

Recipient's information:

Name:	Kinsley
Company:	South African Motherriver Trade Co., Ltd.
Add:	138 Fungirl St. Proteria, South Africa
Tel:	0027-12-991-7777
Fax:	0027-12-991-7778
Website:	www.motherriver.com.
Email:	happykinsley@gmail.com
Business scope:	shoes, garments
Overseas markets:	America, Europe, Asia

Task description

Liang Yixun, on behalf of Jinhua Moonsun International Trade Co., Ltd. (herein called JMIT Co., Ltd.) got the enquiry from Kinsley of South African Motherriver Trade Co., Ltd. (herein called SAMT Co., Ltd.) on July 14. He will send an email to Kinsley for the details of prices, specifications, terms of payment and so on.

Hints

- ◆ make an expression of thanks for the enquiry
- ◆ offer the name of commodities, quality, quantity, shipment
- ◆ offer the details of prices, terms of payment, discounts
- ◆ enclose the copies of the latest catalogue
- ◆ express the wish to get an early reply

Specimen letter 2

From: liangyixun28@hotmail.com (JMIT Co., Ltd.)	
To: happykinsley@gmail.com (SAMT Co., Ltd.)	
Date: April 12, 2013	
Subject: offer	
Attachment: catalogues	

Dear Kinsley,

In reply to your enquiry letter of April 8, we have pleasure in giving you an offer, subject to your reply reaching here by 5 p.m. our time, Thursday, May 5, as follows:

Commodity: Electronic Calculators

Specifications: As per attached list

Packing: As per the buyers option

Color: yellow, brown, red and green

Quantity: 5,000 pcs.

Size: 12×18in

Price: US$5.80 net per piece CIF Lagos
Shipment: June/July, 2013
Payment: Confirmed, irrevocable letter of credit payable by draft at sight to be opened 30 days before the time of shipment.
Under separate cover, we have sent you 2 copies of illustrated catalogue of various brands as per your request.
Please note that we have given you our most favorable price and we trust that the above will be acceptable to you.

Yours sincerely,
Liang Yixun
JMIT Co., Ltd.

Task Practice

Task 1

Description

Sunny Group is one of the largest exporters of electronic products and has been in this line for 30 years with a good reputation.

Bill, a foreign salesperson of Sunny Group has got the enquiry from Mall of ABC Co., Ltd. by fax on February 10. He will send an email to ABC Co., Ltd. for the details of commodities.

Requirements

You are required to send an email to ABC Co., Ltd. as the role of Bill, according to the following tips.

Tips

- make an expression of thanks for the enquiry
- offer the name of commodities, quality, quantity, specifications
- offer the details of prices, terms of payment, shipment
- state the validity of the offer
- wish to get an early order

From: ______________________________

To: ______________________________

Date: ______________________________

Subject: ______________________________

____

____

____

____

____

____

____

____

____

____

Specimen letter 3

Suggested answer for Task 1

From: huaribill11@hotmail.com (Sunny Group)

To: mall88@yahoo.com (ABC Co., Ltd.)

Date: March 22, 2013

Subject: offer

Attachment: latest catalogue

Dear Mall,

HUARI REFRIGERATOR

Thank you for your interest in purchasing 2,800 sets of our Huari refrigerators. We are pleased to know that you are interested in our products.

Complying with the request in your letter dated March 18, we take pleasure in enclosing you our latest catalogue with an offer as follows, provided your reply reaches us 7 days from today:

Specification	Quantity (set)	Price (US$)
HMH 212	1,000	510.00
HMH 175	1,000	580.00
HMH 219	800	495.00

The price is on the basis of CIF Alexandria.
Packing: at buyer's option
Shipment: Total quantity to be delivered by 3 equal monthly shipments, April through June, 2013.
Payment: 100% by irrevocable letter of credit.
We have received a lot of other enquiries for the above sets as well; therefore your early order is absolutely essential.

Yours sincerely,
Bill
Sunny Group

Task 2

Description

ABC Co., Ltd. is a new set-up firm of electronic equipments.

Mall, a foreign salesperson of ABC Co., Ltd. has got the email from Bill of Sunny Group. She will send an email to Bill to make a counter-offer as a reply.

Requirements

You are required to reply an email to Bill as the role of Mall, according to the following tips.

Tips

- ◆ mention the received email and show thanks
- ◆ show one's disagreement to the certain term or terms
- ◆ express one's own idea properly and politely
- ◆ list the reasons for refusal
- ◆ express the wish to accept the counter-offer

From: ______________________________

To: ______________________________

Date: ______________________________

Subject: ____________________

Specimen letter 4

Suggested answer for Task 2—A Reply

From: mall88@yahoo.com (ABC Co., Ltd.)
To: haierbill11@hotmail.com (Sunny Group)
Date: March. 26, 2013
Subject: reply to the offer for Huari Refrigerators
Attachment:

Dear Bill,

We have received your offer No. 198 offering us 2,800 sets for three designs of the subject goods. In reply, we regret to say that your prices are out of line with the current market level. Information here shows that the makes offered by you can be obtained from other sources at prices much lower than yours. Moreover, the market is declining.

We do not deny that we are interested in your products as you know, but the difference in price should, in no case, be so big. To step up the trade, we counter offer as follows, subject to your reply reaching here by 5 p.m. our time, March 28:

US$450.00 for HMH 212
US$500.00 for HMH 175
US$425.00 for HMH 219

It is true that competitive prices will often result in a high market share with great profit in the future.

We wish you to accept our counter-offer.

Yours sincerely,
Mall
ABC Co., Ltd.

Notes

1. In reply to your enquiry letter of December 3rd, we have pleasure in... 对于你方的询盘，我们非常乐意报盘。
   From your email the day before yesterday, we have pleasure in making an offer as following. 对于你方前日的询盘，我们非常乐意报盘如下。类似的表达还有：We appreciate/ thank you for your enquiry... 我们非常感谢你方的询盘。
2. subject to 以……为条件，以……为准
   offer subject to our written acceptance 以我方书面接受为准的报盘；offer subject to goods being unsold 以商品未售出为准的报盘；offer subject to first available steamer 以装第一艘轮船为准的报盘。
3. The offer holds good until... 该报盘有效期至……
   类似的表达还有：Our offers are for × days. 我们的报盘×天有效。
4. We can allow 2% discount on all orders of US$10,000 in value and over.
   价值在 10 000 美元以上的所有订单，我们给予 2%的折扣。
5. as per 按照（仅用于商业书信）
   As per your request, we have marked the cases with gross, tare and net weights.
   我们已经按你方要求在箱上注明毛重，皮重及净重。
6. irrevocable letter of credit 不可撤销的循环信用证
7. by 3 equal monthly shipments 分三个月每次数量相等装货
8. absolutely essential 必要的
9. in no case 在任何情况下，无论如何不，绝不
10. owing to 由于，因为，多亏
11. to step up the trade 为促进贸易
12. counter offer 还盘；还价 也可以写作 counteroffer, counter-offer
    The price you counter offered is not in line with the prevailing market.
    你方还盘价格与市场价不符。

New Words and Expressions

1. offer	*n./v.* 发盘，报盘，报价
2. asterisk	*n.* 星号
3. *The Economist*	《经济学家》杂志

4. exceed　　v. 超过，超出
5. entertain　　n. 接受
6. substitute　　n./v. 取代，代替
7. propose　　v. 提议，建议
8. slightly　　a. 略微的，轻微的
9. keen　　a. 强烈的，敏锐的
10. firm offer　　实盘
11. take advantage of　　利用

Business Link

◆《经济学家》杂志

1843 年创刊于英国。是一份包含新闻、政治经济观点和深度分析的周刊。该杂志所有的文章都不署名，皆由集体创作。

《经济学家》在 20 世纪 20 年代发行量仅有 3 700 份，直到 1970 还未能突破 10 万份大关。如今，杂志分别在 7 个国家印刷，其发行量已超过 70 万份，其中有 4/5 的发行是在英国本土以外，单独在美国的发行量占总量的 1/3。

一个多世纪以来，《经济学家》始终恪守创始人 James Wilson 的办刊思想：“在文章中提出的任何争论和主张必须要经得起事实的考验。”

《经济学家》读者定位为高收入、富有独立见解和批判精神的社会精英，与此相适应，文章始终保持了一种独特的格调：不拘一格、叙述朴实、用词准确和忠于事实。

◆ 发盘

在国际贸易实务中，发盘也称报盘、发价、报价，法律上称之为“要约”。发盘一般是由卖方发出的，是卖方主动向买方提供商品信息，或者是对询盘的答复，是卖方根据买方的来信向买方报盘，其内容可包括商品名称、规格、数量、包装条件、价格、付款方式和交货期限等，但也可以由买方发出，业务称其为“递盘”。

◆ 实盘与虚盘

实盘是发盘人（Offerer）按其提供的条件以达成交易目的的明确表示。实盘具有法律效力，受盘人（Offeree）一旦在有效期限内接受实盘上的条件和内容，发盘人就无权拒绝售货。一项实盘必须具备：

（1）发盘的内容和词句必须肯定，不能用“大约（about）”、“参考价（reference price）”等模棱两可的词。

（2）发盘的内容明确完整，其内容应包括商品品质（Quality）、数量（Quantity）、包装（Packing）、价格（Price）、装运（Shipment）、支付（Payment）、有效期（Validity）等。

（3）发盘中不能有保留条件。如：以我方最后确认为准 subject to our final confirmation; 以货物的未售出为准 subject to goods being unsold.

虚盘是发盘人所作的不肯定交易的表示，凡不符合实盘所具备的上述三个条件的发盘，都是虚盘。虚盘无须详细的内容和具体条件，也不注明有效期。它仅表示交易的意向，不

具有法律效力。

More to Practice

I. Translate the following business terms or expressions into English.

1. 发盘
2. 实盘
3. 以……为准
4. 不受约束的
5. 虚盘
6. 很大的需求
7. 由于
8. 供你参考
9. 给予折扣
10. 导致

II. Translate the following sentences into Chinese.

1. Our offers are for 3 days.
2. We are in a position to offer tea from stock.
3. We can offer you a quotation based upon the international market.
4. My offer was based on reasonable profit, not on wild speculations.
5. This offer is based on an expanding market and is competitive.
6. This offer is subject to your reply reaching here before the end of this month.
7. We have extended the offer as per as your request.
8. This offer is subject to the goods being unsold.
9. The offer is given without engagement.
10. We are unable to entertain any counter-offer.

III. Translate the following sentences into English.

1. 感谢贵方于 4 月 5 日对我产品的询盘。
2. 对于你所要求的产品，我们的报盘如下。
3. 报价单中所有价格以我方确认为准。
4. 我们愿意以此价格为你报实盘。
5. 我们的报价是每套茶壶 300 元人民币，上海离岸价。
6. 除非你们减价 5%，否则我们无法接受报盘。
7. 我们将优先向你们报盘。
8. 由于对该产品的需求增大导致价格上涨。
9. 我们借此机会向贵方报盘类似产品。
10. 很抱歉我们无法提供您所询问产品的报盘。

IV. Writing practice.

Mr. Harry has emailed you and enquired for your products and asked you to make an offer. Please write a letter of making an offer.

Unit 5

Counter-offer

Study Aims

应知目标

1. To know the writing steps of a counter-offer.
2. To know the writing steps of a reply to a counter-offer.
3. To know the knowledge of "Lead in" Part.
4. To know the knowledge of "Business Link" Part.

应会目标

1. To be able to translate a counter-offer properly.
2. To be able to make a counter-offer properly and politely.
3. To be able to translate a reply to counter-offer.
4. To be able to reply to counter-offer properly.

Lead in

- If the buyer does not agree with the specific terms such as price, packing, shipment mentioned in the prior offer from the seller, he will reply the seller with a counter-proposal on those trade terms unacceptable. When a counter-offer is made, the original offer ends.
- Generally speaking, the process of offer and counter-offer is a kind of bargaining in business. Sometimes two parties will repeat the process for several times to complete a transaction. Both parties should pay more attention to the expressions they use to avoid misunderstanding.
- How to reply a counter-offer?

1. No matter you accept it or not, you should send back a punctual, courteous and considerate reply.
2. Explain the reasons for declining the counter-offer in an unfavorable reply.
3. Show the wish of further business.

Writing Skills

Step 1: To express gratitude to the original offer
Step 2: To explain the reasons for inability to accept the offer
Step 3: To put forward a counter-proposal
Step 4: To express the wish for an early reply

Key Sentence Patterns

1. In reply, we very much regret to inform you that our end-users here find your price too high and out of line with the prevailing market level.
2. Our counter-offer is well found.
3. We accept your counter-offer of 25th.
4. The price you counter-offer is unreasonable.
5. I'm afraid we can't accept your counter-offer.
6. I appreciate your counter-offer but find it too low.
7. Our counter-offer is in line with international market.
8. We accept your counter-offer. Please advise us the shipping date.
9. We make a counter-offer to you of $150 per metric ton F.O.B. London.
10. We have managed to maintain the present price despite the increase cost of raw materials.
11. There is no room to make any further reduction in prices.
12. We've already cut down our price to cost level.
13. This is our rock-bottom price.
14. I'm sorry the difference between our price and your counter-offer is too wide.
15. However, such practice will mean no profit to us.

Case Study

Case 1
Business background

Sender's information:

Name:	Mark
Company:	Shaoxing Mark Textile Trade Co., Ltd.
Add:	128 Ziguang Rd. Shaoxing, Zhejiang, P.R.China 323900
Tel:	0086-574-6078000
Fax:	0086-574-6078001
Website:	www.sxmt.com
Email:	coolmark@hotmail.com
Business scope:	textiles, silk products
Overseas markets:	Europe, America

Recipient's information:

Name:	Anna
Company:	Fragrant Household Items Trade Co., Ltd.
Add:	65 Ocean Avenue Apt 6B Brooklyn, NY, USA. 11211
Tel:	001-212--255-6568
Fax:	001-212-255-6569
Website:	www.fragrantcoffee.com
Email:	prettyanna@gmail.com
Business scope:	textiles
Overseas markets:	Asia, Africa

Task description

Mark, on behalf of Shaoxing Mark Textile Trade Co., Ltd. (herein called SMTT Co., Ltd.) met Anna of Fragrant Household Items Trade Co., Ltd. (herein called FHIT Co., Ltd.) at Guangzhou Trade Fair two years ago. He received a counter-offer from Anna 3 days ago. He will send an email to Anna to show his disagreement and put forward a counter-proposal following his standpoint.

Hints

- express gratitude to the original offer
- show one's disagreement to the certain terms
- express the reasons for inability to accept the offer
- put forward a counter-proposal properly
- wish to get an early reply

Specimen letter 1

From: coolmark@hotmail.com (SMTT Co., Ltd.)	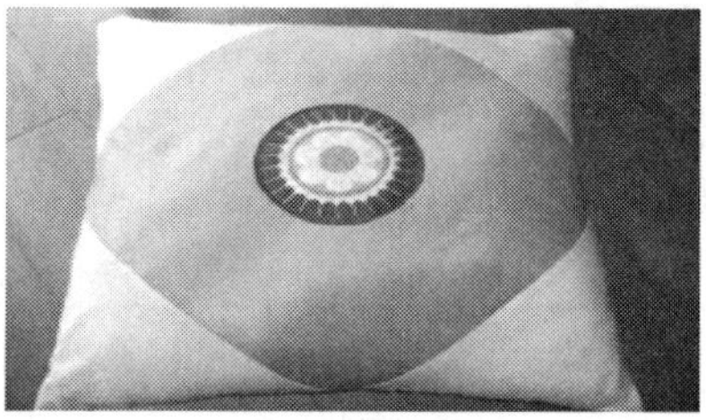
To: prettyanna@gmail.com (FHIT Co., Ltd.)	
Date: Nov 25, 2013	
Subject: embroidered cushion	
Attachment:	

Dear Anna,

We thank you for your offer by fax of Jan 3 for 5,000 pieces of the captioned goods at $9.5 per piece CIF Toronto.

We immediately contacted our customers and they showed great interest in the quality and designs of your products. However they said that your price is 15% higher than the average. They told us if you could reduce your price to $8.5 per piece, they would increase 5,500 pieces to the quantity. We hope you will take advantage of this opportunity so that you will benefit from the expanding market.

If you would reduce your price to that extent, we will also be pleased to place with you an order that will carry us for the rest of this year.

Hope to hear from you soon.

Yours sincerely,

Mark

SMTT Co., Ltd.

Case 2
Business background

Sender's information:

Name:	Steven
Company:	Atlanta Trade Co., Ltd.
Add:	5480 Old National Highway #100, Atlanta, Ga, USA, 30349
Tel:	001-678-557-1188
Fax:	001-678-557-1189
Website:	www.apemountain.net
Email:	badsteven@hotmail.com
Business scope:	textiles
Overseas markets:	China, Japan, Korea

Recipient's information:

Name:	Faith
Company:	Zhejiang Sunshine International Trade Co., Ltd.
Add:	39 Shuguang Rd. Jiangbei District, Hangzhou, Zhejiang, CPR. 315020
Tel:	0086-571-87606666
Fax:	0086-571-87606667
Website:	www.sunshinetrade.com
Email:	wellfaith@gmail.com
Business scope:	textiles
Overseas markets:	America, Europe

Task description

Steven, on behalf of Atlanta Trade Co., Ltd (herein called AT Co., Ltd.) got the offer from Faith of Zhejiang Sunshine International Trade Co., Ltd. (herein called ZJSIT Co., Ltd.) on March 28, 2013. He will send an email to Faith to show his disagreement and put forward a counter-proposal following his point stand.

Hints

- express gratitude to the original offer
- show one's disagreement to the certain term or terms
- express the reasons for inability to accept the offer
- put forward a counter-proposal properly
- wish to get an early reply

Specimen letter 2

From: badsteven@hotmail.com (AT Co., Ltd.)	
To: wellfaith@gmail.com (ZJSIT Co., Ltd.)	
Date: Mar 30, 2013	
Subject: a counter-offer	
Attachment:	

Dear Faith,

We learn from your letter of Mar 8 that you find our offer for the silk scarf too high to be acceptable.

We are sorry to say that there is no possibility of our cutting the price to the extent you indicated, i.e. 15%. As the prices of materials have raised a lot recently, we have to adjust our prices to cover the increasing cost. Moreover, if you put the quality of our goods into consideration, this price is in fact very reasonable. Desirous as we are to do business with you, we regret being unable to entertain your counter-offer for the time being.

If later on you can see any chance to do better, please let us know. In the meantime, please keep us posted of developments at your end. We assure you that all your enquiries will receive our prompt attention.

Yours sincerely,
Steven
AT Co., Ltd.

Task Practice

Task 1

Description

ABC Co., Ltd. is one of the largest importers of foodstuff and has been in this line for 100 years with a good reputation.

Amanda, a foreign salesperson of ABC Co., Ltd. has got the information of BCD Co., Ltd. on September 3. He will send an email to BCD Co., Ltd.

Requirements

You are required to send an email to BCD Co., Ltd. as the role of Amanda, according to the following tips.

Tips

- express gratitude to the original offer
- show one's disagreement to certain terms
- express the reasons for inability to accept the offer
- put forward a counter-proposal properly
- wish to get an early reply

From: ____________________

To: ____________________

Date: ____________________

Subject: ____________________

____

____

____

Specimen letter 3

Suggested answer for Task 1

From: coolamanda@hotmail.com (ABC Co., Ltd.)
To: prettylily@yahoo.com (BCD Co., Ltd.)
Date: Sept 8, 2013
Subject: counter-offer
Attachment:
Dear Lily, We are pleased to receive your offer of September 3, offering us 50 tons of first-class coffee at US$550 per ton CIF New York, on usual terms. We are regretful that our users here find your price too high and out of line with the international market. As goods of similar quality are easily obtainable at a much lower price, we find it hard to persuade our users to accept your offer. If you can reduce your limit by, say, 5%, we might come to terms. In view of our long-standing business relations, we make you the above counter-offer. If your price is favorable, we can place an order with you right away. As the market is declining, we hope you will take it into consideration and email us acceptance at your earliest convenience. Yours sincerely, Amanda ABC Co., Ltd.

Task 2

Description

BCD Co., Ltd. is a firm in the line of photographic equipments with good reputation for 20 years.

Luo, a foreign salesperson of BCD Co., Ltd. has got the email from Amanda of ABC Co., Ltd. He will send an email to Amanda for the counter-offer as a reply.

Requirements

You are required to write an email to Amanda as the role of Luo, according to the following tips.

Tips

- express the gratitude towards the offer
- show one's disagreement to the certain term or terms
- express the reasons for inability to accept the offer
- put forward a counter-proposal properly
- wish to get an early reply

From: ______________________________

To: ______________________________

Date: ______________________________

Subject: ______________________________

____

____

____

____

____

____

____

____

____

____

Specimen letter 4

Suggested answer for Task 2—A Reply

From: shiningluo@yahoo.com (BCD Co., Ltd.)
To: wayamanda@hotmail.com (ABC Co., Ltd.)
Date: Jan 12, 2013
Subject: counter-offer
Attachment:
Dear Amanda, We acknowledge receipt of your offer for "Seagull" Brand cameras dated Jan 8. Regretfully we are unable to accept your offer as your prices are too high. We also have got the quotation from a Japan camera company. Their prices are 8% lower than yours for similar products. We accept that the quality of your cameras is better, but it does not justify such a large difference in price. If you were prepared to reduce your limit by, say 6%, we might come to terms. Otherwise we have to decline your offer. We shall appreciate it very much if you will make a concession and fax us your acceptance ASAP. Yours sincerely, Luo BCD Co., Ltd.

Notes

1. rock-bottom price 最低价，底价
   This is our rock-bottom price, Mr. Smith, we can't make any further concessions.
   史密斯先生，这是我们的底价，我们不能再做任何让步。
2. offering us 600 kgs of first-class coffee at USD60 per kg CIF New York, on usual terms. 按常规条款向我方报盘 600 公斤一等咖啡，成本保险加运费到纽约价为每公斤 60 美元。
3. out of line with the international market 与国际市场状况不符
   类似的表达还有：in line with... 与……相符
4. persuade sb. to do sth. 说服某人做某事
5. in view of 鉴于，由于
6. at your earliest convenience 请尽早，尽快
7. make a concession 做出让步

To reach agreement, we decided to make a concession with honor.
为了达成协议，我们决定做出体面的让步。

8. take advantage of this opportunity 利用这一有利时机
We are glad to take advantage of this opportunity to introduce our various products available to you. 我们很高兴利用这个机会向你方介绍我方可提供的各种产品。
9. ...benefit from/by 从……获益
You will benefit from investing in China.你们将从在中国的投资中获益。
10. entertain your counter-offer 考虑接受你方的还盘

New Words and Expressions

1. regretful	*a.* 后悔的；抱歉的；惋惜的，遗憾的
2. punctual	*a.* 精确的，准时的
3. courteous	*a.* 有礼貌的；谦恭的；客气的
4. metric	*a.* 米制的；公制的；十进制的
5. persuade	*v.* 说服
6. decline	*v.* 下降，下滑；拒绝
7. unfavorable	*a.* 不利的；相反的；令人不快的
8. indicate	*v.* 指示，指明
9. prompt	*a.* 敏捷的，迅速的；即时的
10. acknowledge	*v.* 承认；答谢；报偿
11. parcel	*n.* 一批，一宗
12. appreciate	*v.* 赏识；鉴赏；感激
13. justify	*v.* 证明……是正当的
14. allowance	*n.* 折扣
15. concession	*n.* 让步

Business Link

◆ **还盘**

受盘人不同意发盘中的交易条件而提出修改或变更的意见，称为还盘（Counter Offer），在法律上叫反要约。还盘实际上是受盘人以发盘人的地位发出的一个新盘。原发盘人成为新盘的受盘人。还盘又是受盘人对发盘的拒绝，发盘因对方还盘而失效，原发盘人不再受其约束。还盘可以在双方之间反复进行，还盘的内容通常仅陈述需变更或增添的条件，对双方同意的交易条件无须重复。

◆ **杭州丝绸**

杭州丝绸，历史悠久，质地轻软，色彩绮丽，品种繁多，有绸、缎、绫、绢等十几类品种，最著名的品牌有长城、喜得宝、万事利、凯地、丝煌等。

杭州有“丝绸之府”之称。距今四千七百年的良渚出土丝织物就已揭示了杭州丝绸的历史之久，唐代大诗人白居易“丝袖织绫夸柿蒂，青旗沽酒趁梨花”的诗句又道出了当时杭州丝绸的水准之高，旧时清河坊鳞次栉比的绸庄更见证了丝绸经济的繁荣。

如今杭州常年生产绸、缎、棉、纺、绉、绫、罗等十四个大类，二百多个品种，二千余个花色，图景新颖，富丽华贵，花卉层次分明，人物栩栩如生，许多产品荣获国家部优或省级优质产品奖，远销世界上 100 多个国家和地区。

杭州丝绸著名品牌之一都锦生，都锦生丝绸厂创立于 1922 年，曾是中国最大的丝绸工艺品生产的出口企业之一，主要生产风景画、台毯、靠垫、窗帘及织锦衣料，产品富丽堂皇，雍容华贵，被国际友人誉为“东方艺术之花”。

◆ **海鸥相机**

海鸥品牌代表行业形象，是中国历史最悠久、规模最大，国内唯一一家具有开发、生产制造各类单反相机、数码相机、立体相机、全自动相机及各类照相器材的影像器材制造企业，产品远销美、德、英等三十多个国家和地区。

海鸥目前拥有市级开发中心，形成了数字软件、电路光学、感光等 11 个开发版块，具备 CAD 设计开发和 CAM 辅助加工能力，并从日本、德国引进了先进的精密冲压、精密压铸、精密涂装、先进的设备，引进了国外先进的装配流水线及技术与专利，近年通过与日本美能达等跨国公司建立合资企业，形成了国际相机制造转移载体，形成了雄厚的产品设计生产和成品装配能力。

海鸥立足跨越式发展战略，构筑了传统、数码、立体三足鼎立的产品格局，建立了世界一流的数码相机生产基地。海鸥集 40 年传统照相机制造经验，在对引进技术的消化吸收工作中，开发形成了中国照相机制造最高水平的单镜头反光系列相机和全自动平视取景照相机系列、双镜头反光照相机系列，立体相机及多款定焦、变焦镜头。

◆ **咖啡**

“咖啡”（Coffee）一词源自埃塞俄比亚的一个名叫卡法（Kaffa）的小镇，在希腊语中“Kaweh”的意思是“力量与热情”。茶叶与咖啡、可可并称为世界三大饮料。

咖啡树是属茜草科常绿小乔木，原产于埃塞俄比亚。热带、亚热带的常绿小乔木或灌木。叶长卵形，花白色，结深红色浆果。有小果、中果、大果咖啡等。种子炒熟碾成粉可制饮料，有兴奋作用。

日常饮用的咖啡是用咖啡豆配合各种不同的烹煮器具制作出来的，而咖啡豆就是指咖啡树果实内之果仁，再用适当的烘焙方法烘焙而成。

咖啡是由咖啡豆磨制成粉、用热水冲泡而成的饮品。其味苦，却有一种特殊的香气，是西方人的主要饮料之一。它原产于非洲热带地区，如今在中国云南、广东等省亦有栽培，其种子称“咖啡豆”，炒熟研粉可作饮料，即咖啡。

有知名品牌：高乐雅咖啡、象粪咖啡、麝香猫咖啡、蓝山咖啡、阿里山玛翡咖啡、图兰朵音乐咖啡、摩卡（Mocha）、苏门答腊曼特宁、夏威夷科纳、巴西咖啡、哥伦比亚特级、肯尼亚 AA、哈拉尔咖啡、危地马拉安提瓜、波多黎各尧科等。

More to Practice

I. Translate the following business terms or expressions into English.

1. 到了……的程度
2. 还盘
3. 巨大的价格差距
4. 同类产品
5. 暂时
6. 谢绝还盘
7. 鉴于
8. 达成交易
9. 拒绝你方报盘
10. 让步

II. Translate the following sentences into Chinese.

1. Should you be able to reduce your price by 10%, we can come to terms.
2. There is no possibility to do business unless you reduce your price by 5%.
3. After going into the case carefully, we decided to make a further concession of 5 cents per yard.
4. We have to state that your price is out of line with our market level.
5. You early order is absolutely essential.
6. Since the market is advancing we suggest you place an order with us at once.
7. As the market has strengthened recently, there is no margin left for bargaining in our quotation.
8. The quality of the Sesame Seed is high, but the quantity is not large enough to go round.
9. We have received your offer for T-shirts, but find your price rather high.
10. Our products are of better quality than those from other countries.

III. Translate the following sentences into English.

1. 你方的还价与我方价格相差太多。
2. 相同质量产品的价格相比，我们的价格总是偏低。
3. 因为你方不同意降低价格，我公司将去别处购买。
4. 双方各自坚持自己的价格是不明智的。
5. 如果你方仍然坚持原来的报价，我们只好放弃这笔交易。
6. 在质量方面，其他牌子的商品很难和我们的相比。
7. 鉴于我们长期的贸易关系，我们可以考虑减价 3%。
8. 只有订货数量达到 600 吨时，我们降价才不至于影响土豆的等级。
9. 如果订单在 100 打以上，我们愿意给予 5%的折扣。
10. 如果质量符合要求，我们将来就会再次订购。

IV. Writing practice.

Mr. Bill has received your offer for black tea. He emailed you to make a counter-offer and showed his reasons. Please write a letter of making a counter-offer as the role of Mr. Bill.

Unit 6

Acceptance and Order

Study Aims

应知目标

1. To know the writing steps of a letter of an order.
2. To know the writing steps of a letter of acceptance.
3. To know the writing steps of a letter of confirmation.
4. To know the knowledge of "Lead in" Part.
5. To know the knowledge of "Business Link" Part.

应会目标

1. To be able to translate purchase order.
2. To be able to write a letter of order.
3. To be able to translate a letter of acceptance.
4. To be able to write a letter of acceptance.
5. To be able to translate a letter of confirmation.
6. To be able to write a letter of confirmation.

Lead in

- Acceptance is one of the necessary components in the conclusion of a foreign trade. As stated in United Nations Convention on Contracts for the International Sale of Goods. (Abb. CISG), "A contract is concluded at the moment when an acceptance of an offer becomes effective in accordance with the provisions of the Convention on CISG." Only after acceptance, we can in fact conclude a contract. But according to Chinese law requirements, contracts have to be concluded in written form.
- An order is a request to supply a specified quantity of goods. It may result from an offer or an enquiry. An order is also called a purchase order, which contains a formal offer from an intending buyer to buy from a supplier the goods listed, in the quantities and at an approximate price. Then a contract may come into existence when the supplier sends a formal acknowledgment to the buyer. An order can be sent by a letter, fax, even an email. An order or an order letter should cover the following:

1) Goods description, including name, article No., specifications, quantity etc.
2) Price, total price and payment terms
3) Packing and shipment terms

Of above all, the accuracy and clarity are most important to an order.

Writing Skills

Step 1: To thank the offer
Step 2: To confirm the transaction terms
Step 3: To state one's requirements
Step 4: To express the wish of future business

Key Sentence Patterns

1. We'd like to draw your attention to the fact that the goods should be shipped by the end of Mar, 2007.
2. If the goods we ordered cannot be delivered at that time, we have to cancel the order.
3. We hope this transaction will be satisfactory to both of us.
4. We appreciate your cooperation and are pleased to confirm the order as follows.
5. Enclosed please find our Purchase Order No.123.
6. We'd like to place an initial order with you on the terms and conditions as follows.
7. I'm writing to let you know that your Order No.123 for 1,000 sets computers was shipped yesterday via DHL.
8. Your regular orders are always highly appreciated.
9. Thank you for your cooperation and welcome further business opportunities.
10. Would you please email us your confirmation of our order?
11. We are pleased to place this order with you as a trial.
12. We have cut our price to the limit. So we can't accept any price reduction.
13. We can supply you with 500 MT first class green tea from stock.
14. Thank you very much for your first order of the above products.
15. We look forward to your trial order.

Case Study

Case 1
Business background

Sender's information:

Name:	Jack
Company:	Hangzhou Hollway Trade Co., Ltd.
Add:	118 Wensan Rd Hangzhou, Zhejiang, P.R.China 310000
Tel:	0086-571-82826266
Fax:	0086-571-82826267
Website:	www.hzhlt.com.cn
Email:	jackabc@hotmail.com
Business scope:	kitchenware, flower pots
Overseas markets:	Europe, America, Asia, South America

Recipient's information:

Name:	Mary
Company:	Southafrican Sunflower Trade Co., Ltd.
Add:	227 Long St Capetown, South Africa
Tel:	27-21-3456666
Fax:	27-21-3456667
Website:	www.afslt.com.sa
Email:	maryl@gmail.com
Business scope:	foodstuff
Overseas markets:	America, Europe, Asia, Africa

Task description

Jack, manager of Hangzhou Hollway Trade Co., Ltd. (herein called A Co., Ltd.) contacts Mary of Southafrican Sunflower Trade Co., Ltd. (herein called B Co., Ltd.) on the net. He will send an email to Mary for the first order of coffee pots.

Hints

- thank for offer
- confirm some transaction terms
- state one's shipment requirement
- wish to get an early reply

Specimen letter 1

From: jackabc@hotmail.com (A Co., Ltd.)	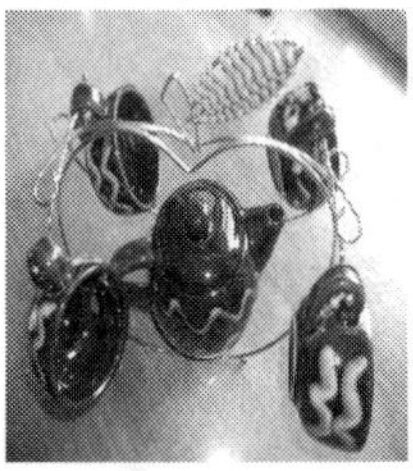 
To: maryl@gmail.com (B Co., Ltd.)	
Date: Dec 5, 2012	
Subject: acceptance	
Attachment:	

Dear Mary:

Thank you for your email of Nov 23, 2012 offering us 20,000 sets of coffee pots at US$7.8 per set CIF Shanghai.

All the terms and conditions are acceptable to us, so please send us your Sales Confirmation ASAP and we can arrange L/C establishment with our bank.

We'd like to draw your attention to the fact that the goods should be shipped by the end of Feb, 2013. If they can not be delivered at that time, we have to cancel the order.

We hope this transaction will be satisfactory to both of us and it will lead to further business opportunity.

Yours sincerely,
Jack
manager
A Co., Ltd.

Case 2
Business background

Sender's information:

Name:	Mike
Company:	Guangzhou Med International Trade Co., Ltd.
Add:	298 Liuhua Rd Guangzhou, Guangdong, P.R.China 318000
Tel:	0086-20-68886666
Fax:	0086-20-68886667
Website:	www.gzmedit.com.cn
Email:	coolmike@hotmail.com
Business scope:	household appliance
Overseas markets:	Japan, Korea, Africa

Recipient's information:

Name:	Johnson
Company:	NKK Trade Co., Ltd.
Add:	228 Long St cape town, South Africa
Tel:	27-3-3456666
Fax:	27-3-3456667
Website:	www.nkk.com.sa
Email:	johnson@gmail.com
Business scope:	household appliance
Overseas markets:	America, Europe, Asia

Task description

Mike, a sales manager of Guangzhou Med International Trade Co., Ltd. (herein called C Co., Ltd.) got the initial order from NKK Trade Co., Ltd. (herein called D Co., Ltd.) last week. He will send an email to Johnson for confirming the details.

Hints

- thank for the customer's first order
- confirm some details
- express desire of further cooperation
- wish to get an early reply

Specimen letter 2

From: coolmike@hotmail.com (C Co., Ltd.)

To: johnson@gmail.com (D Co., Ltd.)

Date: June 8, 2013

Subject: initial order

Attachment:

Dear Johnson:

We'd like to place an initial order with you on the terms and conditions as follows:

Articles: Hisense Brand Air Conditioner

Specifications: HRAP 35 GW

Quantity: 3,000 sets

Unit price: US$280 /set CIF Cape town, South Africa

Total Amt. : US$840,000

Payment: by irrevocable confirmed L/C

Shipment: to be shipped within 30 days after receipt of L/C

Insurance: by seller

Look forward to receiving your confirmation ASAP.

Yours sincerely,
Mike
C Co., Ltd.

Task Practice

Task 1

Description

ABC Co., Ltd. is an import and export company of electronic computer and accessories and has enjoyed a good reputation.

Clark, a foreign salesperson of ABC Co., Ltd. has got a repeat order of 500 sets of PC from BCD Co., Ltd. He will send an email to BCD Co., Ltd. for thanking for regular orders from BCD Co., Ltd.

Requirements

You are required to send an email to BCD Co., Ltd. as the role of Clark, according to the following tips.

Tips

- inform the customer of sending the ordered goods
- thank the customer for their regular orders
- satisfy the customer with fine quality goods at reasonable prices
- wish to get more further business opportunities

From: ____________________

To: ____________________

Date: ____________________

Subject: ____________________

____

____

____

____

Specimen letter 3

Suggested answer for Task 1

From: coolboy@hotmail.com (ABC Co., Ltd.)
To: prettygirl@bcd.com (BCD Co., Ltd.)
Date: Feb 8, 2013
Subject: thanks for your order
Attachment:
Dear Sir or Madam: I'm writing to let you know that your Order No. F1302 for 500 sets personal computers was shipped yesterday via UPS to reach you on or before Mar 5, 2013. Your regular orders are always highly appreciated. We haven't written to you for each purchase, but we'd like to let you know that we make every effort to satisfy your need with fine quality goods at reasonable prices. Thank you very much for your cooperation and welcome further business opportunities. Yours faithfully, Clark ABC Co., Ltd.

Task 2

Description

B Co., Ltd. is an importer of foodstuff in Shanghai, China.

Mary, a foreign salesperson of B Co., Ltd. has made a purchase order of 500 kgs first-class coffee from A Co., Ltd. She will send an email to A Co., Ltd. for confirming this order.

Requirements

You are required to write an email to A Co., Ltd. as the role of Mary, according to the following tips and attached purchase order.

Tips

- thank for email from A Co., Ltd.
- confirm the details of the order
- enclose the purchase order
- state the payment after receipt of the countersigned purchase order
- wish to get an early reply

Attachment 1: purchase order

B CO., LTD.
346 HUAI HAI ROAD SHANGHAI CHINA
TEL: +86-21-56783355 FAX: +86-21-56783355

TO: **A CO., LTD.** **Purchase Order NO.** **123**
Date: **Jan 9, 2013**

Please supply the following:

Commodity	Specification	Quantity	Price	Total
Coffee	First class	500 kgs	US$20 CIF Shanghai	US$10,000

Comments: Insurance made by seller for 110% of invoice value.
Shipment in Mar, 2013
Payment : 30% in advance by T/T, 70% by D/P.
Authorized: *Mary*

From: ______________________
To: ______________________
Date: ______________________
Subject: ______________________

____
____
____
____
____
____

Specimen letter 4

Suggested answer for Task 2

From: prettygirl@yahoo.com (B Co., Ltd.)
To: coolboy@hotmail.com (A Co., Ltd.)
Date: Jan 9, 2013
Subject: order confirmation
Attachment: Purchase order
Dear Sir or Madam: Thank you for your email of Jan 8. We appreciate your cooperation and are pleased to confirm the order as follows: 500 kgs of first-class coffee at US$20 per ton CIF Shanghai, for shipment in Mar, 2013. Enclosed please find our Purchase Order No.123 and return one signed copy ASAP. We are arranging 30% payment of total value by T/T with Bank of China, Shanghai branch, upon receipt of the above mentioned Purchase Order in time. Yours sincerely, Mary B Co., Ltd.

Notes

1. All the terms and conditions are acceptable to us. 我方可接受所有条款及条件。
2. arrange L/C establishment with our bank 安排与我方银行开立信用证
3. draw your attention to the fact that 请贵方关注的事实是……
   类似的表达还有：invite one's attention to…
4. appreciate your cooperation 感谢贵方的合作
5. confirm the order as follows 兹确认订单如下
6. Enclosed please find sth… 是"please find enclosed sth."的倒装形式，商务函电中较常用。表示"随函附上……，请查收。"

7. to place an initial order with you 向某人初次订购……或向某人初次下订单
8. on the terms and conditions as follows 按如下条件及条款……
9. Your regular orders are always highly appreciated. 非常感谢贵方的定期/日常的订单。
10. We make every effort to do sth. 我方尽力去做某事
11. ...satisfy your need with fine quality goods at reasonable prices.
以价格合理、品质优良的货物来满足贵方的需求。

New Words and Expressions

1. acceptance — *n.* 接受、承诺，接受函
2. purchase — *n.*/*v.* 购买，采购
3. order — *n.*/*v.* 订单，订货
4. via — *prep.* 通过
5. initial — *a.* 初次的
6. regular — *a.* 固定的，常规的
7. terms and conditions — 条件及条款
8. Air Conditioner — 空调
9. OSAKA — 大阪，日本一港口
10. confirmation — *n.* 确认书，确认函

Business Link

◆ 关于 Acceptance（接受或承诺）的生效

《联合国国际货物销售合同公约》规定，受要约人做出声明或以其他行为对要约或报盘（Offer）表示同意，即为接受或承诺（Acceptance）。它一旦生效，合同即告成立，对双方当事人有约束力。

关于 Acceptance （接受或承诺）何时生效，各国的法律规定不尽相同。但大致有以下几种原则：

（1）英美法的“投递主义原则”

英美法认为，凡是以信件、函电等做出接受或承诺时，则该接受或承诺一经投递立即生效，合同即告成立。

（2）大陆法的“到达主义原则”

《德国民法典》规定：“对于相对人所做的意思表示，于意思表示到达相对人时发生效力。”因此，接受或承诺的通知必须到达相对人时才生效，合同即告成立。

（3）《公约》的规定

《公约》对于接受或承诺的生效时间，原则上采用“到达主义原则”。

◆ **关于对 offer 做了变更的 acceptance（接受或承诺）的效力**

（1）有效

《公约》19 条第 2 款规定，对要约（offer）表示接受或承诺（acceptance）但附加或变更了一些条件的答复，如这些条件不是实质上变更要约条件，可作为接受或承诺，合同有效。

（2）无效

《公约》19 条第 3 款规定，对要约（offer）表示接受或承诺（acceptance）但附加或变更了一些条件的答复，如这些条件对下列事项做了添加或变更，则是实质上变更要约条件，不能作为接受或承诺，合同无效：

1）货物价格；2）付款；3）货物数量与质量；4）交货时间与地点；5）当事人的责任范围；6）解决争议的办法等。

◆ **UPS**

UPS 是 Universal Parcel Service（美国联合包裹运输公司）的缩写。该公司是于 1907 年在美国成立的一家信使公司，由于明确地定位于支持全球商业的目标，现已经发展成为一家拥有 400 多亿美元资产的全球大型公司。UPS 目前不仅是全世界最大的快递公司，而且还是专业的运输、物流、与电子商务信息的领军企业。

其特点：速度快，范围广，定时定点，全程跟踪，通关便捷。

◆ **答谢客户**

写信感谢客户订货是出口商与客户维护良好关系的妙招。一般来说，客户订货是对出口方的一种恩惠，出口方理应表示感谢。但现实中，不可能每次都写信致谢。故答谢有一定的技巧：对于老客户，不必每次都致谢，可在年底或重要的节假日致信表示感谢，维系良好的合作关系；对于新客户，要重视，首次订货后最好能够及时写信致谢，维护刚刚开始的业务关系。

More to Practice

I. Translate the following business terms or expressions into English.

1. 接受
2. 订单
3. 首次订单
4. 续订单
5. 条件及条款
6. 联合国国际货物销售合同公约
7. 中国银行
8. 定期订单
9. 美国联合包裹运输公司
10. 未来的商机

II. Translate the following sentences into Chinese.

1. If the goods we ordered can not be delivered at that time, we have to cancel the order.
2. We trust the first order will lead to our further cooperation.
3. The above order is urgent need; please effect shipment as soon as possible.
4. If your first order proves satisfactory, we will place regular orders with you.

5. Although your price is on the high side, we will place the order with you in view to keep a long term business relationship.
6. We are looking forward to receiving your first order.
7. We hope the goods will reach you in due course and be satisfactory to you.
8. We have accepted your Order No.123 for 6,000 dozen T-shirts.
9. We are ready to place a large order with you for Haier Brand washing machines if your price is competitive.
10. If your goods are fine in quality and excellent in workmanship at reasonable prices, we are prepared to place regular and large orders with you.

III. Translate the following sentences into English.

1. 很高兴告知贵方我们打算订购 6 000 双红蜻蜓牌男士皮鞋。
2. 如贵方产品质优价廉，我方将长期订购。
3. 我们对贵方的产品质量优良、工艺精湛表示满意。
4. 从贵方 5 月 5 日的电邮中，欣悉贵方打算订购我方的丝绸产品。
5. 很高兴从贵方昨日的传真中得知对首次订单货物满意。
6. 本公司打算大量订购贵方的吉利轿车，由于其具有竞争力的价格。
7. 相信本次订单不但能促进双方未来的贸易而且能增进之间的友谊。
8. 贵方龙井茶品质优良，誉满全球，我们客户非常欣赏。如价格再优惠，我司将大量长期订购。
9. 本公司欲订购贵司浪莎牌男士袜子 5 000 打 CIF Osaka 价，请尽快报价。
10. 兹确认贵方 3 月 8 日订单：2 000 套雅戈尔男士西服每套 CIF London ￡280，6 月装船。

IV. Writing practice.

Please write a letter of initial order according to the following given information.

Sender’s information:
Name: Louis
Company: Green power Equipment Imp and Exp Co., Ltd.
Email: greenidea@hotmail.com
Products: Fuel Economizers

Recipient’s information:
Name: Alice
Company: Green Products Imp and Exp Co., Ltd.
Email: sunnygirl@gmail.com
Subject: the initial order
Date: Jan 8, 2013

Unit 7

Business Contract

Study Aims

应知目标

1. To understand the forms and contents of a Sales/Purchase Confirmation.
2. To understand the forms and contents of a Sales/Purchase Contract.
3. To know the knowledge of "Lead in" Part.
4. To know the knowledge of "Business Link" Part.

应会目标

1. To be able to translate a Sales/Purchase Confirmation.
2. To be able to make a Sales/Purchase Confirmation.
3. To be able to translate a Sales/Purchase Contract.
4. To be able to make a Sales/Purchase Contract.

Lead in

- Once an acceptance is confirmed, it means a deal. In international trade, usually a contract will be made to further specify the rights and obligations of both buyers and sellers for legal purposes. If any conflict between the parties concerned happens later, reference is generally made to the contract in an effort to resolve the misunderstanding. So it is vital that the contract is negotiated with great care so that both buyers and sellers are able to live within its terms and conditions. After signing the contract, the parties concerned are legally bound to honor their agreements.
- There are no specific requirements about the form of contract in international trade, but some often used forms are as follows:

1) Formal contract (Sales Contract, Purchase Contract)
2) Confirmation (Sales Confirmation, Purchase Confirmation)
3) Agreement

Of above all, the first two are more commonly used in international trade in China. Once a transaction is concluded, buyers and sellers may sign a contract (confirmation, agreement) face to face. But in most cases, it is hard for them to do so, while one party can make the contract (confirmation, agreement) and sign two copies, and then send them to the other party for countersignature and return of only one copy for file.

Writing Skills

Step 1: To thank the order

Step 2: To send the relative S/C

Step 3: To state one's requirements

Step 4: To express the wish of good cooperation

Key Sentence Patterns

1. Thank you for your email of Jan 15, 2013 asking us to send the Sales Confirmation.
2. We are sending you our Sales Confirmation No.168 in duplicate.
3. Please countersign the enclosed S/C and send us one copy back.
4. Upon receipt of your covering L/C, we'll effect shipment without any delay.
5. Thank you very much for your sending Purchase Confirmation to us.
6. We are sending the countersigned S/C to you by FedEx, which will reach you in due course.
7. We'd like to stress the importance of punctual shipment of our order within the validity of the L/C.
8. Enclosed please find our S/C No.168 and let us know if everything is acceptable to you.
9. This sales confirmation is made by and between the Sellers and the Buyers.
10. The buyers agree to buy and the sellers agree to sell the under mentioned commodity according to the terms and conditions below.
11. It is mutually agreed that Certificate of Quality issued by public inspection organization at the port of shipment shall be taken as the basis of delivery.
12. Any claim by the Buyers against the goods shipped shall be filed within 30 days after the arrival of the goods at the port of destination.
13. If shipment of the contracted goods is prevented or delayed in whole or in part due to Force Majeure, the Sellers shall not be liable for non-shipment or late shipment of the goods under this Contract.

Case Study

Case 1

Business background

Sender's information:

Name:	Mary
Company:	Southafrican Sunflower Trade Co., Ltd.
Add:	227 Long St Capetown, South Africa
Tel:	27-21-3456666
Fax:	27-21-3456667
Website:	www.afslt.com.sa
Email:	maryl@gmail.com
Business scope:	foodstuff, kitchenware
Overseas markets:	America, Europe, Asia, Africa

Recipient's information:

Name:	Jack
Company:	Hangzhou Hollway Trade Co., Ltd.
Add:	118 Wensan Rd Hangzhou, Zhejiang, P.R.China 310000
Tel:	0086-571-82826266
Fax:	0086-571-82826267
Website:	www.hzhlt.com.cn
Email:	jackabc@hotmail.com
Business scope:	foodstuff, kitchenware, flower pots
Overseas markets:	Europe, America, Asia, South America

Task description

Jack, a sales manager of Hangzhou Hollway Trade Co., Ltd. (herein called C Co., Ltd.) got an S/C from Mary of Southafrican Sunflower Trade Co., Ltd. (herein called D Co., Ltd.) last week. He will send an email to Mary for informing her that the countersigned S/C will be sent today.

Hints

- inform the buyer of receiving the S/C
- send the countersigned S/C
- wish the buyer to rush L/C establishment

Specimen letter 1

From: jackabc@hotmail.com (C Co., Ltd.)	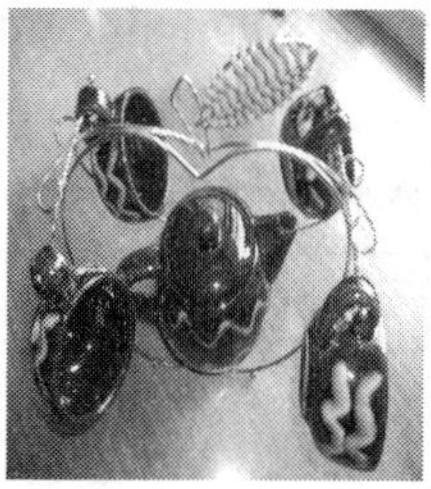 
To: maryl@gmail.com (D Co., Ltd.)	
Date: Dec 5, 2012	
Subject: S/C	
Attachment: S/C	

Dear Mary:

I'm writing to let you know that we have signed the Sales Contract No. 666 and sent to you today.

Please find the enclosed S/C in attachment.

Thank you for your cooperation in rushing L/C establishment.

Yours sincerely,

Jack

C Co., Ltd.

Attachment

Sales Contract

NO. 666

Date: _______ **Place:**_______

Sellers: Southafrican Sunflower Trade Co., Ltd.
Add: 227 Long St Cape town, South Africa

Tel: +27-21-3456666
Fax: +27-21-3456667

Buyers: Hangzhou Hollway Trade Co., Ltd.
Add: 118 Wensan Rd Hangzhou, P.R.China

Tel: + 86-571-82826266
Fax: + 86-571-82826267

This contract is made by and between the Sellers and the Buyers, whereby the buyers

agree to buy and the sellers agree to sell the under mentioned commodity according to the terms and conditions below:

Commodity: porcelain coffee pots

Specifications: HRCR1268

Quantity: 2,000 sets

Unit price: US$7.8 /set CIF Shanghai, China

Total Amt.: US$156,000

Payment: by irrevocable confirmed L/C draft payable at 30 days

Shipment: Jan. /Feb., 2013

Shipping marks: at seller's option

Port of shipment: Cape Town, South Africa

Port of destination: Shanghai, China

Transshipment and partial shipment: allowed

Insurance: by the buyer

Commodity Inspection: It is mutually agreed that Certificate of Quality and Weight issued by public inspection organization at the port of shipment shall be taken as the basis of delivery.

Discrepancy and Claim: Any claim by the Buyers on the goods shipped shall be filed within 30 days after the arrival of the goods at port of destination and supported by a survey report issued by a public surveyor approved by the Sellers. Claims in respect of matters within the responsibility of the insurance company or of the shipping company will not be considered or entertained by the Sellers.

Force Majeure: If shipment of the contracted goods is prevented or delayed in whole or in part due to Force Majeure, the Sellers shall not be liable for non-shipment or late shipment of the goods under this Contract. However the Sellers shall notify the Buyers by fax and furnish the Latter within 15 days by registered airmail with a certificate issued by the local chamber of commerce attesting such event or events.

Sellers (signature): ________________ **Buyers (signature):** ________________

Case 2

Business background

Sender's information:

Name:	Tom
Company:	Hangzhou Hope Trade Co., Ltd.
Add:	128 Wensan Rd Hangzhou, Zhejiang, P.R.China 310000
Tel:	0086-571-88886266
Fax:	0086-571-88886267
Website:	www.hzht.com.cn
Email:	nicetea@yahoo.com
Business scope:	foodstuff, wine, toy, textiles, shoes
Overseas markets:	Europe, America, Asia, South America

Recipient's information:

Name:	Dawn
Company:	American Sunny Trade Co., Ltd.
Add:	227 Hero St New York, US
Tel:	1-21-3456666
Fax:	1-21-3456667
Website:	www.ast.com.am
Email:	coolgirl2@gmail.com
Business scope:	foodstuff
Overseas markets:	Europe, Asia, Africa

Task description

Tom, manager of Hangzhou Hope Trade Co., Ltd. (herein called A Co., Ltd.) has received an email from Dawn of American Sunny Trade Co., Ltd. (herein called B Co., Ltd.) asking him to send an S/C covering 600 kgs of Green tea at US$36 per kg. He will send an email to Dawn for asking her to countersign the S/C, return one copy and arrange L/C establishment ASAP.

Hints

- thank for receiving email
- confirm some transaction terms
- state one's requirement for L/C establishment
- thank for cooperation

Specimen letter 2

From: nicetea@yahoo.com (A Co., Ltd.)

To: coolgirl2@gmail.com (B Co., Ltd.)

Date: Mar 5, 2013

Subject: Sending an S/C

Attachment:

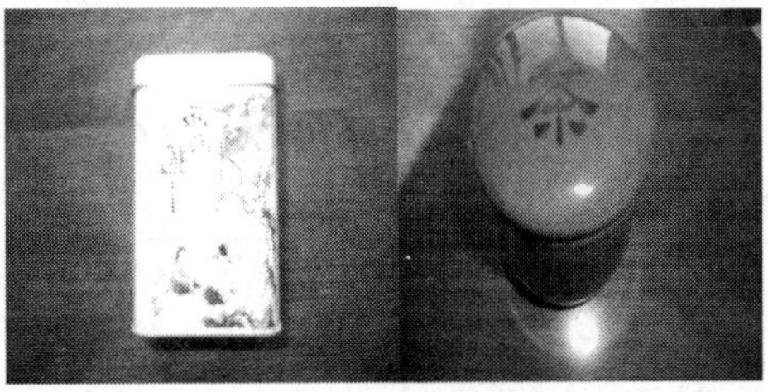

Dear Dawn:

Thank you for your email of Feb 25, 2013 asking us to send the Sales Confirmation covering 600 kgs of first-class Green Tea at US$36 per kg CIF New York.

We are sending you our Sales Confirmation No.335 in duplicate. Please countersign them and send us back one copy.

We hope you can arrange L/C establishment with your bank ASAP.

Upon receipt of your covering L/C, we'll effect shipment without any delay.

Thanks for your full cooperation.

Yours sincerely,

Tom

manager

A Co., Ltd.

Task Practice

Task 1

Description

ABC Co., Ltd. is an import and export company of household appliances and has enjoyed a good reputation.

Mike, a foreign salesperson of ABC Co., Ltd. has got an initial order of 2,500 sets of Hisense Brand air conditioners from BCD Co., Ltd. He has made a sales confirmation and will send an email to BCD Co., Ltd. for confirming it with BCD Co., Ltd.

Requirements

You are required to send an email to BCD Co., Ltd. as the role of Mike, according to the following tips and the S/C.

Tips

- thank the customer for their initial order
- ask the customer to confirm details of the sales confirmation
- ask the customer to sign the S/C and return one copy
- wish to get more further business opportunities

From: ______________________________

To: ______________________________

Date: ______________________________

Subject: ______________________________

____

____

____

____

____

____

____

____

____

Specimen letter 3

Suggested answer for Task 1

From: coolboy@hotmail.com (ABC Co., Ltd.)
To: prettygirl@bcd.com (BCD Co., Ltd.)
Date: Feb 8, 2013
Subject: thanks for your order
Attachment: S/C No.268
Dear Sir or Madam: Thank you very much for your initial order with us. Enclosed please find our S/C No.268 and let us know if everything is acceptable to you. If everything is OK, please sign them and return one copy to us. Thank you very much for your cooperation and welcome further business opportunities. Yours faithfully, Mike ABC Co., Ltd.

Attachment

Sales Confirmation
NO. 268

Sellers: ABC CO., LTD.
Buyers: BCD CO., LTD.
This sales confirmation is made by and between the Sellers and the Buyers, whereby the buyers agree to buy and the sellers agree to sell the under mentioned commodity according to the terms and conditions below:
Commodity: Hisense Brand Air Conditioners
Specifications: HRAP 35 GW
Quantity: 2,500 sets
Unit price: US$300 /set CIF DUBAI
Total Amt. : US$750,000
Payment: by irrevocable L/C
Shipment: to be shipped within 30 days after receipt of L/C
Shipping marks: at seller's option

Port of shipment: China ports
Port of destination: Dubai
Insurance: by seller

Done and signed in ______ on _______.

Task 2

Description

B Co., Ltd. is an importer of foodstuff in New York, US.

Mary , salesperson of B Co., Ltd. has received the S/C of 600 kgs first-class green tea from Jack of A Co., Ltd. She countersigned them in duplicate and sent one copy to A Co.,Ltd. She will send an email to Jack for informing him of above and asking him to urge shipment in time.

Requirements

You are required to write an email to A Co., Ltd. as the role of Mary, according to the following tips.

Tips

- thank for the S/C from A Co., Ltd.
- countersign the S/C and return one copy by FedEx
- open the L/C with Bank of China, New York branch
- state the importance of punctual shipment
- wish to have good cooperation

From: ______________________________

To: ______________________________

Date: ______________________________

Subject: ______________________________

____

____

____

Specimen letter 4

Suggested answer for Task 2

From: prettygirl@yahoo.com (B Co., Ltd.)
To: coolboy@hotmail.com (A Co., Ltd.)
Date: Mar 9, 2013
Subject: order confirmation
Attachment: Purchase order
Dear Jack: Thank you for sending us your S/C covering 600 kgs of first-class Green Tea at US$36 per kg CIF New York. We are sending the countersigned S/C No.335 to you by FedEx, which will reach you in due course. We have opened the L/C in your favor with Bank of China, New York branch. Because of urgent need of the goods, we'd like to stress the importance of punctual shipment of our order within the validity of the L/C. Wish to have good cooperation between us. Yours sincerely, Mary B Co., Ltd.

Notes

1. Thank you for your email of Jan 15, 2013 asking us to send the Sales Confirmation.
   感谢贵方 2013 年 1 月 15 日的电邮，要求我方寄送销售确认书。
   asking sb. to do sth. 请求某人做某事
   covering sth. 关于某物、某事

2. We are sending you our Sales Confirmation No. 168 in duplicate.
   兹寄送编号为 168 的销售确认书一式两份。
   in duplicate 一式两份
   in triplicate 一式三份
   in quadruplicate 一式四份
   in quintuplicate 一式五份
3. Please countersign the enclosed S/C and send us one copy back.
   请会签随函附上的销售确认书并寄回其中一份。
4. Upon receipt of your covering L/C, we'll effect shipment without any delay.
   一收到相关的信用证，我方将立即安排装运。
5. We are sending the counter-signed S/C to you by FedEx, which will reach you in due course.
   我方已通过联邦快递公司寄送已经会签的销售确认书，相信会及时到达贵方。
6. We'd like to stress the importance of punctual shipment of our order within the validity of the L/C. 我方想强调一下贵方在信用证有效期内按时装运的重要性。
7. The buyers agree to buy and the sellers agree to sell the under mentioned commodity according to the terms and conditions below.
   兹经买卖双方同意按如下条款达成下列商品交易。
8. It is mutually agreed that... 兹经双方同意……
9. ...supported by a survey report issued by a public surveyor approved by the Sellers.
   由卖方同意的公证机构出具的检验报告作为支撑材料……
10. Claims in respect of matters ... will not be considered or entertained by the Sellers.
    关于某些方面的索赔，卖方不予受理。
11. ...due to Force Majeure, the Sellers shall not be liable for non-shipment or late shipment of the goods under this Contract. 由于不可抗力导致的……，卖方对于本合同项下货物的没有装运或延迟装运不承担责任。
12. ...the Sellers shall notify the Buyers by fax and furnish the Latter within 15 days by registered airmail with a certificate issued by the local chamber of commerce attesting such event or events. 卖方应该通知买方，并在 15 天内用挂号航空邮件给买方由当地商会出具的事故证明书。

New Words and Expressions

1. conflict	*n.* 冲突，矛盾
2. vital	*a.* 重要的
3. countersign	*v.* 会签
4. inspection	*n.* 检验
5. duplicate	*a.* 完全相同的 *n.* 副本 *v.* 复制
6. at seller's option	由卖方决定

7. in most cases 在大多数情况下
8. in due course 及时
9. Certificate of Quality 品质检验证书
10. discrepancy and claim 异议与索赔
11. Force Majeure 不可抗力
12. attest *v.* 证明

Business Link

◆《联合国国际货物销售合同公约》

《联合国国际货物销售合同公约》是迄今为止关于国际货物买卖的一个重要的国际公约。该公约共分四个部分：（1）适用范围；（2）合同成立；（3）货物买卖；（4）最后条款。全文共 101 条。该公约于 1980 年 3 月在维也纳召开的外交会议上获得通过，并于 1988 年 1 月 1 日起生效。

我国是《联合国国际货物销售合同公约》的最早成员国之一。我国政府曾派代表参加了 1980 年的维也纳会议，并于 1986 年 12 月向联合国递交了关于该公约的核准书，成为该公约的缔约国。但我国在核准该公约时，有两项予以保留：（1）关于采用书面形式的保留；（2）关于公约适用范围的保留。

◆ 合同的形式

交易双方达成一项交易后，应立即签订合同，以保护双方的利益。但不同的交易应选择不同的订立形式。主要包括口头和书面两大类形式。我国涉外经济合同法规定："当事人就合同条款以书面形式达成协议并签字，即为合同成立。通过信件、传真等达成协议，一方当事人要求签订确认书的，签订确认书时，合同成立。"

◆ 外贸书面合同的主要形式

在外贸业务实际中，以下几种是常用的书面合同形式，受法律保护和约束：

a）合同 Contract

正式的销售或购买合同，格式规范，内容详细，对于双方的权利义务以及违约、争议及处理等方面都有详尽的说明。

b）确认书 Confirmation

销售或购买确认书是一种简式合同，只列出交易的主要条款，大多没有对双方的权利义务以及违约、争议及处理等方面详尽的说明。

c）协议书 Agreement

协议书比较灵活，可简可繁。一般用于一些代理等合作方式。

d）订单 Order

订单一般是指买方制作的一种书面购买承诺书，签字后递交卖方并会签。有时也可由卖方制作，买方填写并签字。这事实上也是一种合同，双方当事人均有约束力。

More to Practice

I. Translate the following business terms or expressions into English.

1. 销售确认书
2. 销售合同
3. 购货确认书
4. 购货合同
5. 协议书
6. 一式三份
7. 品质检验证书
8. 数量检验证书
9. 异议与索赔
10. 不可抗力

II. Translate the following sentences into Chinese.

1. Please sign and return one copy of S/C for our file.
2. Upon receipt of your countersigned P/C, we'll arrange L/C with our bank.
3. Upon receipt of your L/C, we'll arrange shipment without any delay.
4. If everything is OK, please sign the S/C as soon as possible.
5. We'd like to let you know that we have sent the S/C to you today by DHL.
6. We are sending you our Sales Confirmation No.225 in duplicate.
7. Please find the enclosed P/C in triplicate in attachment.
8. The buyers agree to buy and the sellers agree to sell the under mentioned commodity according to the terms and conditions below.
9. The Sellers shall not be liable for non-shipment or late shipment of the goods under this Contract.
10. A contract is a formal written agreement, which sets forth rights and obligations of the parties concerned.

III. Translate the following sentences into English.

1. 很高兴告知贵方我们已收到贵方的销售确认书。
2. 如各项条款合适，请尽快会签。
3. 按贵方要求，我方已寄去 123 号销售合同一式两份。
4. 贵方 5 月 5 日的电邮收悉，要求我方寄送相关销售确认书。
5. 请会签 168 号销售合同，并寄回一份以便我方存档。
6. 兹经买卖双方同意按如下条款达成下列商品交易。
7. 索赔由卖方同意的公证机构出具的检验报告作为支撑。
8. 关于保险公司方面的索赔，卖方不予受理。
9. 由于不可抗力，卖方对于本合同项下货物的没有装运或延迟装运不承担责任。
10. 卖方必须及时通知买方并在 15 天内用挂号航空邮件附上由当地商会出具的事故证明书。

IV. Writing practice.

Please make an S/C according to the following Chinese information:

卖方：中国土畜产总公司江苏分公司

买方：布莱特有限公司

品名：中国甜薯片

规格：大路货，水分不超过 10%

数量：10 000 吨 +/–5%

价格：US$180/MT CIF New York

总价：US$1,800,000

支付：不可撤销即期信用证

包装：散装

装运：2007 年 12 月到 2008 年 1 月

唛头：卖方决定

保险：由卖方按发票金额的 110%投保一切险和战争险

检验：品质、数量、重量等以中国出入境检验检疫局出具的证明为最终依据

其他条款：略

Unit 8

Payment

Study Aims

应知目标

1. To know three main terms of payment and their procedures.
2. To know the knowledge of "Lead in" Part.
3. To know the knowledge of "Business Link" Part.

应会目标

1. To be able to translate these terms of payment and procures.
2. To be able to write a letter of payment.

Lead in

Payment is an important issue in international trade. No export transaction can be regarded as successful until the money has been paid for the goods delivered overseas, and the proceeds have been safely credited to the exporter's account.

In international trade, there are major modes of payment that the buyers may adopt namely remittance, collection and letter of credit (L/C).

Payment sometimes is made by collection or remittance. These two modes of payment rely on commercial credit between sellers and buyers. Remittance means the buyer send the payment through bank or other forms to the receiver initiatively. It is divided into three forms of mail transfer (M/T), telegraphic transfer (T/T) and demand draft (D/D). Collection means the creditor issues the bill of exchange and entrusts the bank to collect the payment of the shipment. It has two forms: one is documents against payment (D/P), and the other documents against acceptance (D/A).

L/C is used in cases where the exporter wishes to avoid the risk, and it involves a guarantee of the bank opening the L/C. It is one of the most common forms of payment in international business. A letter of credit is a document issued by a bank (issuing bank) stating its commitment to pay the seller a stated amount of money on behalf of the buyer as long as the seller meets very specific terms and conditions. Letters of credit are more formally called documentary letters of credit, and are with different types.

Writing Skills

Step 1: To mention the contract, goods, etc.
Step 2: To suggest the terms of payment
Step 3: To give out the reason
Step 4: To wish the reader to accept

Key Sentence Patterns

1. After careful study of your proposal, we agree to D/P payment terms for this contract.
2. For future transactions D/P will only be accepted if the amount involved for each transaction is below $5,000.
3. If the amount exceeds that figure, payment by L/C will be required.
4. The consignment 245 will leave Ningbo by S.S. Kunlun, due to arrive at Port Klang sometime in late February.
5. We have drawn on you at 60 days and passed the draft and shipping documents to our branch.
6. The documents will be presented to you by the Citi Bank against your acceptance of the draft.
7. We would appreciate it very much if you could ship the goods to us on T/T basis.
8. Payment by confirmed, irrevocable L/C payable by draft at sight is convenient for us.
9. On receipt of L/C we shall make the necessary arrangement for the shipment of your order.
10. Any request for further assistance or information will receive our immediate attention.

Case Study

Case 1
Business background

Sender's information:

Name:	Jack
Company:	Hangzhou Hollway Trade Co., Ltd.
Add:	118 Wensan Rd Hangzhou, Zhejiang, P.R.China 310000
Tel:	0086-571-82826266
Fax:	0086-571-82826267
Website:	www.hzhlt.com.cn
Email:	jackabc@hotmail.com
Business scope:	foodstuff, kitchenware, flower pots
Overseas markets:	Europe, America, Asia, South America

Recipient's information:

Name:	Mary
Company:	Southafrican Sunflower Trade Co., Ltd.
Add:	227 Long St Capetown, South Africa
Tel:	27-21-3456666
Fax:	27-21-3456667
Website:	www.afslt.com.sa
Email:	maryl@gmail.com
Business scope:	foodstuff, kitchenware
Overseas markets:	America, Europe, Asia, Africa

Task description

Jack of Hangzhou Hollway Trade Co., Ltd. (herein called B Co., Ltd.) contacts Mary, manager of Southafrican Sunflower Trade Co., Ltd. (herein called A Co., Ltd.) on the net. He will send an email to Mary for asking for T/T payment term for waists under No.666 Order with total value of US$15,600.

Hints

- mention the contract No, total value and products
- express thanks for T/T payment
- wish to get an early reply

Specimen letter 1

From: jackabc@hotmail.com (B Co., Ltd.)
To: maryl@gmail.com (A Co., Ltd.)
Date: Dec 5, 2012
Subject: ask for T/T payment
Attachment:
Dear Mary: Reference is made to your contract No. 888 covering coffee pots in the amount of US$15,600. As it is less than US$20,000 in value, we would appreciate it very much if you could ship the goods to us on T/T basis. We hope you will accommodate us in this respect and look forward to your favorable reply soon. Yours sincerely, Jack Manager

Case 2
Business background

Sender's information:

Name:	Mike
Company:	Guangzhou Med International Trade Co., Ltd.
Add:	298 Liuhua Rd Guangzhou, Guangdong, P.R.China 318000
Tel:	0086-20-68886666
Fax:	0086-20-68886667
Website:	www.gzmedit.com.cn
Email:	coolmike@hotmail.com
Business scope:	household appliances
Overseas markets:	Japan, Korea, Africa

Recipient's information:

Name:	Johnson
Company:	Japan NKK Trade Co., Ltd.
Add:	227 Long St Capetown, Japan
Tel:	0086-21-3456666
Fax:	0086-21-3456667
Website:	www.hzfnw.com.cn
Email:	johnson@gmail.com
Business scope:	shoes, garments
Overseas markets:	America, Europe, Asia

Task description

Mike, a sales manager of Guangzhou Med International Trade Co., Ltd. (herein called C Co., Ltd.) got an email from Japan NKK Trade Co., Ltd. (herein called D Co., Ltd.) last week asking for payment terms. He will send an email to Johnson for giving a reply.

Hints

- thank for the customer's first order
- confirm payment terms
- express desire of further cooperation
- wish to get an early reply

Specimen letter 2

From: coolmike@hotmail.com (C Co., Ltd.)
To: johnson@gmail.com (D Co., Ltd.)
Date: June 8, 2013
Subject: L/C payment
Attachment:
Dear Johnson: We're glad to place an initial order with you. As to our terms of payment, it is usually required to be made by an irrevocable letter of credit, payable by draft at sight, reaching us 30 days ahead of shipment, remaining valid for negotiation in China. We hope the above payment terms will be acceptable to you and expect more business opportunities. Look forward to receiving your confirmation ASAP. Yours sincerely, Mike C Co., Ltd.

Task Practice

Task 1

Description

ABC Co., Ltd. is an import and export company of electronic computer and accessories and has enjoyed a good reputation.

Clark, a sales manager of ABC Co., Ltd. got an email from BCD Co., Ltd. last week asking for D/P payment. He will send an email to BCD Co., Ltd. for giving a favorable reply.

Requirements

You are required to send an email to BCD Co., Ltd. as the role of Clark, according to the following tips.

Tips

- inform the customer of receiving requirement for D/P payment
- agree to the payment terms
- state one's usual payment by L/C, only value below $5,000 by D/P
- wish to get more further business opportunities

From: ______________________________

To: ______________________________

Date: ______________________________

Subject: ______________________________

____

____

____

____

____

____

____

____

Specimen letter 3

Suggested answer for Task 1

From: coolboy@hotmail.com (ABC Co., Ltd.)
To: prettygirl@bcd.com (BCD Co., Ltd.)
Date: Feb 8, 2013
Subject: agree to D/P payment
Attachment:
Dear Sir or Madam: We have received your email of Feb 5, asking for D/P terms of payment. Considering long term business relationship, we agree to D/P payment terms for this contract. However, we consider it advisable to make it clear that for future transactions D/P will only be accepted if the amount involved for each transaction is below $5,000. If the amount exceeds that figure, payment by L/C will be required. Thank you very much for your cooperation and welcome further business opportunities. Yours faithfully, Clark ABC Co., Ltd.

Task 2

Description

B Co., Ltd. is an importer of foodstuff in Shanghai, China.

Mary , a foreign salesperson of B Co., Ltd. has received an email from A Co., Ltd. asking for D/A payment terms. She will send an email to A Co., Ltd. informing the buyer of her usual practice of payment by L/C or D/P at sight .

Requirements

You are required to reply an email to A Co., Ltd. as the role of Mary, according to the following tips.

Tips

- thank for email from A Co., Ltd.
- express the understanding of A Co., Ltd.
- state the payment requirements
- wish to get an early reply

From: ______________________________

To: ______________________________

Date: ______________________________

Subject: ______________________________

____

____

____

____

____

____

____

____

____

____

Specimen letter 4

Suggested answer for Task 2

From: prettygirl@yahoo.com (B Co., Ltd.)
To: coolboy@hotmail.com (A Co., Ltd.)
Date: Jan 9, 2013
Subject: order confirmation
Attachment: Purchase order
Dear Sir or Madam: Thank you for your email of Jan, 8 asking for payment by D/A 30 days. Unfortunately, we regret to be unable to accept it.

Payment by irrevocable L/C payable by draft at sight or D/P is convenient for us. We are now awaiting the arrival of your L/C, on receipt of which we shall make the necessary arrangements for the shipment of your order. Any request for further assistance or information will receive our immediate attention.

Yours faithfully,

Mary

B Co., Ltd.

Notes

1. payment terms 支付方式
   意思与 terms of payment 相同，类似的表达还有：modes of payment, methods of payment
2. remittance 汇付
   T/T (Telegraphic Transfer) 电汇
   M/T (Mail Transfer) 信汇
   D/D (Demand Draft) 票汇
3. collection 托收
   D/P (document against payment) 付款交单
   D/A (document against acceptance) 承兑交单
4. L/C (letter of credit) 信用证
   … payment is to be made by a confirmed irrevocable letter of credit payable by draft at sight. 支付用保兑的、不可撤销的凭即期汇票付款的信用证
5. reference is made to… 关于某事
6. ship the goods to sb. on T/T basis 以电汇方式付款的基础上给某人发货
7. in this respect 在这方面
8. make the necessary arrangement for the shipment of your order
   为你方订购的货物做好装运安排

New Words and Expressions

1. payment *n.* 支付，付款
2. proposal *n.* 提议，建议
3. advisable *a.* 可取的，明智的
4. transaction *n.* 买卖，交易
5. exceed *v.* 超过
6. consignment *n.* 货物
7. due *a.* 预定的；应到的
8. draft *n.* 汇票

9. blouse *n.* 女式衬衫
10. accommodate *v.* 照顾，通融
11. adequate *a.* 充足的
12. stock *n.* 贮存，存货
13. warehouse *n.* 仓库
14. receipt *n.* 收到

Business Link

◆ 支付方式

出口商为了适应国际间激烈的竞争，竞相采用各种灵活的贸易方式以扩大出口，特别是在支付条款方面，给予国外进口商以各种优惠待遇。目前出口商较常用的支付方式有：

1. 信用证支付（L/C payment)，其缺点是进口商的费用负担大。进口商到银行开立信用证，不但要付银行手续费，而且要先付垫头（Margin)，损失利息。一般来说，这对扩大外销不利，但收汇相当稳妥。采用信用证支付方式，为了适应竞争，出口商常在价格上给予优惠。

2. 付款交单（D/P)，进口商不开信用证，由出口商开出汇票连同装运单证通过银行向进口商收款，进口商必须付清货款才能取得单证。这种方式属于托收（Collection）方式，也有人把这种方式称作现金支付（on a cash basis)。

3. 承兑交单（D/A)，这也属于托收方式。由出口商开具汇票（Draft）连同装运单证通过银行托收。进口商只需承兑汇票即可取得单证。汇票是远期的，有 30/60/90/120 天期等。进口商在汇票到期日必须付款。在取得单证到付款日期间，进口商取得出口商的商业信用（Commercial Credit)。

4. 赊账方式（Open Account Terms)，出口商将货物赊销给进口商，双方订立契约，说明每季度/半年/年度结算一次，这种方式风险很大。

◆ 汇票

汇票是出票人签发的，委托付款人在见票时或者在指定日期无条件支付确定的金额给收款人或者持票人的票据。从以上定义可知，汇票是一种无条件支付的委托，有三个当事人：出票人、付款人和收款人。按出票人不同，可分成银行汇票和商业汇票。银行汇票，出票人是银行，付款人也是银行。商业汇票，出票人是企业或个人，付款人可以是企业、个人或银行。按是否附有包括运输单据在内的商业单据，可分为光票和跟单汇票。光票指不附带商业单据的汇票。银行汇票多是光票。跟单汇票指附有包括运输单据在内的商业单据的汇票。跟单汇票多是商业汇票。按付款日期不同，汇票可分为即期汇票和远期汇票。

◆ 信用证操作过程简介

1. 进口商和出口商之间签订一个商品买卖合同。

2. 进口商向银行（开证行）递交保证金按合同条款申请开立信用证。信用证内容要求与合同条款一致，如果不同以信用证为准。

3. 经银行（开证行）审核同意开证，银行收取开证费。信用证由开证行用 SWIFT 等

方式到进口商所在地的通知行。

4. 通知行通知出口商取信用证并收取通知费。

5. 出口商按信用证的要求出货和缮制单据。

6. 出口商将全套按 L/C 要求缮制的单据交银行（议付行）结汇。银行收取手续费并将单据寄开证行。

7. 开证行收到单据经审核无误，将货款汇到出口商银行（议付行）账户，并将单据交进口商，凭此单据清关提货。

More to Practice

I. Translate the following business terms or expressions into English.

1. 支付方式
2. 票汇
3. 托收
4. 汇付
5. 付款交单
6. 承兑交单
7. 装运单证
8. 汇票
9. 电汇
10. 不可撤销的信用证

II. Translate the following sentences into Chinese.

1. Our terms of payment are by a confirmed irrevocable letter of credit by draft at sight.
2. Since the total amount is so big and the world monetary market is rather unstable at the moment, we can not accept any terms of payment other than a Letter of Credit.
3. We would suggest that for this particular order you let us have a L/C, on receipt of which we shall ship the goods on the first available steamer.
4. In order to conclude the business, I hope you'll meet me half way. What about 50% by L/C and the balance by D/P?
5. I'd like to discuss the terms of payment with you. I wonder if you would accept D/A.
6. As we must adhere to our customary practice, we hope that you will not think us unaccommodating.
7. We have instructed our bank to open an irrevocable documentary letter of credit in your favor. The amount is $1,300.00.
8. Your request for T/T payment has been considered and we agree to grant you this facility.
9. We'd like you to accept L/C for this transaction and future ones.
10. We shall draw on you at 60 days sight after the goods have been shipped. Please honor our draft when it falls due.

III Translate the following sentences into English.

1. 你想必知道我们要求即期信用证付款吧。
2. 我们通常采用的付款方式是保兑不可撤销的信用证。

3. 关于将来的经常性订货，你们能否同意采用远期信用证呢？
4. 开立信用证会增加我们进口的成本。
5. 不可撤销的信用证会使你方出口商品得到银行的担保。
6. 由于我方向贵国出口一般采用即期信用证付款方式，这次也不能例外。
7. 开立信用证花费很大，这对我们这样的小公司来说，对资金周转影响太大，最好还是采用 D/P 或 D/A 付款方式。
8. 我方将开立以你为受益人的不可撤销信用证，在香港凭装运单据付款交单。
9. 我们通常采用不可撤销的信用证，凭装运单据结汇的付款方式。
10. 我方同意接受以见票 30 天后付款的信用证支付方式。

IV. Writing practice.

Please write a letter of asking for payment by D/P according to the following information.

Sender's information:

Name: Louis

Company: Greenpower Equipment Imp and Exp Co., Ltd.

Email: greenidea@hotmail.com

Products: Fuel Economizers

Recipient's information:

Name: Alice

Company: Green Products Imp and Exp Co., Ltd.

Email: sunnygirl@gmail.com

Subject: the initial order

Date: Jan 8, 2013

Unit 9

Letter of Credit

Study Aims

应知目标

1. To understand main clauses of an L/C.
2. To know the knowledge of "Lead in" Part.
3. To know the knowledge of "Business Link" Part.

应会目标

1. To be able to analyze an L/C.
2. To be able to translate an L/C.

Lead in

The most generally adopted method of payment is L/C, which is reliable and safe. As a usual practice, the L/C is to be established and to reach the seller one month before the date of shipment so as to leave enough time for the seller to arrange shipment.

- Parties in connection with an L/C:

1) **Applicant**: to apply for the issuing bank to issue an L/C. (usually the buyer or importer of a transaction)

2) **Issuing Bank** (Opening Bank): to issue an L/C with the request to the application from the applicant. (be responsible for payment, usually the bank in buyer's location)

3) **Beneficiary**: to get the payment. (usually the seller or exporter of a transaction)

4) **Advising Bank** (Notifying Bank): to notify/inform the beneficiary of the L/C. (usually the bank in seller's location)

5) **Negotiating Bank:** to pay or discount documentary bills from the beneficiary under the L/C. (usually the advising bank in seller's location)

6) **Paying Bank:** to be responsible for payment of the L/C. (usually the issuing bank in buyer's location)

In this unit, urging L/C establishment, L/C application and L/C specimen will be discussed.

Writing Skills

Step 1: To mention the relative contract (order, confirmation)
Step 2: To state the fact that no L/C reaches the seller
Step 3: To urge the buyer to arrange L/C establishment
Step 4: To express the seller's requirements and wish

Key Sentence Patterns

1. We usually accept payment by irrevocable L/C payable against shipping documents.
2. We cannot accept L/C available by draft at 60 days' sight.
3. We would appreciate it very much if you can accept payment by D/A at 30 days' sight.
4. Please arrange for the establishing of an irrevocable L/C in our favor.
5. Please do your utmost to rush the L/C establishment so that we can execute the contract smoothly.
6. As the amount of our Order No. 11 is below US$1,000, please agree to payment by D/P because an L/C will cost us much.
7. Emphasis has to be laid on the point that the L/C must reach us before May 1st.
8. In order to avoid subsequent amendments, please see to it that the L/C stipulations are in exact conformity with the terms and conditions of the S/C 168.
9. Please open the L/C in exact accordance with the clauses of S/C 888 ASAP to avoid future amendment.
10. This L/C will remain valid until Mar 8, 2008, confirmed by Bank of China, Hangzhou branch.
11. Payment is to be made against sight draft drawn under a confirmed, irrevocable letter of credit without recourse.
12. In compliance with your request, we exceptionally accept payment against D/P at sight.
13. Your compliance with our request will be highly appreciated.
14. We are awaiting the arrival of your L/C, on receipt of which we shall make the shipment of your order.
15. We have opened a letter of credit with ABC Bank in your favor, for US$1,000,000, covering your order No. 22, available until April 15.

Case Study

Case 1
Business background

Sender's information:

Name:	Mary
Company:	Southafrican Sunflower Trade Co., Ltd.
Add:	227 Long St Capetown, South Africa
Tel:	27-21-3456666
Fax:	27-21-3456667
Website:	www.afslt.com.sa
Email:	maryl@gmail.com
Business scope:	foodstuff, kitchenware
Overseas markets:	America, Europe, Asia, Africa

Recipient's information:

Name:	Jack
Company:	Hangzhou Hollway Trade Co., Ltd.
Add:	118 Wensan Rd Hangzhou, Zhejiang, P.R.China 310000
Tel:	0086-571-82826266
Fax:	0086-571-82826267
Website:	www.hzhlt.com.cn
Email:	jackabc@hotmail.com
Business scope:	foodstuff, kitchenware, flower pots
Overseas markets:	Europe, America, Asia, South America

Task description

Mary, manager of Southafrican Sunflower Trade Co., Ltd. (herein called B Co., Ltd.) has signed the S/C 666 with Jack, Hangzhou Hollway Trade Co., Ltd. (herein called A Co., Ltd.). But she hasn't received the L/C. She will send an email to Jack for urging the L/C.

Hints

- mention the relative contract
- state not arrival of the L/C
- urge the buyer to arrange L/C establishment
- wish to get an early reply

Specimen letter 1

From: maryl@gmail.com (A Co., Ltd.)

To: jackabc@hotmail.com (B Co., Ltd.)

Date: Dec 5, 2012

Subject: urging L/C

Attachment:

Dear Jack:

With reference to your order No.123 for 2,000 sets coffee pots under S/C 666, we'd like to invite your attention to the fact that we haven't received your L/C until now.

Please do your utmost to rush the L/C establishment so that we can execute the contract smoothly.

In order to avoid subsequent amendments, please see to it that the L/C stipulations are in exact conformity with the terms and conditions of the S/C 666.

We hope to receive your good news soon.

Yours sincerely,

Mary

B Co., Ltd.

Case 2
Business background

Sender's information:

Name:	Mike
Company:	Guangzhou Med International Trade Co., Ltd.
Add:	298 Liuhua Rd Guangzhou, Guangdong, P.R.China 318000
Tel:	0086-20-68886666
Fax:	0086-20-68886667
Website:	www.gzmedit.com.cn
Email:	coolmike@hotmail.com
Business scope:	home apps
Overseas markets:	Japan, Korea, Africa

Recipient's information:

Name:	Johnson
Company:	Japan NKK Trade Co., Ltd.
Add:	227 Sun St Osaka, Japan
Tel:	81-21-3456666
Fax:	81-21-3456667
Website:	www.nkk.com.cn
Email:	johnson@gmail.com
Business scope:	shoes, garments
Overseas markets:	America, Europe, Asia

Task description

Mike, a sales manager of Guangzhou Med International Trade Co., Ltd. (herein called C Co., Ltd.) signed the S/C 888 with Japan NKK Trade Co., Ltd. (herein called D Co., Ltd.) last week. As the date of shipment is approaching, but he has not received the covering L/C. He will send an email to Johnson for urging L/C establishment.

Hints

- thank for the S/C
- state not arrival of the L/C
- express requirements of L/C
- wish to get an early reply

Specimen letter 2

From: coolmike@hotmail.com (C Co., Ltd.)
To: johnson@gmail.com (D Co., Ltd.)
Date: June 8, 2013
Subject: urging L/C establishment
Attachment:

Dear Johnson:

Thank you for your countersigned S/C 888.
We'd like to point out that the date of shipment is approaching, but we have not received your covering L/C.
Please open the L/C in exact accordance with the clauses of S/C 888 to avoid future amendment.
Look forward to receiving your L/C ASAP.

Yours sincerely,
Mike
C Co., Ltd.

Task Practice

Task 1

Description

Jack has signed the S/C 666 with Mary. Mary sent an email informing him of not arrival of the L/C and asking Jack for urging it. He will send an email to Mary for a reply.

Requirements

You are required to send an email to Mary as the role of Jack, according to the following tips.

Tips

- mention the relative contract
- arrange L/C establishment
- state the validity of L/C
- wish to have good cooperation

From: ______________________

To: ______________________

Date: ______________________

Subject: ______________________

____

____

____

____

____

____

____

____

____

____

Specimen letter 3

Suggested answer for Task 1

From: coolboy@hotmail.com (ABC Co., Ltd.)
To: prettygirl@bcd.com (BCD Co., Ltd.)
Date: Feb 8, 2013
Subject: reply to L/C establishment
Attachment:
Dear Mary: Thank you for your S/C 666. I'm writing to let you know that we have asked the Bank of Communications, Hangzhou branch to open an irrevocable L/C in your favor. This L/C will remain valid until Mar 8, 2013, confirmed by Bank of China, Hangzhou branch and they will accept your draft on them at 30 days after sight for the amount of your full invoice value. Thank you for your cooperation and welcome more future business opportunities. Best regards, Jack

Task 2

Description

B Co., Ltd. is an importer of foodstuff in Shanghai, China.

Mary, a foreign salesperson of B Co., Ltd. has made a deal of 500 kgs first-class coffee with A Co., Ltd. Both A and B agree to pay by L/C. Mary has got the news from the seller that no arrival of the L/C. She will send an email to A Co., Ltd. for giving a reply.

Requirements

You are required to write an email to A Co., Ltd. as the role of Mary, according to the following tips.

Tips

- thank for email
- be sorry for not arrival of the L/C
- be arranging L/C establishment in the seller's favor
- wish to have good cooperation

From: ____________________

To: ____________________

Date: ____________________

Subject: ____________________

____

____

____

____

____

____

____

____

____

____

Specimen letter 4

Suggested answer for Task 2

From: prettygirl@yahoo.com (B Co., Ltd.)
To: coolboy@hotmail.com (A Co., Ltd.)
Date: Jan 9, 2013
Subject: reply to L/C establishment
Attachment:
Dear Sir or Madam: Thank you for your email of Jan 25. We're sorry to hear that you haven't received the covering L/C in your favor. We are arranging the L/C establishment with Standard and Chartered Bank, here.

We make every effort to ensure that the L/C stipulations are in exact accordance with the terms and conditions of the S/C 168.

We appreciate your cooperation and understanding.

Yours faithfully,
Mary
B Co., Ltd.

Notes

1. With reference to your order No.123 for 2,000 sets coffee pots under S/C 666...
关于根据你方 123 号订单签订的 666 号销售确认书 2 000 套咖啡壶……
再如：With reference to your email of yesterday, we learn that you are interested in ordering our typewriter No. 2188.
关于贵方昨日的电邮，我方了解到贵方有兴趣订购我方 No. 2188 的打字机。
类似的表达还有：with regard to… 相关，关于……
2. …invite your attention to the fact that we haven't received your L/C until now.
请贵方关注的是我方至今还未收到贵方的信用证。
类似的表达还有：draw your attention to the fact that…
3. Please do your utmost to rush the L/C establishment. 请贵方尽力加速开立信用证。
4. …please see to it that the L/C stipulations are in exact conformity with the terms and conditions of the S/C 168. 请务必做到信用证的规定与 168 号销售合同的条款完全一致。
5. We're sorry to hear that you haven't received the covering L/C in your favor.
很抱歉得知贵方还未收到以贵方为受益人的信用证。
6. We are arranging the L/C establishment with Standard Chartered Bank, here.
我方正在安排与渣打银行开立信用证。
7. We'd like to point out that the date of shipment is approaching, but we have not received your covering L/C. 我方想要指出的是装运期临近，可还未收到贵方的信用证。
8. Please open the L/C in exact accordance with the clauses of S/C 888 to avoid future amendment.
为了避免随后的改证，请完全按照 888 号销售合同的条款开立相关信用证。
9. This L/C will remain valid until Mar 8, 2013, confirmed by Bank of China, Hangzhou branch. 该信用证将于 2008 年 3 月 8 日到期，且由中国银行杭州分行保兑。
10. …they will accept your draft on them at 30 days after sight for the amount of your full invoice value. 他们将接受贵方开出的 30 天期全额发票金额的汇票。

New Words and Expressions

1. applicant	*n.* 申请人
2. beneficiary	*n.* 受益人
3. issuing bank	开证行
4. notifying bank	通知行
5. negotiation bank	议付行
6. paying bank	付款行
7. irrevocable	*a.* 不可撤销的
8. urge	*v.* 催促
9. L/C establishment	信用证开立
10. confirmed	*a.* 保兑的
11. execute	*v.* 执行，履行
12. do one's utmost	尽某人最大努力
13. stipulation	*n.* 规定
14. amendment	*n.* 修改

Business Link

◆ **L/C Specimen 信用证样例**

ISSUE OF A DOCUMENTARY CREDIT

SEQUENCE OF TOTAL	*27 : 1/1
FORM OF DOC. CREDIT	*40 A : IRREVOCABLE
DOC. CREDIT NUMBER	*20 : 00556678
DATE OF ISSUE	31 C :20 080117
EXPIRY	*31 D : DATE 20080308 PLACE CHINA
APPLICANT	*50 : ABC CO., LTD. NO. 58 SHIXIANG ROAD HANGZHOU, ZHEJIANG, CHINA
BENEFICIARY	*59 : BCD CO., LTD. NOVEMRE, 21012 CASSANO ITALY
AMOUNT	*32 B : CURRENCY USD AMOUNT 15,000.00
AVAILABLE WITH/BY	*41 D: BANCA DI ITALIA, MILANO BRANCH BY NEGOTIATION
DRAFTS AT …	42 C : 60 DAYS AFTER SIGHT
DRAWEE	42 D : *BANK OF COMMUNICATIONS, CHINA

*NO.357 YANAN ROAD.
*HANGZHOU

PARTIAL SHIPMENTS 43 P : NOT ALLOWED
TRANSSHIPMENT 43 T : NOT ALLOWED
PORT OF LOADING 44 A : SHANGHAI, CHINA
PORT OF DESTINATION 44 B : MILANO, ITALY
LATEST DATE OF SHIP. 44 C :20080220
DESCRIPT. OF GOODS 45 A :

WATER PUMPS
CIF SHANGHAI, CHINA
AS PER INVOICE NO. 0014719 DATED 20080120.

DOCUMENTS REQUIRED 46 A :

1. ORIGINAL SIGNED COMMERCIAL INVOICE PLUS ONE COPY SHOWING L/C NO.
2. PACKING LIST IN DUPLICATE.
3. CERTIFICATE OF ORIGIN.
4. FULL SET OF CLEAN ON BOARD OCEAN BILLS OF LADING MADE OUT TO ORDER OF SHIPPER, BLANK ENDORSED, MARKED 'FREIGHT PREPAID', AND NOTIFY APPLICANT.

DETAILS OF CHARGES 71 B : ALL BANKING CHARGES AND COMMISSIONS OUTSIDE CHINA ARE FOR BENEFICIARY'S ACCT.

PRESENTATION PERIOD 48 : 15 DAYS
CONFIRMATION *49 : BANK OF CHINA
HANGZHOU BRANCH

INSTRUCTIONS 78 :

PLS FORWARD REQUIRED DOCUMENTS BY SPECIAL COURIER DHL OR SIMILAR TO OUR FOLLOWING ADDRESS:
NO .357 YANAN ROAD
HANGZHOU ZHEJIANG (CHINA)

WE HEREBY ENGAGE OURSELVES TO EFFECT PAYMENT—AT MATURITY DATE—IN COMPLIANCE WITH REMITTING BANK'S INSTRUCTIONS, AGAINST DOCUMENTS FULL COMPLYING WITH CREDIT TERMS

SEND. TO REC. INFO. 72 : THIS IS THE ACTUAL CREDIT SUBJECT TO U.C.P. (2007 REV.) I.C.C. PUB. NO. 600.

◆ **信用证的主要内容**

各家银行开出的信用证格式并不完全一样，但主要内容却大致相似，基本包含如下方面：

（1）信用证本身说明。主要有信用证的性质、号码、币种、金额、开证行、议付行、开证申请人、受益人等信息。

（2）有关货物描述。主要包括品名、规格、数量、价格、包装、唛头、装运、保险等信息，一般详见发票或合同。

（3）有关单据的要求。主要包括发票、提单、装箱单、产地证、检验证、保险单以及各类证明等信息。

（4）开证行付款指示及其他要求。

◆ **SWIFT**

SWIFT，即"环球同业银行金融电讯协会"。它是国际银行同业间的国际合作组织。于 1973 年在瑞典成立，目前全球大多数国家的许多银行使用该系统开立、传递信用证。该系统的使用，为银行的结算提供了安全、快捷、标准化、自动化的电讯业务，提高了银行的结算效率和速度，因此受到各家银行的好评。SWIFT 信用证具有许多优点：密押可靠性、保密性高，传递速度快捷，操作标准化、格式化、自动化。

◆ **催开信用证**

在外贸实际业务中，买方可能由于各种原因未能及时开立信用证。对此，卖方应该催促对方尽快办理开证手续。如下是几种常见的要卖方发出函电提醒和催促对方开立信用证：

（1）合同规定开证到期时，还未收到相关信用证；

（2）合同签约日期与履约日期相隔时间较长，在合同规定开证日之前，发函说明对该笔生意的重视，提醒对方及时开立；

（3）卖方货物备妥待运，可提前装运，可以要求对方提前开立；

（4）得知买方资信欠佳，发函提醒对方重合同，守信用，及时开立。

More to Practice

I. Translate the following business terms or expressions into English.

1. 信用证
2. 信用证开立
3. 跟单信用证
4. 开证行
5. 付款行
6. 开证申请人
7. 受益人
8. 即期信用证
9. 保兑信用证
10. 不可撤销即期信用证

II. Translate the following sentences into Chinese.

1. The applicant is generally the buyer or importer to the bank to issue the L/C.
2. As the goods under S/C No.12 are ready for shipment, please rush your L/C ASAP.
3. We will open an L/C if you promise to effect shipment one month earlier.

4. From your fax of May 19, we learn that the L/C has been arranged, but we haven't received the banker's advice yet.
5. We regret that we have repeatedly urged our clients to issue L/C but without success.
6. It is our usual practice to require sight L/C. We cannot make an exception with this transaction.
7. Having some troubles in opening the L/C, our clients request you to agree to pay by T/T.
8. We find the stipulations in your L/C are not in accordance with the contract.
9. Please open the L/C promptly at the contract price, or we cannot apply for export license.
10. For the sake of convenience, we have issued a revolving L/C in your favor.

III. Translate the following sentences into English.

1. 第 211 号合同项下的货物已备妥，请尽快开立信用证。
2. 如你方信用证不能在 7 月底前开到我方，将被迫撤销订单。
3. 为避免日后修改，请注意信用证的内容要和合同条款完全一致。
4. 尽管再三催请开证，但仍然未收到信用证，请立即开立，否则我方无法交货。
5. 请尽快开立信用证以便我方能够顺利执行订单。
6. 我方的支付条款是凭保兑的、不可撤销的信用证付款。
7. 相关信用证已经开立。
8. 如你方信用证在 8 月初到达，我方将尽快安排装运你方所订的货物。
9. 进口方必须以出口方为受益人开立信用证。
10. 若信用证迟到，卖方对延迟装运不负责任。

IV. Writing practice.

Please write a letter of urging establishment of L/C according to the following information.

Sender's information:
Name: Louis
Company: Greenpower Equipment Imp and Exp Co., Ltd.
Email: greenidea@hotmail.com
Products: Fuel Economizers

Recipient's information:
Name: Alice
Company: Green Products Imp and Exp Co., Ltd.
Email: sunnygirl@gmail.com
Subject: the initial order
Date: Jan 8, 2013

Unit 10

L/C Examination and Amendment

Study Aims

应知目标

1. To know main points of an L/C examination.
2. To know the writing steps of a letter of L/C amendment.
3. To know the knowledge of "Lead in" Part.
4. To know the knowledge of "Business Link" Part.

应会目标

1. To be able to examine an L/C.
2. To be able to translate a letter of L/C amendment.
3. To be able to write a letter of L/C amendment.

Lead in

Upon receipt of the relevant L/C, the beneficiary (seller) of the L/C should, first of all, make a thorough examination to it to find whether the clauses in the L/C are in complete conformity with the terms in the contract. If any discrepancies, the beneficiary (seller) should ask the applicant (buyer) to ask for his issuing bank to amend the L/C accordingly. Moreover, the applicant (buyer) may also ask for amendment.

The following points may be given for reference in the examination of L/C:

(1) Whether the issuing bank is a sound reliable foreign bank or not, whether the currency employed and other reimbursement clauses are clear and in accordance with the regulations in the exporting country.

(2) The L/C should usually be irrevocable without any restrictions, such as "Subject to import license obtainable", etc.

(3) Whether the goods description (specifications, quantity, number, packing, marks, etc.) are in accordance with the sales contract.

(4) The total amount, validity time and date and place of expiry.

(5) Whether the required documents (invoice, c/o, B/L, insurance policy, etc.) are in

accordance with the sales contract.

Writing Skills

Step 1: To thank the arrival of L/C
Step 2: To state the discrepancies between contract and L/C
Step 3: To ask for amendment to the L/C accordingly
Step 4: To express the wish of receiving L/C amendment ASAP

Key Sentence Patterns

1. Please insert the word "about" before the quantity in your L/C No 234.
2. As there is no direct steamer from Shanghai to New York during May, it is necessary for you to delete the clause "by direct steamer".
3. Please amend L/C No.11 to read "This L/C will expire on 20 June 2008 in China .
4. On examination, we find that the amount of your L/C is insufficient.
5. We hope you will see to it that the amendment is faxed without delay.
6. We regretfully find that some points are not in conformity with the terms stipulated in the S/C No. 999.
7. On receipt of your amendment to the L/C, we will arrange for the shipment without any delay.
8. On examination, we find that partial shipment and transshipment are prohibited.
9. We are writing to you today to ask you to extend the shipment date and validity date to May 10 and May 31 respectively.
10. Whether any special clauses or stipulations are mentioned in the L/C regarding shipping documents.
11. Your L/C No. 223 is short established to the amount of US$520. Please increase it according to the contract.
12. We will grant an extension of L/C to June 30 in response to your request.
13. Please amend the L/C to allow transshipment and partial shipment.
14. We are looking forward to receiving the relevant amendment at an early date and thank you in advance.
15. We wish to call your attention to the validity of the L/C, since there is no possibility of L/C extension.

Case Study

Case 1
Business background

Sender's information:

Name:	Mary
Company:	Southafrican Sunflower Trade Co., Ltd.
Add:	227 Long St Capetown, South Africa
Tel:	27-21-3456666
Fax:	27-21-3456667
Website:	www.afslt.com.sa
Email:	maryl@gmail.com
Business scope:	foodstuff, kitchenware
Overseas markets:	America, Europe, Asia, Africa

Recipient's information:

Name:	Jack
Company:	Hangzhou Hollway Trade Co., Ltd.
Add:	118 Wensan Rd Hangzhou, Zhejiang, P.R.China 310000
Tel:	0086-571-82826266
Fax:	0086-571-82826267
Website:	www.hzhlt.com.cn
Email:	jackabc@hotmail.com
Business scope:	foodstuff, kitchenware, flower pots
Overseas markets:	Europe, America, Asia, South America

Hints

- thank for receiving L/C
- state the discrepancies between contract and L/C
- ask for amendment to the L/C accordingly
- wish to get an early reply

Task description

Mary, manager of Southafrican Sunflower Trade Co., Ltd. (herein called B Co., Ltd.) has received the L/C from Jack of Hangzhou Hollway Trade Co., Ltd (herein called A Co., Ltd.). After examing it, she has found some differcences between the L/C and the Contract they signed 30 days ago. She will send an email to Jack for asking amendment for the L/C.

Specimen letter 1

From: maryl@gmail.com (B Co., Ltd.)

To: jackabc@hotmail.com (A Co., Ltd.)

Date: Dec 5, 2013

Subject: asking for L/C amendment

Attachment:

Dear Jack:

We are glad to inform you that L/C No. 556677 issued by the Bank of Communications, Hangzhou branch, China for our S/C No. 666 has just been received.

However, after examining the clauses of the L/C, we regretfully find that some points are not in conformity with the terms stipulated in the S/C No. 666. The discrepancies are as follows:

1. Draft should be 30 days after sight not "60 days";
2. Shipment is to be made during Jan /Feb instead of "by the end of Feb";
3. Transshipment and partial shipment should read "be allowed";
4. The total amount should be USD15,600, not "USD15,800";

So you are requested to amend the L/C accordingly. On receipt of your amendment to the L/C, we will arrange for the shipment without any delay.

Yours sincerely,
Mary
Manager
B Co., Ltd.

Case 2
Business background

Sender's information:

Name:	Mike
Company:	Guangzhou Med International Trade Co., Ltd.
Add:	298 Liuhua Rd Guangzhou, Guangdong, P.R.China 318000
Tel:	0086-20-68886666
Fax:	0086-20-68886667
Website:	www.gzmedit.com.cn
Email:	coolmike@hotmail.com
Business scope:	shoes products
Overseas markets:	Japan, Korea, Africa

Recipient's information:

Name:	Johnson
Company:	Japan NKK Trade Co., Ltd.
Add:	227 Sun St Osaka, Japan
Tel:	81-21-3456666
Fax:	81-21-3456667
Website:	www.hzfnw.com.cn
Email:	johnson@gmail.com
Business scope:	shoes, garments
Overseas markets:	America, Europe, Asia

Task description

Mike, a sales manager of Guangzhou Med International Trade Co., Ltd. (herein called C Co., Ltd.) got No.6788 L/C from Japan NKK Trade Co., Ltd. (herein called D Co., Ltd.) yesterday. But he got a call from the supplier that they could not finish the goods ordered by the end of April. He will send an email to Johnson for asking for extension of shipment date and L/C validity date respectively.

Hints

- thank for receiving L/C No.6788
- state the reasons for shipment delay
- ask for extension of shipment date and L/C validity date
- wish to get an early reply

Specimen letter 2

From: coolmike@hotmail.com (C Co., Ltd.)

To: joinson@gmail.com (D Co., Ltd.)

Date: Apr 8, 2013

Subject: L/C extension

Attachment:

Dear Johnson:

We acknowledge with thanks the receipt of your L/C No. 6788, covering your Order No.123 for 20,000 pairs Model 2356 shoes.

We are sorry that we will be unable to ship the goods by the end of April due to delay of our suppliers.

We are writing to you today to ask you to extend the shipment date and validity date to May 10 and May 31 respectively.

Thank you for your cooperation and understanding in this matter.

Look forward to receiving your confirmation ASAP.

Yours sincerely,

Mike

C Co., Ltd.

Task Practice

Task 1

Description

ABC Co., Ltd. is an import and export company of Electronic computer and accessories and has enjoyed a good reputation.

Clark, a foreign salesperson of ABC Co., Ltd. has got L/C, but after checking it, he found it was not allowed to partial shipment and transshipment. He will send an email to BCD Co., Ltd. for amending it to allow "partial shipment and transshipment".

Requirements

You are required to send an email to BCD Co., Ltd. as the role of Clark, according to the following tips.

Tips

- inform the customer of receiving the L/C No. 668899
- find that partial shipment and transshipment are prohibited
- ask for amending it to "partial shipment and transshipment are allowed" and state the reasons
- wish to get an early reply

From: ____________________

To: ____________________

Date: ____________________

Subject: ____________________

____

____

____

____

____

____

____

____

Specimen letter 3

Suggested answer for Task 1

From: coolboy@hotmail.com (ABC Co., Ltd.)
To: prettygirl@bcd.com (BCD Co., Ltd.)
Date: Feb 8, 2013
Subject: Amending L/C to allow partial shipment and transshipment
Attachment:
Dear Sir or Madam: Thank you for your L/C No. 668899 covering 2,000 sets Haier Brand Air Conditioners. On examination, we find that partial shipment and transshipment are prohibited. We regret to say that we have 1,500 sets available by the end of this month, and the rest 500 sets will be ready by the end of next month. And we have to let you know that no direct ship from Ningbo to your port during Mar/Apr. Such being the case, we hope that you can amend the covering L/C to allow partial shipment and transshipment. Look forward to receiving your amendment ASAP. Yours faithfully, Clark ABC Co., Ltd.

Task 2

Description

B Co., Ltd. is an importer and exporter of foodstuff in Shanghai, China.

Mary, a foreign salesperson of B Co., Ltd. has received the L/C No. STB3126 against Contract No. 246 about 5,000 kgs Frozen Shrimps from A Co., Ltd. After checking the L/C carefully，she has found some discrepancies. She will send an email to A Co., Ltd. to ask for amendment.

Requirements

You are required to write an email to A Co., Ltd. as the role of Mary, according to the following tips.

Tips

- thank for receiving the L/C from A Co., Ltd.
- find some discrepancies between L/C and contract
- state the discrepancies in details
- ask for amendment of the L/C
- wish to get an early reply

From: ______________________________

To: ______________________________

Date: ______________________________

Subject: ______________________________

____

____

____

____

____

____

____

____

____

____

Specimen letter 4

Suggested answer for Task 2

From: prettygirl@yahoo.com (B Co., Ltd.)
To: coolboy@hotmail.com (A Co., Ltd.)
Date: Jan 9, 2013
Subject: Asking for L/C amendment
Attachment:
Dear Sir or Madam: We have received the L/C No. STB3126 against our Contract No. 246. After checking the

L/C carefully, we have found some discrepancies and would request you to make the following amendments:

1. The place of expiry should be “China” instead of “New York”;

2. The correct name of the applicant is “New York Green Food Imp and Exp. Co., Ltd.”, not “New York Food Imp and Exp. Co., Ltd.”;

3. The unit price should be US$2,500 per M.T. in stead of US$2,000 and the total amount both in figure and in words should respectively be “US$12,500” and “(SAY US DOLLARS TWELVE THOUSAND FIVE HUNDRED ONLY)”instead of “US$10,000” and “(SAY US DOLLARS TEN THOUSAND ONLY)”;

4. Please amend the clause “Partial shipments and transshipment are prohibited” to read “Partial shipments are allowed, transshipment is prohibited”;

5. Please amend “90% of the invoice value” to read “full invoice value”;

6. The contracted goods are “Frozen Shrimps”, not “Fresh Shrimps”.

We hope you will send us your amendment advice without any delay so as to enable us to effect shipment in time.

Yours faithfully,
Mary
B Co., Ltd.

Notes

1. We are glad to inform you that L/C No. 556677 issued by the Bank of Communications, Hangzhou branch, China for our S/C No. 666 has just been received.
   我方很高兴告知贵方按照编号 666 销售合同，由中国交通银行杭州分行开立的编号为 556677 的信用证已收悉。
   再如：We inform you that we have sent our latest catalogue.
   告知贵方我方已寄送我们最新产品目录。
2. …after examining the clauses of the L/C, we regretfully find that some points are not in conformity with the terms stipulated in the S/C No. 666.
   经审核信用证相关条款，我们很遗憾地发现一些条款与 666 号销售合同的条款不一致。
3. The discrepancies are as follows: 不符点如下：
4. Shipment is to be made during Jan /Feb instead of “by the end of Feb”.
   装运应该是在 1 到 2 月而非截至 2 月底。
5. So you are requested to amend the L/C accordingly. 故请贵方对信用证做相应的修改。
6. On receipt of your amendment to the L/C, we will arrange for the shipment without any delay. 一收到贵方寄来的信用证修改书，我方将立即安排装运。
7. Such being the case, we hope that you can amend the covering L/C to allow partial

shipment and transshipment.
在这种情况下，我方希望贵方能够修改相关信用证为允许分批装运和转运。

8. We acknowledge with thanks the receipt of your L/C No.6788, covering your Order No.123 for 20,000 pairs Model 2356 shoes.
兹收到按 123 号订单关于 20 000 双 2356 样式的鞋子开出的 6788 号信用证，深表感谢。

9. We are writing to you today to ask you to extend the shipment date and validity date to May 10 and May 31 respectively.
我方今日特致此函请求贵方延期装运期和信用证效期分别为 5 月 10 日和 5 月 31 日。

New Words and Expressions

1. inform	*v.* 通知，告知
2. branch	*n.* 分行，分公司
3. examine	*v.* 审核，检验
4. be in conformity with	一致，相符
5. discrepancy	*n.* 不符点
6. stipulate	*v.* 规定
7. respectively	*ad.* 分别地，各自地
8. expiry	*n.* 到期，终止
9. acknowledge	*v.* 告知收到
10. available	*a.* 可供的
11. extend	*v.* 延期，扩展
12. validity date	到期日
13. prohibit	*v.* 禁止
14. Bank of Communications	中国交通银行
15. such being the case	在这种情况下，情况如此

Business Link

◆ **信用证修改通知书样例**

BANK OF CHINA

BANK OF CHINA HANGZHOU BRANCH
ADD: NO.358 YANAN ROAD
TELEX: 86736 DHT CN
SWIFT BAKCHCNBRC A 863
FAX:86-571-86878899

NOTIFICATION OF AMENDMENT

2008/06/30

Continued

<table>
<tr><td colspan="2">TO:
ABC CO., LTD.
NO.667SHIXIANG ROAD, HANGZHOU, CHINA</td><td colspan="2">WHEN CORRESPONDING　ASS200Z00085
PLS QUOTE OUR REF.NO.</td></tr>
<tr><td colspan="2">ISSUING BANK 9800358
BARCLAYS BANK PLC
LONDON BRANCH
NO.776 AVE LONDON UNITED KINGDOM</td><td colspan="2">TRANSMITTED TO US THROUGH
REF. NO.</td></tr>
<tr><td>L/C NO.
NBC00667788LC2008</td><td>L/C DATED
2008/06/10</td><td>L/C TTL AMT
GMP 5,000</td><td>EXPIRY PLACE
LOCAL</td></tr>
<tr><td>EXPIRY DATE
2008/08/15</td><td>TENOR
0 DAYS</td><td>CHARGE
RMB 200.00</td><td>CHARGE BY
BENEFICIARY</td></tr>
<tr><td>RECEIVED VIA
SWIFT</td><td>AVAILABLE
VALID</td><td>TEST/SIGN
YES</td><td>CONFIRM
NO</td></tr>
<tr><td>AMEND NO,
1</td><td>AMEND DATE
2008/06/30</td><td>INCREASE AMT
GBP 300</td><td>DECREASE AMT
GBP 0.00</td></tr>
<tr><td colspan="4">DEAR SIR,
WE HAVE PLEASURE IN ADVISING YOU THAT WE HAVE RECEIVED FROM THE A/M BANK (AN) AMENDMENT TO THE CAPTIONED L/C CONTENTS OF WHICH ARE AS PER ATTACHED SHEETS.
THIS AMENDMENT SHOULD BE ATTACHED TO THE CAPTIONED L/C ADVISED BY US. OTHERWISE THE BENEFICIARY WILL BE RESPONSIBLE FOR ANY CONSEQUENCES ARISING TRERFORM.</td></tr>
<tr><td colspan="4">THIS AMENDMENT CONSISTS OF SHEET(S), INCLUDING THE COVERING LETTER AND ATTACHMENTS.
KINDLY TAKE NOTE THAT THE PARTIAL ACCEPTANCE OF THE AMENDMENT IS NOT ALLOWED.
THIS AMENDMENT IS ADVISED SUBJECTED TO ICC UCP PUBLICATION NO.600.
YOURS FAITHFULLY,
BANK OF CHINA</td></tr>
</table>

◆ **信用证“三个期”**

信用证一般有“三个期”，即装运期、交单期和有效期。

装运期指信用证中规定的最后装运日期，即提单签发日期。

交单期指信用证项下要求的各类单据议付时最后提交日期。

有效期指信用证的到期日。

一般来说，装运期最早，至少与到期日相距 2 周以上，否则缮制各类单据就非常紧张，另外，即使在信用证有效期内，银行议付时也不接受提单签发日后 21 天以后的单据，因此向银行议付时要计算这二者中最近的一个日期作为交单期，才是明智稳妥之举。

◆《UCP 600》

UCP 是 Uniform Customs and Practice for Documentary Credits 的缩写，翻译成为《跟单信用证统一惯例》。它是国际商会制定的关于协调跟单信用证有关各方矛盾，对各方权利、责任、条款的定义和术语的统一解释和公认标准。目前已被世界上大多数国家和银行广泛采纳和应用。

《跟单信用证统一惯例》第 500 号出版物自 1993 年修订本使用十多年后，随着全球经济与贸易的不断发展，已经出现了一些不能与时俱进的问题。因此，自 2007 年第 600 号出版物取而代之。

◆ **几家知名银行简介**

中国银行
Bank of China

中国银行，全称中国银行股份有限公司，是中国四大国有商业银行之一。业务范围涵盖商业银行、投资银行和保险领域，旗下有中银香港、中银国际、中银保险等控股金融机构，在全球范围内为个人和公司客户提供全面和优质的金融服务。中国银行主营商业银行业务，包括公司、个人金融、资金业务和金融机构等业务。按核心资本计算，2005 年中国银行在英国《银行家》杂志“世界 1000 家大银行”排名中列第十八位。

中国交通银行
Bank of Communications

交通银行始建于 1908 年，是中国历史最悠久的商业银行之一。新中国成立后，交通银行香港分行继续营业，内地行业务并入中国人民银行和中国人民建设银行。1987 年 4 月 1 日，经国务院批准重新组建的交通银行正式对外营业，总行设在上海。

交通银行是我国首家全国性的国有股份制商业银行。在全国 137 个城市拥有近 2 600 个分支机构，并在香港、纽约、东京、新加坡、首尔设立了分行，在伦敦、法兰克福开设了代表处。

英国渣打银行
Standard Charted Bank

渣打银行有 150 多年的历史，致力于在全球高增长市场的发展。渣打银行在亚太、南亚、中东、非洲、英国及美洲等 56 个国家和地区拥有 1 400 多家分支机构。

作为世界上国际化程度最高的银行之一，渣打银行拥有来自全球 100 多个国家和地区的近 60 000 名雇员。随着世界经济的持续一体化，这种多元化特色充分反映在渣打银行的核心价值观中并支持着渣打银行的进一步发展。

现在渣打银行已经成功确立了其在亚洲、非洲和中东等新兴贸易走廊的地位。

More to Practice

I. Translate the following business terms or expressions into English.

1. 审核信用证
2. 修改信用证
3. 如合同所规定
4. 与……相符
5. 有效期
6. 装运单据
7. 毫无延迟
8. 修改通知
9. 务必做到
10. 到期日

II. Translate the following sentences into Chinese.

1. Such being this case, we would request you to amend your L/C to allow partial shipment and transshipment.
2. You are asked to increase the amount of the L/C No. 12 by US$800 according to our fax statement of December 15, 2007.
3. Please delete from the L/C the clause, "All charges are for beneficiary's account". Such should be paid by the importing party only.
4. The L/C has been amended as required. Please do your best to effect shipment before next month.
5. Your L/C has been received. It has been found that the amount is US $500 short of the total value in the S/C.
6. You are requested to notify your client to increase the L/C amount to RMB￥1,000.
7. The commission for this transaction is 3% as clearly stipulated in our S/C, but we find that your L/C demands a commission of 8%.
8. We shall be grateful if you can instruct your bank to amend it to 3%.
9. Owing to the delayed arrival of the scheduled steamer, we have failed to effect shipment within the date stipulated in our L/C.
10. Please extend the shipment date and validity date to May 10 and May 31 respectively, thus enabling us to effect shipment of the goods in question.

III. Translate the following sentences into English.

1. 请把上述信用证条款匹长 40 码改为 50 码。
2. 请插入条款“在宁波转船”。
3. 请通知银行修改信用证第 123 号使之成为可以转船。
4. 请修改信用证第 1288 号使之成为“本信用证将于 2007 年 9 月 8 日在中国到期”。
5. 经核查我方发现你方的信用证金额不足，请将总金额增至 50 000 美元。
6. 请修改你方信用证第 3466 号，在数量和金额项下插入“溢短 5%”。
7. 单价已修改为每个 5 美元而非原来的单价每个 4 美元。
8. 请修改信用证插入下列条款“允许数量多于或少于 5%”。

9. 感谢你方指出我方信用证第 3466 号的错误，随信附加一份信用证修改通知。
10. 期待你方信用证修改通知早日到达。

IV. Writing practice.

Please write a letter of requesting L/C amendment according to the following information.

1. 对方的信用证金额不足，请将总金额增至 100 000 美元；
2. 装运港是上海，目的港是纽约，而非装运港是纽约目的港是上海；
3. 请从信用证中删去此条款：“禁止分批装运和转运”；
4. 提单上标注“运费已付”而非“运费到付”；
5. 在数量条款前插入单词“about”。

Sender’s information:
Name: Louis
Company: Greenpower Equipment Imp and Exp Co., Ltd.
Email: greenidea@hotmail.com
Products: Fuel Economizers

Recipient’s information:
Name: Alice
Company: Green Products Imp and Exp Co., Ltd.
Email: sunnygirl@gmail.com
Subject: the initial order
Date: Jan 8, 2013

Unit 11

Shipment

Study Aims

应知目标

1. To know main means of transportation in international trade and their advantages and disadvantages.

2. To know the writing steps of a letter of shipment.

3. To understand contents of a B/L.

4. To know the knowledge of "Lead in" Part.

5. To know the knowledge of "Business Link" Part.

应会目标

1. To be able to translate articles of shipment.

2. To be able to translate a letter of shipment.

3. To be able to write a letter of shipment.

4. To be able to analyze articles of a B/L.

Lead in

- Proper control of shipment is very important in the exporting and importing. Indispensable terms as this part, it means the seller's fulfillment of the obligation to make delivery of the goods. As we know, a delayed shipment may mean losing the order and the customer's trust. As to the shipment of goods, we should pay attention to the following contents: 1) modes, 2) time, 3) place of shipment and destination, 4) partial shipment and transshipment, 5) shipping instruction sent by the buyer and shipping advice by the seller.
- When it comes to shipment, it includes such procedures as clearing the goods through the Customs, booking shipping space or chartering a ship, completing shipping documentation, dispatching shipping advice. There are three parties involved in the movement of goods:

1) The consignor or the shipper
2) The carrier
3) The consignee

Writing Skills

Step 1: To mention the relative order or contract
Step 2: To state the importance of immediate shipment
Step 3: To urge the seller to ship the goods early
Step 4: To wish the goods to arrive in good condition

Key Sentence Patterns

1. How long does it take you to make delivery?
2. When can we collect the goods?
3. Our terms of payment are by irrevocable L/C payable by sight draft against presentation of shipping documents.
4. I'm very sorry for delay in delivery.
5. What sort of delivery periods did you have in mind?
6. When can you make the balance shipment?
7. We have booked a direct steamer, which is due to sail to your port next month.
8. We have to remind you that shipment of our Order No. 365 is rapidly becoming overdue.
9. How about making Guangzhou the port of shipment instead of Zhuhai?
10. We would like to remind you to open the covering L/C.
11. We feel extremely sorry for our inability to advance the shipment.
12. Please ensure that we'll get tight shipping documents before the arrival of the goods.
13. As the goods you ordered are now in stock, we will ship them without delay.
14. We must insist on immediate delivery, otherwise we shall be compelled to cancel the order.
15. We require that transshipment be allowed.

Case Study

Case 1
Business background

Sender's information:

Name:	Jeff Shao
Company:	Sums Trade Co., Ltd.
Add:	81 HuiGui Rd Hangzhou, Zhejiang, P.R.China 310000
Tel:	0086-571-81819999
Fax:	0086-571-81819998
Website:	www.Sumsco.com.cn
Email:	crystal@hotmail.com
Business scope:	porcelain, quartz, glass, wood
Overseas markets:	Europe, America, Asia, South Africa

Recipient's information:

Name:	William Hunter
Company:	Hex Trade Co., Ltd.
Add:	150 Federal Street, Boston
Tel:	617-951-8000
Fax:	617-951-8000
Website:	www.Mahex.com.
Email:	returning@yahoo.com
Business scope:	porcelain, quartz, glass, wood
Overseas markets:	Europe, America, Asia, Africa

Task description

Jeff Shao, on behalf of Sums Trade Co., Ltd. (herein called A Co., Ltd.) will send an email to Mr. Hunter from Hex Trade Co., Ltd. (herein called B Co., Ltd.) for explaining the reasons for shipping delay.

Hints

- thank for enquiry about the shipment
- explain the reasons for shipping delay
- enclose shipping documents
- express desire to follow up closely

Specimen letter 1

From: crystal@hotmail.com (A Co., Ltd.)
To: returning@yahoo.com (B Co., Ltd.)
Date: 23 May 2013
Subject: shipping advice
Attachment: our documents

Dear William:

Thank you for your enquiry about the shipment of your order under Contract 4456. We are so sorry for the delay which has been caused by the unavailability of shipping space from Ningbo to Liverpool. We enclose one set of shipping documents comprising:

1. One non-negotiable copy of the Bill of Lading.
2. Commercial Invoice in duplicate.
3. One copy of the Certificate of Quality.
4. One copy of the Certificate of Quantity.
5. One copy of the Insurance Policy.

We are glad to execute your order as contracted. We trust the goods will reach you in time. I will personally ensure that you receive our prompt and careful attention at all times.

Yours sincerely,
Jeff Shao
A Co., Ltd.

Case 2
Business background

Sender's information:

Name:	Chris Zhang
Company:	Hangzhou Meijiawu Tea Co., Ltd.
Add:	248 Longjing Rd Hangzhou, Zhejiang, P.R.China 310000
Tel:	0086-332-5367198
Fax:	0086-332-5367198
Website:	www.meijiawutea.com.cn
Email:	meijiawutea@hotmail.com
Business scope:	tea products, tea sets
Overseas markets:	Europe, USA, Asia

Recipient's information:

Name:	Thomas E. Peckham
Company:	Albers & Viets Trade Co., Ltd.
Add:	200N. Broadway St Louis, USA
Tel:	1-314-231-7318
Fax:	1-314-231-7318
Website:	www. Albers & Viets.com
Email:	tepackham@gmail.com
Business scope:	tea, tea sets
Overseas markets:	America, Europe, Asia

Task description

Chris who works for Hangzhou Meijiawu Tea Co., Ltd. (herein called C Co., Ltd.) will send an email to Thomas from Albers & Viets Trade Co., Ltd. (herein called D Co., Ltd.) for urging the shipment of goods.

Hints

- point out the Contract No
- explain the reasons for urging goods
- express desire of receiving goods
- wish to get an early reply

Specimen letter 2

From: meijiawutea@hotmail.com (C Co., Ltd.)
To: tepackman@gmail.com (D Co., Ltd.)
Date: June 8, 2013
Subject: urging shipment
Attachment:
Dear Thomas: We refer to the previous Contract No. 4632 which covering 320 cartons of Green Tea Pots. We wish to draw your attention to the fact that up to now no news comes from you about shipment of the goods. As we mentioned in our last letter, we are badly in need of the goods and we may be compelled to seek an alternative source of supply. Please understand how urgent it is for us to resolve this matter. Your cooperation will be highly appreciated. Truly yours, Chris Zhang Meijiawu Tea Co., Ltd.

Task Practice

Task 1

Description

Mondo Co., Ltd. which is an importer of leather briefcases and travel Bags is going to exhibit at a trade fair later this year. So it is badly in need of the Italian leather products from Berkshire Co., Ltd. which is purchased previously.

Ding Qi, a salesman of Mondo Co., Ltd. will send an email to Berkshire Co., Ltd. for urging early shipment.

Requirements

You are required to send an email to Berkshire Co., Ltd. as the role of Ding Qi, according to the following tips.

Tips

- point out the Contract No
- express desire of receiving goods early
- explain the reasons for urging goods
- express regret of causing inconvenience
- wish to get an early reply

From: ______________________________

To: ______________________________

Date: ______________________________

Subject: ______________________________

____

____

____

____

____

____

____

____

Specimen letter 3

Suggested answer for Task 1

From: qiqiding@hotmail.com (Mondo Co., Ltd.)
To: berkshire@yahoo.com (Berkshire Co., Ltd.)
Date: May 7, 2013
Subject: urging early shipment
Attachment:
Dear Sir or Madam: Referring to our previous Purchase Contract No. 999, delivery is scheduled for Aug 2013. We would now like an early delivery June/July 2013. We regret to bring the inconvenience for you due to the urgent demand for the trade fair. In view of our long-standing, cordial commercial relationship, we would be very grateful if you would make a special effort to comply with our request. We look forward to your early reply. Yours faithfully, Ding Qi Mondo Co., Ltd.

Task 2

Description

Fior Co., Ltd. trades in the garden furniture which are designed and made in the UK.

Cheng Yin, a salesperson of Fior Co., Ltd. has got the early shipping email from Mike of Amber Co., Ltd. She will send an email to Mike for refusing the early shipment.

Requirements

You are required to write an email to Mike as the role of Cheng Yin, according to the following tips.

Tips

- mention the last email
- point out the Contract No
- refuse the request
- explain the reason for refusing
- express the desire to be forgiven

From: ____________________

To: ____________________

Date: ____________________

Subject: ____________________

____
____
____
____
____
____
____
____
____

Specimen letter 4

Suggested answer for Task 2—A Reply

From: Fiorgirl@yahoo.com (Ficr Co., Ltd.)
To: mikeboy@hotmail.com (Amber Co., Ltd.)
Date: Dec 9, 2013
Subject: reply to early shipping
Attachment:
Dear Mike: We are in receipt of your letter dated May 18, 2013 requesting earlier delivery of goods under your Purchase Contract No. 339. We immediately contacted the shipping company but we regretted to tell you that we were

unable to comply with your request because of no available shipping space on ships sailing from here to your port before 8 June.

We are very sorry that we are unable to advance shipment. We will, however, do everything possible to ensure that the goods are shipped within the contracted time.

Your kind comprehension in this respect will be highly appreciated.

Yours sincerely,

Cheng Yin

Fior Co., Ltd.

Notes

1. non-negotiable copy of the Bill of Lading 不可转让的提单副本
   unsigned Bill of Lading are non-negotiable (未经签署的提单不可转让)
2. Commercial Invoice in duplicate 商业发票一式两份
3. One copy of the Certificate of Quality 质量检验书副本一份
4. One copy of the Insurance Policy 保险单副本一份
5. refer to =with regard to 关于
6. draw your attention to 引起你们注意
7. up to now 到目前为止
8. be badly in need of 迫切需要，非常需要
9. in view of our long-standing, cordial commercial relationship
   考虑到我们长期诚恳的合作关系
10. do everything possible 尽力

New Words and Expressions

1. unavailability	*n.* 无效，没有利用率
2. execute	*v.* 执行，实行；完成
3. compell	*v.* 强迫，迫使，强要
4. comprise	*v.* 包含
5. alternative	*a.* 选择性的，二中择一的
6. cooperation	*n.* 合作，协作
7. schedule	*v.* 确定时间
8. delivery	*n.* 递送，交付
9. longstanding	*a.* 长时间的
10. cordial	*a.* 热忱的，诚恳的
11. comprehension	*n.* 理解；包含
12. comply	*v.* 顺从；答应；遵守

Business Link

◆ **交货**

交货是指卖方按照同买方约定的时间、地点和运输方式将合同规定的货物交付给买方或其代理人。装运一般是指将货物装上运输工具，它与交货是两个不同的概念。但是，在国际商务中，由于采用 F.O.B、C.F.R 和 C.I.F 三种价格术语，卖方只要根据合同的有关规定将货物装上船，取得提单，就算交货。提单签发日期亦即为交货日。因此，装运一词常被用来代替交货的概念。这种凭单交货被称为象征性交货。（实际交货是指货物运抵目的地，因而，装运时间与交货时间是并不一致的。）凭单交货时，装运期和交货期是一致的。在买卖合同中，合理地规定装运期（交货期）是很重要的。

◆ **欧洲主要港口（European Main Ports）**

EMP (European Main Ports)，一般指欧洲主要港口，包括伦敦港（英国）、马赛港（法国）、汉堡港（德国）、鹿特丹港（荷兰）、热那亚港（意大利）、安特卫普港（比利时）以及哥本哈根港（丹麦）等港口。下面选取其中两个做一个简介：

* **伦敦港 LONDON**

港口性质：河口海港、设有企业区

航线：西欧

位于英国东南沿海泰晤士（THAMES）河下游的南北两岸，从河口开始向上游伸延经蒂尔伯里（TILBURY）港区越过伦敦桥，直至特丁顿（TEDDINGTON）码头。沿河两岸有许多用于装卸货物的船坞、油码头、河岸码头及修船坞等。港口始建于公元前 43 年，16 世纪海运昌盛，18 世纪已发展成为世界大港之一，19 世纪成为全国贸易和金融中心，而且是世界航运中心，集中了世界各地的船舶和船公司的代表机构。有世界上最大的保险组织——劳合社（LLOYD'S）。伦敦是英国的首都，全国政治、经济、文化、交通的中心，又是全国最大的海港，并且是英国最主要的制造业城市，以通用机械与电机著称。还有飞机、精密仪器、汽车、炼油、化学、服装、造纸、印刷、食品、卷烟等工业均很发达。

* **鹿特丹港 ROTTERDAM——世界货运第一大港**

港口性质：河口海港、设有保税仓库、基本港

航线：西欧

位于荷兰西南沿海莱茵河和马斯河两大河流入海汇合处所形成的三角洲上。始建于 13 世纪末，当时仅是一个小型海港和贸易中心。1600 年开始发展成为荷兰第二大商港。1870 年港口直通北海的航道得到整治后发展迅速。自 20 世纪 60 年代以来一直是世界货运第一大港，是莱茵河流域的进出门户。现为荷兰第二大城市，水、陆、空的交通枢纽，重要的商业和金融中心。鹿特丹现为世界货物吞吐量最大的港口，又是西欧的商品集散中心，也是欧洲最大的集装箱港口。主要工业有炼油、造船、石油化工、钢铁、食品和机械制造等。这里有大型炼油厂，其炼油能力占荷兰总能力的一半以上，是世界三大炼油中心之一，由于鹿港的许多著名建筑都是现代化的，因此，鹿港被誉为欧洲最现代化的城市。

该港作为商品集散中心，不仅是荷兰的国际贸易门户，而且是整个欧洲的物流基地，对整个欧洲的经济发展起着十分巨大的作用。此外，美国向欧洲出口货物的 43%，日本向

西欧市场出口货物的 34%都经过鹿特丹中转。德国经过鹿特丹的进出口货物几乎超过了其国内港口的总吞吐量，鹿特丹之所以被人们这样重视并建成如此规模，是因为它面临大海，背后腹地辽阔，内陆交通干线极为发达，通过高速公路网可进行国际间的汽车长途运输。在以鹿特丹为中心，半径为 500km 的范围内，用 24 小时便可将货物运至目的地。该范围包括荷兰全部领土、比利时全部、连巴黎在内的法国北半部、德国的北部等等。从鹿特丹到欧洲各大城市之间都有定期的集装箱列车，还可进行铁路、公路间的集装箱联运。

More to Practice

I. Translate the following business terms or expressions into English.

1. 发货
2. 装运标志
3. 载货能力
4. 直达船
5. 已装船通知
6. 装船通知单，装货/运单
7. 分批装运
8. 船期表
9. 整箱货
10. 拼箱货
11. 途经香港
12. 码头收据

II. Translate the following sentences into Chinese.

1. I'm sorry that we can't advance the time of shipment.
2. The order is so urgently required that we must ask you to expedite shipment.
3. The earliest shipment we can make is early March.
4. The goods ordered are all in stock and we assure you that the first steamer will make the shipment available in November.
5. Please see to it that the goods are shipped per PEACE sailing on or about October 15th.
6. Shipment by the middle of October will be too late for us.
7. We are confident of being able to ship the goods to you by the end of next month.
8. Could you possibly advance shipment further more?
9. How long will the delivery take from here to Canada by sea freight?
10. I don't think I can promise you any January shipments.

III. Translate the following sentences into English.

1. 请注意做到包装既要经济节约，又能经受长途海运。我们向贵方保证我们的产品质优价廉。
2. 考虑到目前拥挤的运输状况，请务必提前定舱位。
3. 如果第一批船货令我方客户满意，我将保证大量续订。
4. 若货物在装运期过后到达，我们将拒收并保留索赔的权利。
5. 我希望你们能在收到我方信用证后马上装运。
6. 及时装运对买方极具重要性，否则他们赶不上销售季节会亏本。

7. 我方将尽全力履行此订单，将于 10 月 15 日前安排这些货物装船。
8. 特此通知这批货物（你方订单号码是 No.123）昨天已装运，航空货物的领取号码是 No.123。
9. 我想知道你们能否在九月份装运。
10. 万一你方没有在 12 月 12 日或之前收到货物，请告知我方。

IV. Writing practice.

Please write a letter of urging early shipment with the information given below.

1. 有关第 3387 号合同订购的 800 副羽毛球拍事宜，至今尚未收到贵公司运货通知。
2. 上次已去信贵公司，表示急需此批货物。如贵公司未能供应此货，本公司或需寻求其他货源。
3. 因此，在 8 月 18 日到期的第 1796 号信用证无法再作延期。
4. 烦请于一周内传真贵公司的装运通知。

Unit 12

Insurance

Study Aims

应知目标

1. To know purposes of covering insurance.
2. To know premium and its calculation.
3. To know the writing steps of a letter of insurance.
4. To know the knowledge of "Lead in" Part.
5. To know the knowledge of "Business Link" Part.

应会目标

1. To be able to translate a letter of insurance.
2. To be able to write a letter of insurance.
3. To be able to analyze an insurance policy.
4. To be able to translate articles of insurance.

Lead in

- If your business is new to international trade, it is important to assess and plan for the different risks you will invariably face. As well as physical loss or damage to goods, you need to plan for problems of cash flow or non-payment by your customers. In some cases you also need to plan for risks associated with faulty goods or services.
- As an exporter of goods or services you need to insure against the risks of:

1) loss of or damage to goods in transit
2) a fault that causes and end-customer to sue
3) non-payment for your goods or services

If you are an importer, you may need to take the following into account:

1) possible loss of or damage to goods in transit
2) supplier problems, including failure to supply
3) transport delays and potential hold-ups at ports
4) the risk of performance or health and safety problems
5) import duties
6) storage of goods in bonded warehouses

7) currency fluctuations

Writing Skills

Step 1: To state the contract, goods and so on

Step 2: To suggest the terms of the reason and payment

Step 3: To express one's ideas including agreeing or refusing

Step 4: To state the goods will be insured and sent soon

Key Sentence Patterns

1. I want to discuss the level of insurance coverage you've requested for your order.
2. I believe that we have requested an amount twenty-five percent above the invoice value.
3. We have no problem in complying with your request, but we think that the amount is a bit excessive.
4. We've had a lot of trouble in the past with damaged goods.
5. The normal coverage for goods of this type is to insure them for the total invoice amount plus ten percent.
6. We would feel more comfortable with the additional protection.
7. If you want to increase the coverage, we will have to charge you extra for the additional cost.
8. But the insurance was supposed to be included in the quotation.
9. But we quoted you normal coverage at regular rates.
10. But I suggest you contact your insurance agent there and compare rates.
11. Fax me whatever rates you find there and I'll compare them with what we can offer.
12. According to international practice, we do not insure against such risks unless the buyers call for them.

Case Study

Case 1

Business background

Sender's information:

Name:	Xu Feng
Company:	Hangzhou Longjin Tea Trade Co., Ltd.
Add:	134 Shifeng Rd Hangzhou, Zhejiang, P.R.China 310000
Tel:	0086-571-85555566
Fax:	0086-571-85555567
Website:	www.hzlongjin.com.cn
Email:	xufenglongjin@hotmail.com
Business scope:	green tea, black tea, oolong tea
Overseas markets:	Europe, America, Asia, South Africa

Recipient's information:

Name:	Kent
Company:	Mystic Brew Fine Tea & Coffee Co., Ltd.
Add:	294 high St Orpington, UK
Tel:	01689-829-112
Fax:	01689-829-112
Website:	www.mbftc.co.uk
Email:	mbkent@gmail.com
Business scope:	black tea, green tea, coffee
Overseas markets:	Europe, America, Asia, Africa

Task description

Xu Feng, on behalf of Hangzhou Longjin Tea Trade Co., Ltd. (herein called A Co., Ltd.) will send an email to Kent from Mystic Brew Fine Tea & Coffee Co., Ltd. (herein called B Co., Ltd.) about insurance.

Hints

- mention the last email about quotation for CIF terms
- express desire of our CFR quotation
- explain our position
- wish to get an early reply

Specimen letter 1

From: xufenglongjin@hotmail.com (A Co., Ltd.)
To: mbkent@gmail.com (B Co., Ltd.)
Date: Jan 8, 2013
Subject: About the Insurance
Attachment:
Dear Kent: This is to acknowledge receipt of your email of 8 January, quoting us for 100 metric tons of black tea; your quotation is for CIF terms. We regret to say that we prefer to have your quotation and offers on CFR terms. Our position is that we have taken out an open policy with Lawes of Plymouth. According to the policy, when we arrange the shipment, all we have to do is to advise them of the particulars. However, We want to know the scope of cover handled by your usual insurance company for our reference. We look forward to hearing from you. Yours sincerely, Xu Feng Hangzhou Longjin Tea Co., Ltd.

Case 2
Business background

Sender's information:

Name:	Mike
Company:	Ningbo BeilunTrade Co., Ltd.
Add:	98 Nanguo Rd Ningbo, Zhejiang, P.R.China 318000
Tel:	0086-572-68822266
Fax:	0086-572-68822267
Website:	www.nbbl.com.cn
Email:	mikeningbo@hotmail.com
Business scope:	garments
Overseas markets:	USA, Korea, UK

Recipient's information:

Name:	Jeff
Company:	Newbury Trade Co., Ltd.
Add:	66 Treverby Road St Austell, Cornwall, UK
Tel:	0845-22-58347
Fax:	0845-22-58346
Website:	www.newbuery.co.uk
Email:	jeffnewbury@gmail.com
Business scope:	shoes, garments
Overseas markets:	America, Europe, Asia

Task description

Ningbo Beilun Trade Co., Ltd. (herein called C Co., Ltd.) has a garment dealing with Newbury Trade Co., Ltd. (herein called D Co., Ltd.). Mike, the salesman from C Co., Ltd. will send an email to Jeff who is the salesman from D Co., Ltd. for asking for insurance.

Hints

- ask for a marine insurance policy
- give the name of the company
- give the claim payable
- give the insured amount and items
- give the mark, quantity & description of merchandise

Specimen letter 2

From: mikeningbo@hotmail.com (C Co., Ltd.)
To: jeffnewbury@gmail.com (D Co., Ltd.)
Date: June 8, 2013
Subject: asking for insurance
Attachment:

Dear Jeff,

Please issue a Marine Insurance Policy in the name of Ningbo Beilun Trading Company.

Claims payable at Shanghai.

Amount of Insurance required: US$30,000.

Against the risk of All Risk & War Risk.

Quantity & Description of Merchandise:

Shirts: 3,000 dozen packed in three cases, 1,000 dozen each.

Marks: GTCC

Shanghai

No. 1/25

Voyage from Plymouth to Shanghai per "Peace" sailing on or about 1st February, 2013.

Mike

Ningbo Beilun Trade Co., Ltd.

Task Practice

Task 1

Description

Bright Co., Ltd. is an exporter of bamboo products and has dealings with Austell Co., Ltd. for many years.

Ye Ming, a salesperson of Bright Co., Ltd. will send an email to Austell Co., Ltd. for the insurance for the order No.159.

Requirements

You are required to send an email to Austell Co., Ltd. as the role of Ye Ming, according to the following tips.

Tips

- inform to ship the goods of order No. 159
- give the time to ship
- mention the insured items
- explain the reasons for choosing this type of coverage

From: ______________________________

To: ______________________________

Date: ______________________________

Subject: ______________________________

____

____

____

____

____

____

____

____

____

Specimen letter 3

Suggested answer for Task 1

From: realbright@yahoo.com (Bright Co., Ltd.)
To: hotaustell@hotmail.com (Austell Co., Ltd.)
Date: Jan 8, 2013
Subject: insurance
Attachment:
Dear Sirs: We are glad to inform you that your order No.159 will be shipped per S/S Sunshine due to leave here at the end of this month. Unless otherwise instructed, we will arrange to take out an All Risks insurance policy for you on your order. This type of coverage is, in our opinion, necessary for a cargo of this nature. Yours sincerely, Ye Ming Bright Co., Ltd.

Task 2

Description

Cornwall Co., Ltd. is a dealer in straw Products, Native Products & Arts & Crafts.

Shen Hang, a salesperson of Cornwall Co., Ltd. has got the email from Monica Co., Ltd. about a few questions on insurance. She will send an email to Monica Co., Ltd. for answering these questions.

Requirements

You are required to write an email to Monica Co., Ltd. as the role of Shen Hang, according to the following tips.

Tips

- mention the last email
- explain all-risks
- explain breakage
- explain value to be insured
- wish to get an early reply

From: ______________________________

To: ______________________________

Date: ______________________________

Subject: ______________________________

____

____

____

____

____

____

____

____

____

Specimen letter 4

Suggested answer for Task 2—A Reply

From: shenhang@yahoo.com (Cornwall Co., Ltd.)
To: monicaeu@hotmail.com (Monica Co., Ltd.)
Date: Aug 1, 2013
Subject: reply to insurance
Attachment:
Dear Sir or Madam: Answering your email of July 31 in regard to insurance, we would like to inform you of the following: **All Risks**: Generally we cover insurance WPA & War Risk in the absence of definite instructions from our clients. If you do desire to cover All Risks, we can provide such

coverage at a slightly higher premium.

Risk of Clash and Breakage: Breakage is an additional risk, for which an extra premium will have to be charged. The present rate is about 0.5%. Claims are payable only for that part of the loss, that is over 4%.

Value to be insured: We have due attention to the fact that you wish us to insure shipment to you for 10% above invoice value.

We trust the above information will serve your purpose and await your further news.

Yours faithfully,

Shen Hang

Cornwall Co., Ltd.

Notes

1. open policy 预约保单，而非字面的意思，不可翻译成“开发的政策”。
2. for our reference 供我方参考
3. Marine Insurance Policy 海运保险单
4. Against the risk of All Risk & War Risk. 投保一切险以及战争险。
5. Marks：GTCC. 装箱标志为 GTCC。
6. Unless otherwise instructed. 如不另行通知。
7. a cargo of this nature 这种类型的货物
8. take out 投保
9. In the absence of definite instructions from our clients… 在没有客户的具体指示下……
10. Risk of Clash and Breakage 碰损破碎险
11. Claims are payable only for that part of the loss, that is over 4%.
    索赔仅限损失超过 4%的时候。
12. value to be insured 投保金额，即“保额”，也可说：amount of insurance
13. …await your further news. 期待贵方进一步消息。await=wait for

New Words and Expressions

1. oolong *n.* 乌龙茶
2. premium *n.* 保险费
3. particular *n.* 细节
4. cover *v.* 投保
5. payable *a.* 可付的
6. policy *n.* 保险单
7. coverage *n.* 险别
8. rate *n.* 费率

9. shipment n. 船货，货物
10. marks n. 唛头
11. await v. 等待
12. scope n. 范围；机会，余地
13. breakage n. 破损，破碎

Business Link

◆ **进出口货物运输险种类**

按承保保险责任的大小，可分为若干种不同的险别，具体分类如下：

1. 海运条款：平安险（FPA）、水渍险（WPA）、一切险（ALL RISKS）

2. 陆运条款：

陆运险（OVERLAND TRANSPORTATION RISKS）

陆运一切险（OVERLAND TRANSPORTATION ALL RISKS）

3.航空条款：

空运险（AIR TRANSPORTATION RISKS）

空运一切险（AIR TRANSPORTATION ALL RISKS）

4.邮包条款：

邮包险（PARCEL POST RISKS）

邮包一切险（PARCEL POST ALL RISKS）

5. 海运冷藏条款：

海运冷藏险（RISKS FOR FROZEN PRODUCTS）

海运冷藏一切险（ALL RISKS FOR FROZEN PRODUCTS）

陆运冷藏货物、海运散装桐油及活牲畜、家禽保险条款没有险别大小的分类。

◆ **海上货物运输险附加险种简介**

一般附加险：

a) TPND 偷窃提货不着险
b) FWRD 淡水雨淋险
c) Risk of Shortage 短量险
d) Risk of Leakage 渗漏险
e) Risk of Clash and Breakage 碰损破碎险
f) Risk of Odour 串味险
g) Risk of Rust 锈损险
h) Hook Damage 钩损险
i) Risk of Intermixture and Contamination 混杂玷污险
j) Breakage of Packing 包装破碎险
k) Damage Caused by Sweating and Heating 受潮受热险

特殊附加险：

a) War Risk 战争险

b) Strikes Risk 罢工险

◆ **免赔额、免赔率（franchise）**

Franchise，在海上货物运输保险中，指免赔额或免赔率。在某些情况下，当损失在一定额度或比例下，保险公司不必赔偿，但当超过这一额度或比例时，必须全部赔偿，其目的是不鼓励非常小额的赔偿要求。例如，保单或合同规定“5% franchise”，当货物损失 4%时，保险公司不予赔偿；但如损失达到 6%时，则保险公司要赔偿 6%。

◆ **海上保险的起源**

海上保险究竟起源与何时何地，学界存在着不同的看法，但可以大致归纳为两种观点：一种观点认为是起源于公元前 2000 年出现在地中海一带的共同海损分摊原则，它强调损失分摊；另一种观点认为是起源于公元前 800—700 年流行在古希腊雅典地方的船货抵押借款制度，它强调损失补偿。一般来说，人们把共同海损分摊原则看做是“海上保险的萌芽”，而把船货抵押借款制度看做“海上保险的初级形式”。

More to Practice

I. Translate the following business terms or expressions into English.

1. 保险费
2. 保险费率
3. 保险金额
4. 中国人民保险公司
5. 一切险
6. 水渍险
7. 保险经纪人
8. 保险承保人
9. 保险范围
10. 保险条款

II. Translate the following sentences into Chinese.

1. We have covered insurance on 1,000 cases of beer for 110% of the invoice value against all risks.
2. If you desire us to insure against a special risk, an extra premium will have to be charged.
3. This risk is coverable at a premium of 0.25%.
4. The insurance company insures this risk with 5% franchise.
5. After loading the goods on board the ship, you must go to the insurance company to have them insured.
6. We can serve you with a broad range of coverage against all kinds of risks for sea transport, such as Free of Particular Average (F. P.A.), With Particular Average (W.P.A.), All Risks and Extraneous Risks.
7. W.P.A. plus Risk of Breakage suit your consignment.
8. The premium is calculated according to the premium rate or rates for risks to be covered.
9. They will undertake to compensate you for the losses according to the risks insured.
10. We are able to cover all kinds of risks for transportation by sea, land and air.

III. Translate the following sentences into English.

1. 我们不能投保此项险别，因为海洋运输条款中没有包括这一险别。
2. 除了水渍险和战争险外，你们还保其他险吗？
3. 按常规，额外保险费应由买方负责。
4. 请注意我们的保险范围只是发票金额的 110%。
5. 保险责任的起讫期限有多长？
6. 我们采用国际保险中常用的“仓至仓”的责任条款。
7. 破碎险是一种特别险，需收取额外保险费。
8. 因为这些不是易碎易损的货物，航行中不大可能被损坏。
9. 二月份发运到马尼拉的那批货物破碎严重。
10. 破碎损失超过这批货物的 30%。

IV. Writing practice.

Please write an insurance letter according to the following particulars.

1. 收到你方 8 月 3 日来信，要求我们投保 500 公吨龙井茶综合货物险。
2. 我方已经向中国人民保险公司投保了 1 000 美元的综合险。
3. 保险单下周内会寄给你们。
4. 我们已经安排阳光号装运这些茶叶，将于 9 月 1 日运往你处。

Unit 13

Packing

Study Aims

应知目标

1. To know the functions and types of packing.
2. To know the requirements of packing in international trade.
3. To know the writing steps of a letter of packing.
4. To know the knowledge of "Lead in" Part.
5. To know the knowledge of "Business Link" Part.

应会目标

1. To be able to translate a letter of packing.
2. To be able to write a letter of packing.

Lead in

- Packing is of particular importance in foreign trade because goods have to travel long distance before reaching their destination. Goods must be well packed in every process of international trade so that the business can go on smoothly. Hence, packing is one of the key terms in business communication and negotiation.
- Generally we divide packing into transport packing (or outer packing) and sales packing (or inner packing). Dealers should choose different packing containers according to the material of the goods.
- Packing Containers:

Bag: May be made of strong paper, linen, canvas, rubber, etc.

Sack: A large bag of strong, coarse material for holding objects in bulk, commonly used for powder and granular materials.

Carton: Made of light but strong cardboard or fiberboard, widely used in export packing because it is light, cheap and resilient. The carton is double walled or triple walled.

Case: A strong container made of wood used for small, heavy items.

Box: A small case, which may be made of wood, cardboard or metal.

Crate: A slatted wooden case not fully enclosed, used for storing or shipping, usually used for large and heavy objects like machines.

Drum: A cylinder-shaped container for carrying liquids, chemicals, paint, powders, etc., made of metal, wood or cardboard.

Writing Skills

Step 1: To inform the buyer that the order is ready

Step 2: To show the details in packing

Step 3: To express the hope of buyer's confirmation

Key Sentence Patterns

1. The next thing I'd like to bring up for discussion is packing.
2. We'd like to hear what you say concerning the matter of packing.
3. You'd like to know something about the packing of the drugs. Is that right?
4. The packing must be strong enough to withstand rough handling.
5. We have especially reinforced out packing in order to minimize the extent of any possible damage to the goods.
6. These goods didn't sell well merely because of the poor packing.
7. We agree to use cartons for outer packing.
8. The piece goods are to be wrapped in kraft paper, and then packed in wooden cases.
9. Please make the fruit jar airtight.
10. Ten bottles are put into a box and 100 boxes into a carton.
11. I'm afraid the cardboard boxes are not strong enough for ocean transportation.
12. The canned goods are to be packed in cartons with double straps.
13. Shirts are to be packed in plastic-lined water-proof cartons.
14. We will mark the packages the same as before.
15. Every 100 dozen should be packed in a wooden case marked TM and numbered from No. 1 upward.

Case Study

Case 1

Business background

Sender's information:

Name:	Alan
Company:	Shanghai Aosong Wine Trade Co., Ltd.
Add:	1588 Lian Rd Minghang, Shanghai, P.R.China 310000
Tel:	0086-021-54889999
Fax:	0086-021-54886999
Website:	www.aosongwine.com.cn
Email:	magic@hotmail.com
Business scope:	grape wine
Overseas markets:	Europe, Asia

Recipient's information:

Name:	Chloe
Company:	Rare Wine Trade Co., Ltd.
Add:	115 Berk St Salt Lake City, USA
Tel:	1-801-994243
Fax:	1-801-994253
Website:	www.rarewine.com.
Email:	cholegirl@gmail.com
Business scope:	wines
Overseas markets:	Europe, America, Asia, Africa

Task description

Alan, the salesman from Shanghai Aosong Wine Trade Co., Ltd. (herein called A Co., Ltd.), will imform the buyer—Rare Wine Trade Co., Ltd. (herein called B Co., Ltd.) that their order is ready and the wine will be packed in cartons.

Hints

- inform them the order is ready
- give the packing way
- explain the reasons for this kind of packing way
- enclose a photo of packed sample
- ask about other special requirement

Specimen letter 1

From: magic@hotmail.com (A Co., Ltd.)
To: cholegirl@gmail.com (B Co., Ltd.)
Date: May 8, 2013
Subject: packing
Attachment: a photo of packed sample
Dear Chloe: We are pleased to inform you that your order of 8,000 bottles of grape wine is ready. We shall pack them in cartons because cartons are comparatively light and compact, more convenient to handle. Furthermore cartons will prevent pilferage, for the traces of pilferage will be more in evidence. We have enclosed a photo of packed sample for you. We hope you will accept our carton packing and assure you of our sincere cooperation. Please let us know if you have special requirement. Yours sincerely, Alan A Co., Ltd.

Case 2
Business background

Sender's information:

Name:	Eric
Company:	Barolo Food Trade Co., Ltd.
Add:	298 Fu Chun Rd Hangzhou, Zhejiang, P.R.China 318000
Tel:	0086-577-88886666
Fax:	0086-577-88886667
Website:	www.barolofood.com.cn
Email:	fantasy@yahoo.com
Business scope:	food, wine
Overseas markets:	USA, Korea, Europe

Recipient's information:

Name:	Mario
Company:	Della Food Trade Co., Ltd.
Add:	227 Campeche St Utah, USA
Tel:	1-821-3456666
Fax:	1-821-3456667
Website:	www.dellafood.com.cn
Email:	superma@gmail.com
Business scope:	food, wine
Overseas markets:	America, Europe, Asia

Task description

Eric, on behalf of Barolo Food Trade Co., Ltd (herein called C Co., Ltd.) got an email from Mario, the salesman of Della Food Trade Co., Ltd (herein called D Co., Ltd.) for packing. So he will reply an email to Mario.

Hints

- mention the last email
- disapprove of their packing way
- express desire of changing the packing way
- explain the reasons for changing
- wish to get an early reply

Specimen letter 2

From: fantasy@yahoo.com (C Co., Ltd.)
To: superma@gmail.com (D Co., Ltd.)
Date: May 10, 2013
Subject: reply to the packing
Attachment:
Dear Mario: Thank you for your email of May 8 about the packing details. I immediately approached our clients about the packing. After our repeated explanation, they insist on packing the grape wine in wooden cases instead of cartons. The reason is that the cartons used are not seaworthy. We think you will understand that our frank statements are made for our mutual benefits as packing is a sensitive subject, which often leads to trade disputes. Kindly let us know whether the requirement could be met. Yours sincerely, Eric C Co., Ltd.

Task Practice

Task 1

Description

Globes Food Co., Ltd. is an importers and merchant of food since 1989. It has many deals with a Chinese company named Changyu International Trade Co., Ltd.

Hunk, a salesperson of Globes Food Co., Ltd. has got the email of Changyu Co., Ltd. on inquiring about the packing and shipping marks. He will send an email to Changyu Co., Ltd. for offering the opinion about the packing details.

Requirements

You are required to send an email to Changyu Co., Ltd. as the role of Hunk, according to the following tips.

Tips

- mention the last email
- confirm the packing details
- offer the opinion about shipping marks
- wish to get an early reply

From: ____________________

To: ____________________

Date: ____________________

Subject: ____________________

____

____

____

____

____

____

____

____

Specimen letter 3

Suggested answer for Task 1

From: wisdom@yahoo.com (Globes Food Co., Ltd.)
To: fortune@hotmail.com (Changyu Food Co., Ltd.)
Date: June 8, 2013

Subject: packing
Attachment:
Dear Sir or Madam: We thank you for your email of June 6 inquiring about the packing and shipping marks of the goods under the S/C No. GB135. We'd like to confirm as follows: All powders are wrapped in POLY bags and packed in tins, the lids of which are sealed with adhesive tape. Twenty tins are packed in a wooden case, which is nailed and secured by metal strap. As far as the shipping marks outside the wooden case, in addition to gross and net weights, the wording "Made in China" is also stenciled. If you have any specific requirements, please let us know ASAP. Yours faithfully, Hunk Changyu Food Co., Ltd.

Task 2

Description

Conrad Machine Co., Ltd. is North America's oldest manufacturer of machine tools and metal fabricating equipment.

Ken, a salesperson of Conrad Machine Co., Ltd. has got the email from Minister Machine Co., Ltd. about the order of 20 cases of machine parts. He will reply the email to Minister Machine Co., Ltd. for giving the packing details.

Requirements

You are required to write an email to Minister Machine Co., Ltd. as the role of Ken, according to the following tips.

Tips

- mention the last email
- give the plan for packing
- explain the reasons for packing way
- thank for cooperation

From: ____

To: ____

Date: ____

Subject: ____

____

____

____

____

____

____

____

____

____

Specimen letter 4

Suggested answer for Task 2—A Reply

From: happiness@hotmail.com (Conrad Machine Co., Ltd.)
To: luckyboy@yahoo.com (Minister Machine Co., Ltd.)
Date: Oct 10, 2013
Subject: packing
Attachment:

Dear Sir or Madam:

We've received your email of October 9, regarding our trial order of 20 cases of machine parts.

Please see to it that as machine parts are susceptible to shocks, they must be wrapped in soft materials and firmly packed in seaworthy cases to avoid any movement inside the cases. The unvarnished ferrous metal parts should be well greased to prevent rusting.

We trust that you can meet the above requirements and thank you in advance for your cooperation.

Yours faithfully,
Ken
Conrad Machine Co., Ltd.

Notes

1. light and compact 轻便结实
2. in evidence 明显的，显著的

3. assure sb. of sth. 使某人相信某事，向某人保证
4. approached our clients 联系我们的客户
5. insist on... 坚持……
6. mutual benefits 互惠互利
7. sensitive subject 敏感问题
8. trade disputes 贸易争端
9. S/C 是“Sales Contract 销货合同”的缩写。
10. shipping marks 发货标记，运输标志，唛头
11. in addition to gross and net weights 除了毛重和净重
12. trial order 试订货
13. The unvarnished ferrous metal parts should be well greased to prevent rusting.
   未油漆的含铁金属零件应涂上润滑油以免生锈。

New Words and Expressions

1. comparatively	*ad.* 比较地，相当地
2. pilferage	*n.* 行窃，偷盗
3. approach	*v.* 接近，动手处理
4. insist	*v.* 坚持
5. seaworthy	*a.* 适于海运的，经得起航海的
6. frank	*a.* 坦诚的，直白的
7. sensitive	*a.* 敏感的，灵敏的
8. dispute	*n.* 争论，辩论，争端
9. wrap	*v.* 包装，卷，缠绕，包
10. POLY	*n.* 聚乙烯
11. adhesive tape	胶带
12. metal strap	铁箍，金属条
13. stencil	*v.* 印刷，用……刷
14. susceptible	*a.* 易受影响的，易感动的
15. unvarnished	*a.* 未涂漆的，原样的
16. ferrous	*a.* 铁的，含铁的
17. grease	*v.* 涂脂于
18. rust	*n./v.* 铁锈，（使）生锈

Business Link

◆ 包装标志的分类

包装标志是包装上不可或缺的重要部分，一般分为三类：

1. 运输标志

即通常所说的唛头（Marks），它一般包括四部分：（1）收货人缩写或代号；（2）参考号，如订单号，发票号码等；（3）目的地；（4）件数号码。

2. 指示性标志

它是提示人们在装卸、搬运、保管过程中应该注意的事项，一般由简洁明了的文字或图案组成。

3. 警告性标志

它又被称为危险品包装标志，一般是针对某些易燃易爆物品、某些化学物品、有毒物品、放射性物品等特种物品的运输标志以警示人们做好防护措施。

◆ 常见外包装指示性标志

This side up	此面朝上
Handle with care	小心轻放
Keep from moisture	防潮
No hook	禁止钩挂
Keep dry	保持干燥
Keep cool	保持阴凉

◆ 绿色包装的"3R1D"原则

一是实行包装减量化（Reduce）。包装在满足保护、方便、销售等功能的条件下，应是用量最少。

二是包装应易于重复利用（Reuse），或易于回收再生（Recycle）。通过生产再生制品、焚烧利用热能、堆肥化改善土壤等措施，达到再利用的目的。

三是包装废弃物可以降解腐化（Degradable）。最终不形成永久垃圾，进而达到改良土壤的目的。

◆ 部分国家对于包装的特殊规定

新西兰对于农产品的进口包装禁止使用稻草、麦草、干草、土壤、泥灰等做材料。

希腊规定出口到该国的产品必须在包装上用希腊文注明公司名称、产品名称、数量、质量等信息。

利比亚对进口产品的包装禁止使用猪和女性人体等图案。

德国对进口产品的包装禁止使用类似纳粹或军团等图案。

More to Practice

I. Translate the following business terms or expressions into English.

1. 相对轻便结实
2. 便于搬运
3. 保持阴凉
4. 包装
5. 小心轻放
6. 保持干燥
7. 互惠互利
8. 禁止钩挂
9. 贸易争端
10. 用铁条钉牢

II. Translate the following sentences into Chinese.

1. We require neutral packing, so please stencil shipping marks and some warning marks on the packing.
2. The unique design of the packing will help you promote the sale of drugs.
3. The new packing of the porcelain is in Chinese national style and suitable for display in supermarkets.
4. Please note that the 500 tea sets under our Order No. 456 should be packed in paper padded with foamed plastic.
5. The machines must be well protected against dampness, moisture and shock.
6. Normally, packing charge is included in the contract price.
7. I'm sure the new packing will give your clients satisfaction.
8. A packing that catches the eye will help us push the sales.
9. Thank you for your packing instructions, but regret our inability to comply with your requirement for special packing.
10. The goods must be packed in plastic bags before they are put into the cartons.

III. Translate the following sentences into English.

1. 在外包装上请标明“小心轻放”字样。
2. 每个箱角都用金属角加固。
3. 包装也影响产品的声誉。
4. 包装费用占货物总值的 3%。
5. 钢笔 10 支装一盒，200 盒装一木箱。
6. 为了避免货物在箱子内移动，箱内必须用塑料衬垫填充。
7. 我们有特殊方法包装服装。
8. 青豆可以散装，也可以麻袋装。
9. 纸箱内都衬有塑料布，是防水的，由于箱子是硬纸板的，所以在搬运的时候就会小心处理。
10. 容器上不能出现国家名和商标名。

IV. Writing practice.

买方写信告诉卖方发往新加坡的 100 箱男士衬衣中，有 10 箱严重受潮，希望今后注重商品的包装。应每件装一塑料袋，每打装一纸盒，每 20 盒装一适合海运的纸板箱，箱内衬塑料布。

请卖方告知是否能满足这些要求。

Unit 14

Complaints and Claims

Study Aims

应知目标

1. To know the types of a claim.
2. To know how to solve a complaint and settle a claim.
3. To know the writing steps of a letter of complaint and a claim settlement.
4. To know the knowledge of "Lead in" Part.
5. To know the knowledge of "Business Link" Part.

应会目标

1. To be able to translate a letter of complaint or claim.
2. To be able to write a letter of complaint or claim.

Lead in

- A claim letter is a demand from a customer for something that is due or owed, or something that is a correction of a problem. Complaints and claims are usually raised by buyers. However, sellers may also raise claims against buyers for non-establishment of L/C or breach of contract, etc. A claim should be made as quickly as possible for it can be rejected if it is too late. Some companies may have a deadline for claims.
- In the international trade, complaints and claims often happens because of shortage of quantity, the delivery of wrong goods, the delivery of damaged or defective merchandise or delay of delivery and improper packing, etc. After receiving the complaints or claims, the seller will make immediate investigations and settle the problem as soon as possible. That is called the adjustment.

Writing Skills

Step 1: To state the problem in detail

Step 2: To present the loss or inconvenience that is made by this error

Step 3: To present the evidence to support your complaints and claims

Step 4: To present the way you want to settle the problem

Key Sentence Patterns

1. We received the Order No. 456 last week.
2. We have received our Order No. 0990 for digital cameras.
3. We require you refund the invoice amount and inspection fee of the goods amounting to RMB3,000,000.00.
4. In support of our claim, we will send you a survey report issued by CIQ.
5. All the expenses will be for you account.
6. On opening the cases we noticed that we had received the wrong goods.
7. Please advise us when we can expect to receive our order.
8. Upon examination of the goods against your invoice, we discovered a shortage in the number of Apple MP3.
9. We notify you that we reserve the right to claim on you for the shortage.
10. Ship the additional 100 sets of Apple MP3 on the earliest possible flight from California at your expense.
11. We have not yet received notification that the order has been delivered till now.
12. Please let us know whether the order has been delivered.
13. Please inform us of the arrival date in Ningbo.

Case Study

Case 1

Business background

Sender's information:

Name:	Yang Yuan
Company:	Hanghzou Sunlife Trade Co., Ltd.
Add:	55 Wuling Rd Hangzhou, Zhejiang, P.R.China 310000
Tel:	0086-571-89824531
Fax:	0086-571-89824531
Website:	www.hzwp.com.cn
Email:	coolboy@hotmail.com
Business scope:	digitals, CD players, cameras
Overseas markets:	US, America, Asia, South Africa

Recipient's information:

Name:	Mary
Company:	US Digital Trade Co., Ltd.
Add:	35 Diamond St New York, US
Tel:	001-21-347 581
Fax:	001-21-347 581
Website:	www.new.com
Email:	prettygirl@gmail.com
Business scope:	digitals, CD players, Cameras
Overseas markets:	Europe, America, Asia, Africa

Task description

Yang Yuan, on behalf of Hcngzhou Sunlife Trade Co., Ltd. (herein called ABC Co., Ltd.) met Mary of US Digital Trade Co., Ltd. (herein called BCD Co., Ltd.) in the United States Digital Products exhibition in New York last Nov. He will send an email to Mary to complain about the CD players' quality.

Hints

- mention the exact products you are complaining about
- tell about the exact problem
- express the number of claim
- enclose the relevant evidence of complaint
- wish to get an early reply

Specimen letter 1

From: coolboy@hotmail.com (ABC Co., Ltd.)
To: prettygirl@gmail.com (BCD Co., Ltd.)
Date: Jan 8, 2013
Subject: claim for low quality CD players
Attachment: a survey report issued by CIQ

Dear Mary:

We received the CD players of the Order No. 456 last week and are sorry to tell you that the quality of it is very bad. Half of them could not work properly.

As so many products are of low quality, we require you refund the invoice amount and inspection fee of the goods amounting to RMB30,000,000.00. In support of our claim, we will send you a survey report issued by AQSIQ.

We hope you will settle this claim immediately. As soon as it is settled down, we will send the goods back to you. All the expenses will be for your account.

Yours sincerely,

Yang Yuan

ABC Co., Ltd.

Case 2
Business background

Sender's information:

Name:	Mary
Company:	Ningbo Skyline Trading Co., Ltd.
Add:	14 Caihong Rd Ningbo, Zhejiang, P.R.China 318000
Tel:	0086-574-5374 3366
Fax:	0086-574-5374 3366
Website:	www.ningbost.com
Email:	prettygirl@yahoo.com
Business scope:	MP3, CD players, Cameras
Overseas markets:	UK, Korea, South Africa

Recipient's information:

Name:	Lin
Company:	UK New Technology Co., Ltd.
Add:	57 Ding St London, UK
Tel:	0044-20-3946 712
Fax:	0044-20-3946 712
Website:	www.newtec.com.cn
Email:	coolboy@hotmail.com
Business scope:	MP3, digital products
Overseas markets:	America, Europe, Asia

Task description

Mary, on behalf of Ningbo Skyline Trading Co., Ltd. (herein called BCD Co., Ltd.) writes an email to Lin from UK New Technology Co., Ltd. (herein called ABC Co., Ltd.) to complain about the wrong product number in the last order transportation. And she asks him to make up the shortage.

Hints

- mention the order number
- give the exact number of product shortage
- express desire of receiving the shortage earlier
- specify whose account for the extra expense
- wish to get an early reply

Specimen letter 2

From: prettygirl@yahoo.com (BCD Co., Ltd.)
To: coolboy@hotmail.com (ABC Co., Ltd.)
Date: Jan 11, 2013
Subject: complaint about insufficient delivery of MP3
Attachment:

Dear Lin:

We received on June 10 three cases of goods under our Order No. 859. Upon examination of the goods against your invoice, we discovered a shortage in the number of Apple MP3. Whereas 500 sets were ordered, we received only 400 sets.

The cases are intact, the shortage may be due to confusion in packing and we notify you that we reserve the right to claim on you for the shortage.

Please investigate this matter carefully and ship the additional 100 sets of Apple MP3 on the earliest possible flight from London at your expense.

Yours sincerely,

Mary

BCD Co., Ltd.

Task Practice

Task 1

Description

BCD Co., Ltd. is one of the largest exporters of elevators and has been in this line for 20 years with a good reputation.

Clark, a foreign salesperson of ABC Co., Ltd. has ordered two Hitachi elevators in August. And it was requested to be delivered before September 25. but he hasn't received any information of delivery notification till now.

Requirements

You are required to send an email to BCD Co., Ltd. to complain about the late delivery of Order No. 998 according to the following tips.

Tips

- mention the order number
- give a brief introduction of the order content
- express the complaint of late delivery
- emphasize the delivery time
- wish to get an early reply

From: ______________________________

To: ______________________________

Date: ______________________________

Subject: ______________________________

____

____

____

____

____

____

____

____

Specimen letter 3

Suggested answer for Task 1

From: coolboy@hotmail.com (ABC Co., Ltd.)
To: prettygirl@yahoo.com (BCD Co., Ltd.)
Date: Sep 23, 2013
Subject: complaint about late delivery of Order No. 998
Attachment:
Dear Wei Hong: As you know, we placed an order with you for two Hitachi elevators in August. It was requested to be delivered before September 25. We have not yet received notification that the order has been delivered till now. Please let us know whether the order has been delivered. If so, please inform us of the arrival date in Ningbo. We are really anxious to get this order. We look forward to receiving your early reply. Yours sincerely, Clark ABC Co., Ltd.

Task 2

Description

ABC Co., Ltd. is a large company exporting cameras worldwide.

Mary, a foreign salesperson of BCD Co., Ltd. has placed an order with ABC Co., Ltd. for some digital cameras with the type of IXUS 75 under Order No. 0990. As a matter of fact, they have received IXUS 60 instead of IXUS 75.

Requirements

You are required to send an email to Mr. Lin of ABC Co., Ltd. for the complaint of wrong products received according to the following tips.

Tips

- mention the order No.
- give a brief statement of the products received
- require to receive the right product
- need to know how to deal with the products received
- wish to get an early reply

From: ____________________

To: ____________________

Date: ____________________

Subject: ____________________

____

____

____

____

____

____

____

____

____

____

Specimen letter 4

Suggested answer for Task 2—A Reply

From: prettygirl@yahoo.com (BCD Co., Ltd.)
To: coolboy@hotmail.com (ABC Co., Ltd.)
Date: Jan 8, 2013
Subject: complaint about wrong digital cameras
Attachment:
Dear Mr. Lin: We have received our Order No.0990 for digital cameras. On opening the cases, we noticed that we had received the wrong goods.

We received IXUS 60 instead of the IXUS 75 that we ordered.
Please advise us when we can expect to receive our order. And we would like to know what we should do with the items now in our possession.
Yours sincerely,
Mary
BCD Co., Ltd.

Notes

1. complaint *n.* 投诉，申诉；抱怨，不满
   make a complaint against … 向……投诉
   complain *v.* 投诉
   Many customers complain about the products. 许多客户投诉该产品。
2. claim *n.* 索赔
   表示索赔原因、金额，后接介词 for。
   表示索赔对象，后接 against somebody 或 on goods。
   accept a claim 同意索赔
   reject a claim 拒绝索赔
   settle a claim 解决索赔
   claim *v.* 索赔
   to claim a compensation of … from somebody for something 为某事向某人索赔若干金额
3. CD player CD 播放器
4. be of low quality 低质
5. inspection fee 检验费
6. survey report 检验报告
7. AQSIQ (General Administration of Quality Supervision, Inspection and Quarantine of the People's Republic of China) 中华人民共和国国家质量监督检验检疫总局（简称国家质检总局）
8. All the expenses will be for sb.'s account. 相关费用由某人负担。
   类似的表达方式还有 Expenses will be at one's expense.
9. be due to 因为，由于
10. reserve the right to do sth. 保留做某事的权利
11. place an order with sb. for sth. 向某人订某物
12. Hitachi elevator “日立牌”电梯
13. inform sb. of sth. 通知某人某事
14. arrival date 到达日期
15. in our possession 我方手头的货

New Words and Expressions

1.	complaint	*n.* 投诉、申诉
2.	quality	*n.* 质量
3.	refund	*v.* 退款，偿还
4.	invoice	*n.* 发票
5.	inspection	*n.* 检验
6.	amount	*n.* 金额，数量
7.	issue	*v.* 发出，出具
8.	digital camera	数码照相机
9.	shortage	*n.* 短缺，缺乏
10.	set	*n.* 套，只
11.	intact	*a.* 完好无损的
12.	confusion	*n.* 混乱
13.	packing	*n.* 包装
14.	California	加利福尼亚（美国州名）
15.	investigate	*v.* 调查
16.	notification	*n.* 通知

Business Link

◆ **国家质检总局 AQSIQ**

中华人民共和国国家质量监督检验检疫总局 General Administration of Quality Supervision Inspection and Quarantine of the People's Republic of China（简称国家质检总局，AQSIQ）是国务院主管全国质量、计量、出入境商品检验、出入境卫生检疫、出入境动植物检疫、进出口食品安全和认证认可、标准化等工作，并行使行政执法职能的正部级国务院直属机构。

为履行出入境检验检疫职能，国家质检总局在全国 31 省(自治区、直辖市）共设有 35 个直属出入境检验检疫局，海陆空口岸和货物集散地设有近 300 个分支局和 200 多个办事处，共有检验检疫人员 3 万余人。质检总局对出入境检验检疫机构实施垂直管理。

◆ **索赔过程介绍**

当出口货物遭受损失，对方（进口方）向保险单所载明的国外理赔代理人提出索赔申请。中国人民保险公司在世界各主要港口和城市，均设有委托国外检验代理人和理赔代理人两种机构，前者负责检验货物损失。收货人取得检验报告后，附同其他单证，自行向出单公司索赔，后者可在授权的一定金额内，直接处理赔案，就地给付赔款。

进口方在向我国外理赔代理人提出索赔时，要同时提供下列单证：

（1）保险单或保险凭证正本；

（2）运输契约；

（3）发票；

（4）装箱单；

（5）向承运人等第三者责任方请求补偿的函电或其他单证，以及证明被保险人已经履行应办的追偿手续等文件；

（6）由国外保险代理人或由国外第三者公证机构出具的检验报告；

（7）海事报告。海事造成的货物损失，一般均由保险公司赔付，船方不承担责任；

（8）货损货差证明；

（9）索赔清单；等。

被保险人在办妥上述有关索赔手续和提供齐全的单证后，即可等待保险公司审定责任，给付赔款。在我国，保险公司赔款方式有两种：一是直接赔付给收货单位；二是集中赔付给各有关外贸公司，再由各外贸公司与各订货单位进行结算。

◆ 佳能数码照相机

佳能是全球领先的生产影像与信息产品的综合集团。自 1937 年成立以来，佳能已将自己的业务全球化并扩展到各个领域。目前，佳能的产品系列共分布于三大领域：个人产品、办公设备和工业设备，主要产品包括照相机及镜头、数码相机、打印机、复印机、传真机、扫描仪、广播设备、医疗器材及半导体生产设备等。佳能总部位于日本东京，并在美洲、欧洲、亚洲及日本设有四大区域性销售总部，在世界各地拥有子公司 200 家，雇员超过 10 万人。

◆ 苹果公司

美国苹果股份有限公司，简称苹果公司，英文名 Apple, Inc.，原称苹果电脑(Apple Computer)，在 2007 年 1 月 9 日于旧金山的 Macworld Expo 上宣布改名。总部位于美国加利福尼亚的库比提诺，核心业务是电子科技产品，目前全球电脑市场占有率为 3.8%。苹果的 Apple II 于 1970 年代助长了个人电脑革命，其后的 Macintosh 接力于 20 世纪 80 年代持续发展。最知名的产品是其出品的 Apple II、Macintosh 电脑、iPod 数位音乐播放器和 iTunes 音乐商店，它在高科技企业中以创新而闻名。

More to Practice

I. Translate the following business terms or expressions into English.

1. 索赔
2. 投诉
3. 低质
4. 发票
5. 短装
6. 包装
7. 延迟出运
8. 到达日期
9. 向某人提出索赔
10. 检验费用

II. Translate the following sentences into Chinese.

1. We regret to know that you did not receive the ten sets of Sony TV sets you wanted.
2. We have arranged for the 10 sets of Sony TV sets to be dispatched to you at once.

3. On examination we have found not all the goods correspond with your original samples.
4. We regret to inform you that the Case No. 9 is broken, and the goods within the case were badly damaged owing to improper packing.
5. In view of the fact that the price of raw materials has risen recently, we have to adjust part of the price.
6. We received your consignment of toys under our Order No. 626 yesterday.
7. We regret to hear of the breakages which occurred in transit.
8. We pack our shipments with great care but there are occasions when the merchandise is mishandled along the way.
9. A shortage of 60 tons is a big loss for us. We have no alternative but to lodge a claim against you.
10. We are lodging a claim for inferior quality.

III. Translate the following sentences into English.

1. 我们感到遗憾的是，箱内仅装了 30 台电视机，而不是发票上写明的 36 台。
2. 我们不能向客户供应从你处收到的如此劣质的货物。
3. 对于所遭受的损失，我们不得不要求你方负责。
4. 我们仔细核查了此事，得到的唯一解释是标签弄混了。
5. 发错货物是由于你方包装人员的失误造成的。
6. 我们将在卸货完毕之后检查此货。
7. 无论如何，我们要求你方采取措施，防止类似事件再次发生。
8. 经检验，箱内缺少 17 件货物。
9. 我方到现在还未收到任何货物已出运的通知。
10. 请告知我们抵达宁波港的时间。

IV. Writing practice.

Please write an email to lodge a claim for a damaged delivery.

Unit 15

Integrated Business Negotiation Skills Practice

Study Aims

应知目标

1. To know the writing steps of an enquiry.
2. To know the writing steps of a firm offer.
3. To know the writing steps of a counter-offer.
5. To know the writing steps of a letter of an order.
6. To know the writing steps of a letter of acceptance.
7. To understand the form and content of a Sales Confirmation.
8. To understand the form and content of a Sales Contract.

应会目标

1. To be able to make an enquiry.
2. To be able to make a firm offer.
3. To be able to make a counter-offer.
4. To be able to write a letter of an order.
5. To be able to write a letter of acceptance.
6. To be able to write a letter of confirmation.
7. To be able to make an order.
8. To be able to make a Sales Confirmation.
9. To be able to make a Sales Contract.

Situation Practice

- Seller: Electronics Co., Ltd.
- Buyer: Rose Co., Ltd.
- Goods: MP4 watches
- The buyer gets the seller's information from a magazine named *International Business* and sends an enquiry to the seller.
- The seller gives the buyer an offer.

- The buyer makes the seller a counter-offer.
- The seller accepts the counter-offer.
- The buyer places an initial order with the seller.
- The seller sends a sales contract to the buyer and asks for **countersignature.**
- In international trade, usually a contract will be made to further specify the rights and obligations of both parties for legal purposes. After signing the contract, the parties concerned are legally bound to honor their agreement.

Please write six letters as the roles of buyer and seller according to the Chinese clues:

外贸业务洽谈流程：询盘→报盘→还盘→接受→下订单→签订合同

Sample Letters

Letter 1 Enquiry

From: nicetea@yahoo.com (Rose Co., Ltd.)
To: coolboy@hotmail.com (Electronics Co., Ltd.)
Date: Jan 28, 2013
Subject: Enquiry for MP4 watches
Attachment:
Dear Sir or Madam: We learn from *International Business* that you are a leading exporter of electronic products in your country. We are in the market for MP4 watches and would appreciate your sending us catalogues and sample books if possible. Will you please quote us your lowest price CIF New York, inclusive of terms of payment? We hope this will be a good start for further business relations between us. Yours faithfully, Johnson Rose Co., Ltd.

Letter 2 Offer

From: coolboy@hotmail.com (Electronics Co., Ltd.)
To: nicetea@yahoo.com (Rose Co., Ltd.)
Date: Jan 29, 2013
Subject: Offer for MP4 watches

Attachment: catalogue
Dear Sir or Madam: Thank you for your email of Jan 28, enquiring for our MP4 watches. We are glad to make you an offer as follows, subject to your reply reaching us before Feb 6th, 2013: Commodity: MP4 watches Specifications: as per catalogue Quantity: min 2,000 pieces Unit price: US$20 /pc CIF New York Payment: by irrevocable L/C at sight Shipment: to be shipped within 30 days after receipt of L/C Shipping marks: at seller's option We're looking forward to your early reply. Yours faithfully, Mike Electronics Co., Ltd.

Letter 3 Counter-offer

From: nicetea@yahoo.com (Rose Co., Ltd.)
To: coolboy@hotmail.com (Electronics Co., Ltd.)
Date: Feb 5, 2013
Subject: MP4 watches
Attachment:
Dear Sir or Madam: Thank you for your email of Jan 29, 2013 offering us your MP4 watches on CIF New York basis. We appreciate your products very much, but can we earn some discount if we order 2,500 pieces? It would be highly appreciated if you could agree to pay by T/T in advance for 20% of the total value and by L/C for the balance. Your early reply will be highly appreciated. Yours faithfully, Johnson Rose Co., Ltd.

Letter 4 Acceptance

From: coolboy@hotmail.com (Electronics Co., Ltd.)
To: nicetea@yahoo.com (Rose Co., Ltd.)
Date: Feb 8, 2013
Subject: MP4 watches
Attachment:
Dear Sir or Madam: Thank you for your email of Feb 5, 2013. In order to build our long-term business relationship, we are glad to offer you our best price: US$18/pc CIF New York. Meanwhile, we can not entertain any reduction in price. As to payment, we can only accept L/C at sight. We hope the above will be acceptable to you and await your order. Yours faithfully, Mike Electronics Co., Ltd.

Letter 5 Order

From: nicetea@yahoo.com (Rose Co., Ltd.)
To: coolboy@hotmail.com (Electronics Co., Ltd.)
Date: Mar 3, 2013
Subject: P.O. No.156
Attachment: P.O. No.156
Dear Sir or Madam: Thank you for offering us your best price on CIF New York basis and we are pleased to give you our order No. 156 in the attachment. Please send us your sales contract. As we are in urgent need of the goods, we'd like to stress the importance of punctual shipment of our order. Yours faithfully, Johnson Rose Co., Ltd.

Attachment 1: P.O. No.156

ROSE CO., LTD.
208 BENNETT ROAD, NEW YORK, U.S.A.
TEL: +1-212-56783355 FAX: +1-212-56783355

TO: **Electronics Co., Ltd.**

Purchase Order NO. 156
Date: Mar. 3, 2013

Please supply the following:

Commodity	**Specification**	**Quantity**	**Unit Price** CIF New York
MP4 Watches	Art. No. Am688	3,000 pcs	US$18 per pc
Comments :	Payment by L/C at sight To be shipped during May 2013		

Authorized: *Johnson*

Letter 6

From: coolboy@hotmail.com (Electronics Co., Ltd.)
To: nicetea@yahoo.com (Rose Co., Ltd.)
Date: Mar 8, 2013
Subject: P.O. No.156
Attachment: Sales Contract No. 348
Dear Sir or Madam: Thank you for your initial order No. 156. As requested, we have made out our Sales Contract No. 348. Enclosed please find the S/C and return us one copy countersigned. We appreciate your cooperation and are looking forward to your establishment of the L/C. Yours faithfully, Mike Electronics Co., Ltd.

Attachment 2: Sales Contract No. 348

Sales Contract

NO. 348

Date: _______

Place:_______

Sellers: Electronics Co., Ltd.	**Buyers:** Rose Co., Ltd.
Add: No. 58 Cicheng Road	**Add:** 208 Bennett Road
Cixi, Ningbo	New York
Zhejiang, China	U.S.A.
Tel:+ 86-574-68877556	**Tel:+1-212-56783355**
Fax: +86-574-68877556	**Fax: +1-212-56783355**

This contract is made by and between the Sellers and the Buyers, whereby the buyers agree to buy and the sellers agree to sell the under-mentioned commodity according to the terms and conditions below:

Commodity: MP4 watches

Specifications: Art No. Am688

Quantity: 3,000 pcs

Unit Price: US$18 /pc CIF New York

Total Amount. : US$54,000

Terms of Payment: By irrevocable L/C at sight

Shipping Marks: At seller's option

Time of Shipment: To be shipped during May 2013

Port of Shipment: China port

Port of Destination: New York

Transshipment and Partial Shipment: Allowed

Insurance: To be covered by the seller for 110% of the invoice value against all risks and war risk

Commodity Inspection: It is mutually agreed that Certificate of Quality and Weight issued by public inspection organization at the port of shipment shall be taken as the basis of delivery.

Discrepancy and Claim: Any claim by the Buyers on the goods shipped shall be filed within 30 days after the arrival of the goods at port of destination and supported by a survey report issued by a public surveyor approved by the Sellers. Claims in respect of matters within the responsibility of the insurance company or of the shipping company will not be considered or entertained by the Sellers.

Force Majeure: If shipment of the contracted goods is prevented or delayed in whole or in

part due to Force Majeure, the Sellers shall not be liable for non-shipment or late shipment of the goods under this Contract. However the Sellers shall notify the Buyers by fax and furnish the Latter within 15 days by registered airmail with a certificate issued by the local chamber of commerce attesting such event or events. **Sellers(signature)** ____________ **Buyers(signature)** ____________

Writing Practice

Fill in the following contract form according to some business letters exchanged between the buyer and the seller.

(1) Enquiry

From: greenidea@hotmail.com (Green Products Imp and Exp Co., Ltd.)
To: sunnygirl@yahoo.com (Sunshine Products Co., Ltd.)
Date: June 6, 2013
Subject: Energy saving lamps
Attachment:
Dear Sir or Madam: We have got your name and address from Canton Fair. After carefully studying your catalogue, we are interested in your energy saving lamps. We will appreciate it very much if you will quote us your lowest price CIF New York for 2,000 pieces energy saving lamps of Style No. 2U (12W), indicating your payment terms. Meanwhile, would you please send us some samples of energy saving lamps? We are looking forward to your early reply. Yours faithfully, Clark Green Products Imp and Exp Co., Ltd.

(2) Offer

From: sunnygirl@yahoo.com (Sunshine Products Co., Ltd.)
To: greenidea@hotmail.com (Green Products Imp and Exp Co., Ltd.)
Date: June 7, 2013
Subject: Energy saving lamps
Attachment:

Dear Sir or Madam: Thank you for your email of June 6 enquiring for energy saving lamps. We are pleased to make you an offer as follows, subject to your acceptance reaching us not later than June 15: 2,000 pieces energy saving lamps of Style No. 2U (12W), packed in boxes of one piece each, twenty boxes to a carton, at US$4 per pc CIF New York, for shipment from any Chinese port within 30 days after receipt of L/C. As to terms of payment, we usually require L/C at sight. Today we have sent three samples of different styles to you by DHL, and they will reach you soon. We await your initial order with keen interest. Yours faithfully, Mary Sunshine Products Co., Ltd.

(3) Acceptance & Order

From: greenidea@hotmail.com (Green Products Imp and Exp Co., Ltd.)
To: sunnygirl@yahoo.com (Sunshine Products Co., Ltd.)
Date: June 12, 2013
Subject: Energy saving lamps
Attachment: P.O. No. 331
Dear Sir or Madam: Many thanks for your quotation of June 7 and the samples sent to us. We are satisfied with the quality and accept your price. As payment by L/C will cost us a lot, we suggest payment by D/P at sight for this small-sized order. Enclosed please find our order No. 331 for shipment during December. Insurance is to be covered by you against All Risks and War Risk for 110% of the invoice value. Please kindly let us have your confirmation soon. Yours faithfully, Clark Green Products Imp and Exp Co., Ltd.

以下是 2013 年 6 月 14 号在杭州签订的合同：

Sales Contract

NO. 452
Date:
Signed at:

Sellers:
Buyers:
This contract is made by and between the Sellers and the Buyers, whereby the buyers agree to buy and the sellers agree to sell the under-mentioned commodity according to the terms and conditions below:
Commodity:
Specifications:
Quantity:
Unit price:
Total amount :
Packing:
Terms of payment:
Shipping marks:
Time of shipment:
Port of shipment:
Port of destination:
Transshipment and partial shipment:
Insurance:

Sellers(signature) Buyers(signature)

__________________ __________________

Skills Training

Skills Training for Unit 1 技能训练 1

I. Vocabulary and Grammar Using Skills Training.

Please fill in the following blank with the best answer.

1. We look forward to ______ from you soon.

   A. here　　B. hearing　　C. heard　　D. be heard

2. Your name and address ______ to us by your Chamber of Commerce.

   A. have given　　B. give　　C. have been given　　D. was given

3. We are sending you the samples ______ requested.

   A. be　　B. are　　C. as　　D. for

4. While ______ an enquiry, you ought to enquire into quality specification and price etc.

   A. making　　B. offering　　C. sending　　D. giving

5. If your sample meets our requirement, we will ______ a large order.

   A. place　　B. place you　　C. make　　D. send you

6. I would appreciate your ______ me a booklet.

   A. airmail　　B. enclose　　C. sending　　D. enclosing

7. I would appreciate ______ me an up-to-date price list for your building materials.

   A. it if you would sent　　B. you sent

   C. that you would sent　　D. your sending

8. We are very glad to quote you as ______.

   A. follows　　B. following　　C. follow　　D. below

9. We accept your offer ______ black tea.

   A. with　　B. in　　C. of　　D. by

10. ______ the price quoted by us is reasonable, we trust this will be ______ by you.

    A. As...acceptable　　B. As...accepted

    C. Because...acceptable　　D. Because...satisfied

II. Please write a business letter in one of three mentioned layouts according to the following message.

1. Sender's information:

   PACIFIC CO., LTD.

   Add: POWELL, 234 SAN FRANCISCO CALIFORNIA　U.S.A.

   Tel: + 01-21-88995566　　Fax: +01-21-88995566

2. Receiver's information:
   CATHY　CO., LTD.
   Add: NO.89　YUNSA ROAD HEFEI, ANHUI, P.R.C
   Tel: +86-891-77441233　Fax: +86-891-77441233
3. Date: Oct 10, 2008
4. Subject: Establishing business relations
5. The message:
   Thank you for your letter of Oct 8.
   We are one of the largest importers of silk products in our city and glad to establish business relations with your company.
   At present we are interested in Art. No 168 in your catalogue sent us.
6. Signature: MICKEY

III. Address the following envelope in Chinese.

STAMP

SUNNY CO., LTD.
NO21 BROADWAY,　NEW YORK
U.S.A
Tel: +1-02-6699586
Fax: +1-02-6699586

THE NORTH CO., LTD
NO.58 GUANGA ROAD BEIJING,
P. R.C
Tel: +86-10-28877556
Fax: +86-10-28877556

Airmail

IV. Comprehensive Language Using Skills Training.

Supply the missing words in the blanks of the message.

Dear Sir or Madam,

We have o__1__ your name and address from the M__2__ of Commerce of the People's Republic of China. We were i__3__ that you are one of the largest i__4__ of tea in UK and you are now in the m___5___ for tea. We take this opportunity to approach you in the hope of e___6___ business relations with you.

To give you a g___7___ idea of our products, we enclose a copy of our brochure. If you are i___8___ in any of our products, please contact us with your requirements. We look f___9___ to providing you with high q___10___ products.

Yours faithfully,

V. Business Letters Translation Skills Training.

Please translate the following business letter into Chinese.

Dear Sir or Madam:

Thank you to mail us the latest price list for Peace bicycles. We are very interested in bicycles both for men and women.

There is a heavy demand for bicycles in this country，where cycling has become very popular. If the quality of your bicycles proves satisfactory and your quotation is competitive，we are ready to conclude business with you.

Your early reply will be much appreciated.

Yours faithfully,

VI. Writing Skills Training.

Please write a business letter in one of three mentioned layouts according to the following message.

1. The sender: China National Industrial Products Imp& Exp Corp.
128 Huangpu Road,
Shanghai, China
Tel：+86-21-64468726
2. The receiver: Madison Square
Melbourne E.C.2.
Australia
Tel：+61-2-70525345
Fax：+61-2-75667132
3. Date: Oct 15, 2008
4. Subject: Establishing business relations
5. The message:
Your firm has been recommended to us by Messrs. Freemen & Co. Ltd.，with whom we have done business for many years.
We specialize in the export of Chinese cotton piece goods，which have enjoyed great popularity in world market. We enclose a copy of our catalogue for your reference and hope that you would contact us if any item is interesting to you.

As to our financial standing，you could approach the Bank of China，New York for any information.

We are looking forward to your early reply.

6. Signature: Clark

Skills Training for Unit 2 技能训练 2

I. Vocabulary and Grammar Using Skills Training.

Please fill in the following blank with the best answer.

1. We thank you for your letter of March 12 and the ________catalogue.

   A. sent　B. enclosed　C. given　D. presented

2. We trust that you will find our goods_________.

   A. attracting　B. to be attractive

   C. attract your attention　D. attractive

3. We are willing to establish business relations with you on the _________ of equality and mutual benefit.

   A. basis　B. base　C. based　D. bases

4. We would not allow you a discount _________ you could place a large order.

   A. until　B. except　C. unless　D. besides

5. We wish to introduce ourselves ________ a state-run corporation deal in foodstuffs.

   A. in　B. with　C. as　D. for

6. We owe your name and address ________ your Chamber of Commerce.

   A. from　B. by　C. with　D. to

7. We are a specialized corporation, ________ the import of textiles.

   A. dealing　B. handling　C. dealing with　D. dealt in

8. We are sending you the samples________ requested.

   A. be　B. are　C. as　D. for

9. As the item ________ the scope of our business activities, we shall be pleased to establish trade relations with you.

   A. lies within　B. fall within　C. come under　D. be within

10. We are ________ in the import of chemicals.

    A. interesting　B. interest　C. of interest　D. interested

II. English-Chinese Translation Skills Training.

Please translate the following sentences into Chinese.

1. We owe your name and address to BCD Company.
2. As soon as we receive your specific enquiry，we will send you the catalogue and sample book.
3. Their chief line is the export of personal computers.

4. Our silk has long been a best seller in your market.
5. This product is being marketed in all European countries.
6. Your email of May 5 has been transferred to us for attention from our Head Office in Shanghai.
7. We have been in this line for more than 30 years.
8. We can supply leather shoes in a wide range of styles and sizes.
9. The trade between us is based on the principle of equality.
10. There are two forms of international transaction. One is to trade in goods，the other is in service.

III. Chinese-English Translation Skills Training.

Please translate the following sentences into English.

1. 我们是日本化工产品主要生产商之一，打算和贵公司建立业务关系。
2. 我们专营中国自行车出口业务，想与贵公司在这一行业进行贸易。
3. 浙江凯瑞公司已将贵公司名称及地址转交我方。兹欣然去函与贵司联系，愿与你们建立贸易关系。
4. 感谢贵方 5 月 5 日电邮，我们很高兴与你方探讨扩大贸易的可能性。
5. 我们的最新产品在日本很畅销。
6. 我们愿意在平等互利的基础上与贵公司建立业务关系。
7. 我们经营这一行业已经二十多年了。
8. 我们可供应各种款式和尺码的丝绸睡衣。
9. 我们是一家经营各类空调的大出口商，现特去函自我介绍。
10. 为了促进我们之间的贸易，我们将尽快安排 DHL 公司寄送样品给贵方。

IV. Comprehensive Language Using Skills Training.

Supply the missing words in the blanks of the message.

Dear Sir or Madam,

Thank you for your letter of May 12, i__1__ us that you are in the m__2__ for Chinese bicycles.

To give you a general idea of the goods we are dealing i__3__, we are sending you by air a complete set of our s__4__ books together with full details of our export prices and t__5__ terms.

Our goods are enjoying good reputation in many countries for their fine q__6__ and reasonable p__7__ in spite of the rise in the cost of raw materials. We are glad to say that all the goods listed in our sample books can be supplied f__8__ stock.

Should any of the i__9__ be interesting to you, please send us your s__10__ enquiry, upon receipt of which, we will make an offer by fax.

Yours faithfully,

V. Business Letters Translation Skills Training.

Please translate the following business letter into Chinese.

Dear Sir or Madam:

Your company has been kindly introduced to us by Mr. Black, the president of ABC Company, as prospective buyers of Chinese Agricultural Machines. As this item falls within the scope of our business activities, we shall be pleased to enter into direct business relations with you at an early date.

To give you a general idea of the various kinds of products we handle, we enclose a brochure and a price list. Quotation and sample books will be airmailed to you on receipt of your specific enquiry.

We look forward to your favorable reply.

Yours truly,

VI. Writing Skills Training.

You are asked to write a letter to a foreign company for establishing business relations. The letter should cover at least the following points.

1. Where have you got the information?
2. What is your desire?
3. What is your business scope?

Skills Training for Unit 3 技能训练 3

I. Vocabulary and Grammar Using Skills Training.

Please fill in the following blank with the best answer.

1. Generally speaking, enquiries are made by the____________.
   A. sellers　B. buyers　C. managers　D. government
2. __________, our prices are given on FOB basis.
   A. as a rule　B. for a rule　C. by the rule　D. as the rule
3. ________please find our catalogue.
   A. Enclosing　B. Enclose　C. Enclosed　D. Having enclosed
4. As soon as the price picks up, enquiries will ________.
   A. revive　B. review　C. recur　D. recover
5. We wish to place an order ________ you ________ your goods if prices are reasonable.
   A. in…with　B. with…for　C. as…for　D. for…with
6. Your enquiry is too vague to enable us ________ you.
   A. reply　B. replied　C. replying　D. to reply
7. We want to know how soon you can ________ delivery of our order.
   A. get　B. give　C. make　D. lodge
8. The quality of our goods is superior ________ those from India.
   A. than　B. with　C. to　D. for

9. Here is our ________ catalogue.
   A. latest B. latter C. last D. laster
10. I wish to talk with the person________ of this deal.
   A. in the charge B. be in the charge C. be in charge D. in charge

II. English-Chinese Translation Skills Training.

Please translate the following sentences into Chinese.

1. Could you please send us your latest catalogue and price sheet of the goods?
2. Heavy enquiries witness the quality of our machines.
3. We are sorry that we cannot take care of your enquiry at present.
4. To make an enquiry about our Chinese walnut, a representative of the Indian company paid us a visit.
5. We are really interested in your silk scarves but we need to have further detailed information about the costs before making a final decision.
6. We are in the market for the woolen blankets in your catalogue No. 11.
7. Please tell us the goods we enquire about are available or not?
8. Please inform us of your best terms and discount for cash.
9. We would appreciate receiving details regarding the commodities.
10. We shall be pleased to receive your enquiries for our machineries.

III. Chinese-English Translation Skills Training.

Please translate the following sentences into English.

1. 我们的客户对你方的真皮皮鞋特别感兴趣，请寄样品及报价单。
2. 请报最低价及现货供应的最大量。
3. 请告知贵公司可供应的上等砂糖的价格。
4. 由于这一次订购是合同的组成部分，请提供最好的条件。
5. 请寄该产品最新的样品。
6. 请报新疆棉 50 包、11 月份交货的最低价格是多少?
7. 请告知最好的装货（船）条件。
8. 为使贵方对我们的产品有所了解，现附寄我们的产品目录供你方参考。
9. 请告知我方厦门离岸价、折扣以及付款条件的详情。
10. 我们已经对你们产品询价，可否尽快给予答复？

IV. Comprehensive Language Using Skills Training.

Supply the missing words in the blanks of the message.

Dear Sir or Madam,

We have l__1__ from Black and company of Birmingham that you m__2__ a range of high-fashion handbags in a v__3__ of leathers. We operate a q__4__ retail business and although our sales v__5__ is not large, we obtain high p__6__ for our goods. Would you please send me a copy of your handbag c__7__ with details of your prices and p__8__ terms?

We would find it most helpful if you could also supply s__9__ of the various skins f__10__ which the handbags are made.

Yours faithfully,

V. Business Letters Translation Skills Training.

Please translate the following business letter into Chinese.

Dear Sir or Madam:

We have learnt from Mr. Smith that you are a leading exporter of textile in your country and have enjoyed a good reputation from your customers.

We have a large demand for the supply of 50,000 meters purple serge, whose sample is enclosed to show you the shade and quality we require.

Please send your samples corresponding to our samples with the most reasonable price C.I.F. Hong Kong if you can supply within three months from now.

Looking forward to receiving your reply as soon as possible.

Yours faithfully,

VI. Writing Skills Training.

You are asked to write a letter to a foreign company to make an enquiry for their goods. The letter should cover at least the following points.

1. Where have you got the information?
2. What's your business line?
3. Inquire detailed information about payment, discount, quantities of the goods available.

Skills Training for Unit 4 技能训练 4

I. Vocabulary and Grammar Using Skills Training.

Please fill in the following blank with the best answer.

1. You'll see that our offer compares _________with the quotations you can get elsewhere.
   A. favorable B. favorably C. favor D. favorite
2. We can't accept your offer unless the price is reduced ________ 5%.
   A. by B. for C. to D. with
3. This offer is based on an _________ market and is competitive.
   A. expanded B. extensive C. expanding D. extending
4. Let me make you a ________ offer.
   A. especial B. particular C. special D. specialized
5. We offer ________ for reply 11 a.m. tomorrow.

A. favorable B. well C. non-firm D. firm

6. This offer is ________ to the goods being unsold.

A. valid B. subject C. good D. firm

7. The offer is given without ________.

A. engagement B. force C. limitation D. condition

8. Buyers do not welcome offers made at ______ intervals.

A. regular B. few C. irregular D. wide

9. Our offers are ________ 3 days.

A. by B. within C. for D. after

10. The offer _________ good until 5 o'clock p.m. 23rd of June, 1997, Beijing time.

A. draws B. reaches C. gets D. holds

II. English-Chinese Translation Skills Training.

Please translate the following sentences into Chinese.

1. We can offer you this in different levels of quality.
2. Referring to your enquiry of May 9 for our products, we offer as follows.
3. We'll let you have the official offer tomorrow.
4. I'm afraid I don't find your price competitive at all.
5. Our offer is USD30 per set of teapot, CIF.
6. We cannot make any headway with your offer.
7. The offer holds good until 5 p.m. December 23, 2008, Beijing time.
8. This offer is based on an expanding market and is competitive.
9. All prices in the price list are subject to our confirmation.
10. I'm afraid the quotation is unacceptable.

III. Chinese-English Translation Skills Training.

Please translate the following sentences into English.

1. 我给你一个特别优惠价。
2. 我想知道你们有关 6 号产品的报盘。
3. 我们的报价要求不少于 3 000 件订货。
4. 我们的价格包含了邮资和包装。
5. 价格很可能不久就要上涨。
6. 我们希望付款方式为保兑不可撤销信用证。
7. 我们可以现货供应。
8. 我们不能保证能按你询盘中规定的日期内交货。
9. 报价单中所有价格以我方确认为准。
10. 我们保证会尽快处理您的订单。

IV. Comprehensive Language Using Skills Training.

Supply the missing words in the blanks of the message.

Dear Sir or Madam,

Thank for your e__1__ of April 5. We are pleased to q__2__ you our best price with our terms as f__3__:

P__4__: by T/T or irrevocable and confirmed L/C at sight in our f__5__.

Terms: FOB Xiamen.

D__6__: within 15 days after the r__7__ of your order.

V__8__: days from the date hereof.

P__9__:

Item No. 2: USD 12 per unit

Item No. 4: USD 16 per unit

P__10__: wooden case, 12 units per case

We hope you can accept the offer and wait for your favorable reply.

Yours faithfully,

V. Business Letters Translation Skills Training.

Please translate the following business letter into Chinese.

Dear Sir or Madam:

Thank you for your letter of 10th December. We are pleased to receive your request for men's and women's raincoats on approval.

As we have not previously done business together, perhaps you will kindly agree to supply either the usual trade references, or the name of a bank to which we may refer. As soon as these enquiries are satisfactorily settled, we shall be happy to send you the items you mention in your letter.

We sincerely hope this will be the beginning of a long and pleasant business association. We shall do our best to make it so.

Yours truly,

VI. Writing Skills Training.

You are asked to write a letter to a foreign company to reply an enquiry and make an offer. The letter should cover at least the following points.

1. Price of the goods.
2. Shipment.
3. Validity of the offer.

Skills Training for Unit 5 技能训练 5

I. Vocabulary and Grammar Using Skills Training.

Please fill in the following blank with the best answer.

1. We can't accept your offer ________ the price is reduced by 5%.

   A. until B. unless C. till D. if

2. Your counter-offer is much more______ than mine.
   A. modest B. model C. modern D. modify
3. We hope to further develop our business relations by________ efforts.
   A. joining B. joined C. joint D. join
4. If the price is higher than that, we'd rather call the whole deal ____.
   A. on B. off C. for D. in
5. This is the ________price that we can offer.
   A. bottom B. low C. reasonable D. favorite
6. Our price is in line ________ the international market.
   A. to B. at C. on D. with
7. My friends in business circles all seem to be of the ________that the Chinese corporations have changed a lot in doing business recently.
   A. agreement B. suggestion C. opinion D. argument
8. There is more detailed information to ________ to.
   A. be attended B. attend
   C. have been attended D. attended
9. We'll have a hard time ________ the customers at your price.
   A. to convince B. being convinced C. convincing D. convince
10. Few can compare ________ ours either for flavor or color.
   A. to B. about C. on D. with

II. English-Chinese Translation Skills Training.

Please translate the following sentences into Chinese.

1. There is no possibility to do business unless you reduce your price by 3%.
2. We look forward to replying to our offer in the form of counter-offer.
3. I appreciate your counter-offer but find it too low.
4. Our price is in line with the international market level.
5. We make a counter-offer to you of US$15 per unit F.O.B. Xiamen.
6. I'll respond to your counter-offer by reducing our price by two dollars.
7. Let's meet each other halfway.
8. With your price I'm afraid you'll stand very little chance of obtaining the business.
9. I think that the price of your products is on high side.
10. Your price is acceptable, provided you increase the quantity of your order to 3,000 units.

III. Chinese-English Translation Skills Training.

Please translate the following sentences into English.

1. 我们的价格与国际市场上的价格相比还是合理的。
2. 我认为要达成这笔交易，你至少要降价 5%。

3. 我们已经把价格压到生产费用的边缘了。
4. 没有别的买主的出价高于此价。
5. 此价格比我们给其他供货人的出价要高。
6. 你方报价高于上次。
7. 我们最近的报价大多数都在 100 元以下。
8. 相信我们上周的报价是最好的。
9. 我看你们的报价毫无竞争性。
10. 很抱歉，我们不得不拒绝你方报盘。

IV. Comprehensive Language Using Skills Training.

Supply the missing words in the blanks of the message.

Dear Sir or Madam,

In r__1__ to your email of March 9, we cannot make a better offer than the one we suggested to you, we feel that offer itself is most g__2__ under the c__3__.

In checking our books, we find that you have p__4__ from us twice as much the first three months of this year as you did in the first three months of last year. This i__5__ to us that you have been s__6__ in retailing our m__7__.

We hope that upon r__8__ you will be able to accept our o__9__. We have been very pleased to have you on our list of a__10__.

Yours faithfully,

V. Business Letters Translation Skills Training.

Please translate the following business letter into Chinese.

Dear Sir or Madam:

Thank you for your letter of December 20, 2008. We are disappointed to hear that our price for Dahu cigarette lighters is too high for you to work on. You mention that Japanese goods are being offered to you at a price approximately 10% lower than that quoted by us.

We accept what you say, but we are of the opinion that the quality of the other makes does not measure up to that of our products.

Although we are keen to do business with you, we regret that we cannot accept your counter offer or even meet you halfway.

The best we can do is to reduce our previous quotation by 2%. We trust that this will meet with your approval. We look forward to hearing from you.

Yours faithfully,

VI. Writing Skills Training.

You are asked to write a letter to a foreign company to make a counter-offer. The letter should cover at least the following points.

1. Your desire to do the business with the seller.

2. Your opinion on the price offered by the seller.
3. What's the acceptable price for you?

Skills Training for Unit 6 技能训练 6

I. Vocabulary and Grammar Using Skills Training.

Please fill in the following blank with the best answer.

1. We cannot supply the order because it is ______ stock.
   A. from B. out C. out of D. in
2. As agreed upon in our negotiations, payment______ L/C.
   A. by B. will by C. will be made by D. is by
3. We regret ______ unable to accept your order.
   A. being B. not to be C. be D. having been
4. If you have specific enquiry, please do not ______ to tell us.
   A. feel free B. hesitate C. free D. hesitating
5. We can supply the goods required ______ stock.
   A. in B. out of C. out D. from
6. Should the position ______ in future, we will ______ you immediately.
   A. improve, note B. improve, notify C. improved, note D. improved, notify
7. We will ______ you ______ the least possible delay.
   A. contact, with B. contact with, with C. contact, for D. contact with, for
8. As the market is ______, we recommend your immediate ______.
   A. declining, accepting B. decline, accept
   C. decline, acceptance D. declining, acceptance
9. We cannot ______ clear to entertain your counter-offer.
   A. see our way B. see our C. look our way D. look way
10. ______ your request, we enclose a quotation sheet for your reference.
   A. As pet B. As C. As for D. As to

II. English-Chinese Translation Skills Training.

Please translate the following sentences into Chinese.

1. The quality of the order should be exactly the same as that of the sample you left with us.
2. We find both price and quality satisfactory and are glad to return you the completed order form.
3. As items under your order are beyond our business scope, we can hardly accept your order.
4. If you can improve your price by 5%, we shall be prepared to sell you a large quantity.
5. If your prices are reasonable, we believe we could conclude substantial business with you.
6. In reply to your email of March 8 quoting us the prices of writing paper, we are pleased to place a trial order.

7. As the automobile market is declining，we can hardly conclude the business unless you reduce the price by 10%.
8. We trust that this initial order will lead to further dealings between us.
9. As our factories are fully committed for these months, we regret our inability to entertain any fresh orders.
10. Your order is receiving our immediate attention and we will keep you informed of the progress.

III. Chinese-English Translation Skills Training.

Please translate the following sentences into English.

1. 欢迎贵公司成为我们尊贵的客户之一。
2. 希望货物能及时到达你方，并盼你方的进一步订单。
3. 感谢你方试订，我们将保证你方订单会得到及时、认真的处理。
4. 感谢贵方 5 月 5 日的续订单，我们一定及时处理。
5. 因订单承接过多，我们目前只能接受 10 月份及以后船期的订单。
6. 如能及时处理此订单，我们不胜感激。
7. 很遗憾我们无法按贵方所报价格接受订单。
8. 鉴于我们之间的长期业务关系，我们才按此价格接受订单。
9. 我们愿意按每打 20 美元的价格接受你的订单。
10. 很遗憾，我们目前不能向贵公司续订货。

IV. Comprehensive Language Using Skills Training.

Supply the missing words in the blanks of the message.

Dear Sir or Madam,

In r__1__ to your email of Mar 6, we have pleasure in c__2__ your order for 500 Chinese bicycles.

Our bicycles are enjoying good r__3__ in your country for their fine q__4__ and reasonable p__5__. In v__6__ of our l__7__ standing relationship, we accept your o__8__ at your price.

E__9__ you will find Sales Confirmation No.1236 in duplicate, a copy of which should be returned to us after your c__10__.

Yours faithfully,

V. Business Letters Translation Skills Training.

Please translate the following business letter into Chinese.

Dear Sir or Madam:

Re: Flying Brand Sewing Machines

Thank you for your faxes of July 3 and 9. We appreciate your cooperation and have pleasure in confirming the revised order as follows:

"400 sets Flying Brand Sewing Machines, US$80 per set CFR New York, for shipment in Oct"

Our Sales Confirmation has been sent to you in duplicate.

We look forward to receiving your countersigned S/C.

Yours truly,

VI. Writing Skills Training.

You are asked to write a letter of order. The letter should cover at least the following points.

1. 感谢贵方来函，订购某产品。
2. 对方所订产品目前无货可供，表示遗憾。但推荐替代产品，价格便宜 10%。
3. 随寄一附插图的最新产品介绍。
4. 期待对方订单。

Skills Training for Unit 7 技能训练 7

I. Vocabulary and Grammar Using Skills Training.

Please fill in the following blank with the best answer.

1. We have the pleasure ______ receiving your letter of Dec 5, ______ you inform us that you are satisfied with our goods.
   A. in, which　B. of, in which　C. from, from which　D. on, on which
2. ______ stock shoes, we are enclosing a list for your perusal.
   A. As　B. For　C. Regarding　D. Regards
3. Thank you for your goods shipped to us ______ S/S Peace.
   A. by　B. from　C. in　D. with
4. ______ the said goods are not available from stock, we will have to turn to other suppliers.
   A. In this case　B. In case　C. Under this case　D. For the case
5. Following your order ______ 400 pieces of electronic toys last year, we are pleased to receive your order No. 456 ______ the same quantity.
   A. for, of　B. of, of　C. of, for　D. with, for
6. Should your price ______ competitive, we will place an initial order____ you.
   A. be, with　B. is, with　C. are, from　D. is, from
7. We place an order provided your goods can be supplied ______ stock.
   A. out of　B. out　C. in　D. from
8. We are quite ______ with the shipment.
   A. satisfactory　B. satisfied　C. satisfy　D. satisfaction
9. We shall provide you ______ large quantities of textiles.
   A. with　B. for　C. of　D. in

10. We hope the goods will give you every ______.
   A. satisfactory B. satisfied C. satisfy D. satisfaction

II. English-Chinese Translation Skills Training.

Please translate the following sentences into Chinese.

1. As you know, our foreign trade policy is to trade with every country all over the world on the basis of equality and mutual benefit.
2. Owing to the reasonable price and good quality, our cotton underwear products sell fast.
3. This contract is made by and between the buyer and seller according to the terms and conditions stipulated below.
4. Once entered into, a contract is binding and enforceable by law.
5. Any party who fails to fulfill his obligations must make compensation for the other party's losses.
6. Excellent in workmanship and novel in designs, our products have enjoyed a ready market in Norway.
7. If the shipment comes up to our expectations, substantial orders will follow.
8. In view of the recent increase in the price of raw material, we have to adjust some of our own prices.
9. Since we have reached an agreement on all the details, we can sign the contract now.
10. We are not satisfied with the consignment, because the quality is different from that of the samples.

III. Chinese-English Translation Skills Training.

Please translate the following sentences into English.

1. 我们认为贵方产品市场前景光明，故希望能委托我方为贵公司销售代理。
2. 若贵公司给予我方在中国的独家代理权，我们将不遗余力地促进贵方在中国的贸易利益。
3. 经过再三考虑，我们决定委托你方为我们自行车在德国的总代理商。
4. 如我们双方能达成交易，我方保证每年订购至少 5 000 件。
5. 我们有信心使今年的年销售量超过去年的。
6. 我们愿意在平等互利的基础上与贵公司做生意。
7. 销售确认书应该由买卖双方会签。
8. 除非贵方修订交易条款，否则我们认为无法成交。
9. 合同一旦签订必须严格履行。
10. 合同是一种书面协议，其对有关各方的权利和义务细节做出规定。

IV. Comprehensive Language Using Skills Training.

Supply the missing words in the blanks of the message.

In import and export business, if the seller makes an offer and the buyer accepts that offer, it means a d__1__. A written contract is usually made.

An import and export c__2__ contains the following t__3__ and conditions:

1. The name of the c__4__ and specifications, the quantity and packing.

2. D__5__ of shipment and destination port: The goods must be shipped before or on the stipulated date of shipment and must arrive at the stipulated destination port.

3. The quoting of p__6__: The way to quote a price in foreign trade is different from what we do domestically. In quoting prices in foreign trade, trade terms are added to the unit price.

4. Terms of p__7__: That refers to mode of payment. In international trade the letter of credit is the main mode of payment.

5. I__8__: In international trade, insurance is essential. It should be indicated in the contract whether the seller or the buyer covers insurance on the goods.

6. C__9__: If there is any quality, quantity or weight discrepancy of the goods, the buyer may raise a claim against the seller within a stipulated period of time.

7. A__10__: In case no settlement can be reached through negotiation, dispute may be submitted to arbitration.

8. Shipping documents required.

Other terms:

V. Business Letters Translation Skills Training.

Please translate the following S/C into Chinese.

Sales Contract

S/C No. _________

Signed at _____ on_______

Sellers: China Greenpower Food Imp. And Exp. Co., Ltd.

Buyers: Sunshine Farm Products Co., Ltd.

The undersigned Sellers and Buyers have agreed to close the following transaction according to the terms and conditions stipulated below:

Name of Commodity: Chinese Potatoes

Specifications: FAQ

Quantity: 5,000 metric tons with 5% more or less both in amount and quantity allowed at the Sellers' option

Unit Price: US$180/MT CIF Tokyo

Total Value: US$900,000.00 (SAY US DOLLARS NINE HUNDRED THOUSAND ONLY)

Packing: All in bulk

Time of Shipment: During November and December, 2008

Port of Shipment & Destination: From China ports to Tokyo, transshipment & partial shipments are not allowed

Insurance: To be covered by the Sellers for 110% of the invoice value against ALL RISKS.

Terms of Payment: By Irrevocable, Letter of credit to be available by sight draft

Shipping Mark: At the Sellers' option

Inspection: Quality, quantity and weight Certificates issued by Entry-Exit Inspection and Quarantine of People's Republic of China are to be taken as final.

Other Terms: …

VI. Writing Skills Training.

You are asked to make a Sales Contract according to the following Chinese particulars.

卖方：浙江海盐标准件有限公司

买方：新加坡麦田有限公司

商品：螺母

数量：100 000 套

单价：US$8 CIF Singapore

唛头：卖方决定

保险：水渍险

启运港：上海

最迟装运期：2008 年 6 月 30 日

付款：不可撤销即期信用证

异议与索赔：如买方对货物质量有任何问题，请于货物到港后 30 天提出并出具经卖方同意的公正机构的检验报告。

争端与解决：双方友好协商，协商不成提交浙江中国国际贸易促进委员会对外经济贸易委员会处理。

注意：合同的格式、必要组成部分

Skills Training for Unit 8 技能训练 8

I. Vocabulary and Grammar Using Skills Training.

Please fill in the following blank with the best answer.

1. We will open a confirmed, irrevocable letter of credit ________ your order.
   A. to B. against C. by D. at
2. We enclose our check for $799 __________ your invoice No. 89.
   A. in payment of B. by payment at
   C. to payment on D. for payment in
3. We will draw ________ you by our documentary draft at sight on collection basis.
   A. on B. at C. for D. to
4. We inform you that we have opened an irrevocable letter of credit ________ the Bank of China in your favor.
   A. at B. in C. by D. with

5. As agreed upon in our negotiations, payment ________L/C.
   A. by　B. is by　C. will be　D. will by
6. In order to promote business relations between us, we shall consider ________payment by D/P.
   A. accepting　B. accept　C. to accept　D. acceptance
7. We can supply the goods you require ________.
   A. from stock　B. in stock　C. out of stock　D. just the stock
8. Taking into consideration our long standing business relations with you, we accept ________ by D/A.
   A. enquiries　B. invitations　C. installment　D. payment
9. We thank you very much for your L/C and shipping instructions ________ your trial orders.
   A. being covered　B. to be covered
   C. covering　D. covers
10. We shall be glad if you agree to ship the goods to us ________ Cash Against Documents basis.
    A. with　B. during　C. in　D. on

II. English-Chinese Translation Skills Training.

Please translate the following sentences into Chinese.

1. Payment by L/C is the safest method, but rather complicated.
2. That is our usual practice, because we're sure we'll get the right amount of money, that way.
3. Our company only allows us to do business by irrevocable L/C.
4. Payment by sight L/C is quite usual in international trade.
5. I'll open the L/C 30 days before the date of shipment.
6. It should be valid for 15 days after the date of shipment.
7. A complete set of bills of lading, three invoices, six packing lists, an export license, an insurance policy, an a certificate of inspection.
8. You can be assured that all these documents will be provided in line with your requirements.
9. We only accept payment by irrevocable letter of credit payable against shipping documents.
10. Consult your bank please and see if they can reduce the required deposit to a minimum.

III. Chinese-English Translation Skills Training.

Please translate the following sentences into English.

1. 最终发票的价值是货物卖出时的价格。
2. 实在没有必要继续找第三家银行进行保兑，从而增加我们的成本。
3. 我们就把“保兑”字样从条款中删掉吧。
4. 由于生产这种设备需要垫付一些资金，所以我们要求用见单即付的即期信用证。
5. 我感到很高兴我们能再次全部达成协议。

6. 我们愿意使用付款交单的付款方式。
7. 这笔交易的金额很大，为开立信用证所需的利息和银行费用很高，这会增加工程的开支。
8. 我们自己的钱会陷在你们的设备上，而我们又不得不向总公司支付所借钱的利息。
9. 这与国际贸易的惯例并不矛盾。
10. 你可以放心，我们会承兑期票，并到期付款的。

IV. Comprehensive Language Using Skills Training.

Supply the missing words in the blanks of the message.

Dear Sir or Madam,

We are pleased to receive your letter dated May 2. And we a__1__ your intention to push the sale of our products at your end.

As our usual practice, p__2__ is to be made by a c__3__, irrevocable letter of credit p__4__ by draft at sight, to be o__5__ 30 days before the time of s__6__ and to r__7__ valid for negotiation in China within 15 days after the date of s__8__

E__9__ is a price list for the items you mentioned.

We hope the terms on the list will be a__10__ to you and wish to enter into business with you.

Yours faithfully,

V. Business Letters Translation Skills Training.

Please translate the following business letter into Chinese.

Dear Sir or Madam:

We are pleased to inform you that your Order No. 9000 is in production and almost for shipment. We shall appreciate it if you can establish irrevocable, confirmed L/C in our favor valid until June 4.

After receiving your L/C, we will dispatch the goods immediately and send you the shipping documents soon.

Yours truly,

VI. Writing Skills Training.

You are asked to write a letter to a foreign importer and ask them to pay by L/C. The letter should cover at least the following points.

1. What are the goods they bought?
2. How would you like them to pay?
3. Why do you like them to pay by L/C?

Skills Training for Unit 9 技能训练 9

I. Vocabulary and Grammar Using Skills Training.

Please fill in the following blank with the best answer.

1. As arranged, we would ask you to open an irrevocable credit in ______ favor and shall hand over shipping documents ______ acceptance of our draft.
   A. your, against B. your, for C. our, against D. our, for
2. We request you to ______ that an L/C is opened by cable whenever an order is placed with us.
   A. see to it B. see it C. see D. see for
3. Payments should be made ______ sight draft.
   A. at B. upon C. by D. after
4. Mr. Yin could agree ______ L/C payment terms.
   A. with B. to C. in D. over
5. 80% of the credit amount must be paid ______ the presentation of documents.
   A. at B. by C. against D. when
6. We shall be glad if you agree to ship the goods to us as before ______ sight D/P basis instead of sight L/C.
   A. with B. during C. in D. on
7. We have opened an L/C in your favor ______ the amount of RMB20,000.
   A. on B. in C. by D. at
8. With ______ to Contract No.1239, we agree to L/C payment ______.
   A. regards, term B. regard, terms C. regarding, terms D. regard, term
9. As agreed upon in our negotiation, payment ______ L/C.
   A. is by B. will be C. by D. will by
10. It is important that you ______ the relative L/C not later than Mar 8, 2009.
    A. open B. must open C. opens D. has to open

II. English-Chinese Translation Skills Training.

Please translate the following sentences into Chinese.

1. We must apologize to you for not having established the relative L/C in time.
2. We regret to inform you that we have not received your L/C covering the S/C No. 23434 till today.
3. We are glad to inform you that L/C No. 123 for the amount of USD5,000 has been opened in your favor.
4. Failure to establish the L/C in time will affect the fulfillment of the order.
5. Our S/C No. 23423 stipulates for establishment of the L/C before May 12.
6. As the amount of our Order No. 232 is below USD1,000, please agree to pay by D/P.

Because an L/C will cost us a lot.

7. L/C at sight is what we request for all our clients.
8. We will open the L/C if you promise to effect shipment before May 15.
9. L/C is the normal terms of payment in international trade.
10. It's our usual practice to do business with payment by L/C instead of D/A.

III. Chinese-English Translation Skills Training.

Please translate the following sentences into English.

1. 我方提请你方注意开证期限已逾 1 周，而该信用证尚未到达。
2. 如信用证不能于 5 月 10 之前开到我方，我方只好取消这次合同。
3. 第 1123 号合同项下货物的信用证开证期就要到了。
4. 如你方信用证能在本月底开到我方，我方将尽快安排装运。
5. 根据信用证的相关规定，不允许转运。
6. 信用证内容必须与合同的规定严格一致。
7. 我方下订单的条件是你方接受付款方式为保兑的、不可撤销的信用证。
8. 鉴于双方的友好关系，我方接受 90 天期信用证。
9. 销售合同第 111 号项下的货物已备妥，请尽快开立相关信用证。
10. 很高兴通知贵方按 128 号销售合同由中国银行开立的 SMOU2378 号信用证已收悉。

IV. Comprehensive Language Using Skills Training.

Supply the missing words in the blanks of the message.

The letter of credit is one of m__1__ of p__2__. It is i__3__ by a bank, i.e. opening bank, at the r__4__ of an i__5__, i.e. applicant.

This mode of payment is c__6__ used in f__7__ trade today. G__8__ speaking, the buyer should o__9__ a letter of credit in f__10__ of seller several months before the time of shipment.

When the L/C reaches the seller, i.e. beneficiary, it is necessary for him to check the stipulations of L/C carefully with the clauses of the contract.

V. Business Letters Translation Skills Training.

Please translate the following business letter into Chinese.

Dear Sir or Madam:

We thank you for your Order No. 888 for 600 metric tons of white cement but regret being unable to accept your terms of payment mentioned therein.

In our last letter we sent you a copy of our specimen contract in which the general sales terms and conditions are contained. If you have gone through the specimen contract you will see that our usual terms of payment are by irrevocable letter of credit in our favor, available by draft at sight, reaching us one month ahead of shipment, remaining valid for negotiation in China till the 21st day after the prescribed time of shipment，and allowing transshipment and partial shipments.

We look forward to your favorable reply.

Yours truly,

VI. Writing Skills Training.

You are asked to write a letter to a foreign company for payment. The letter should cover at least the following points.

1. 感谢对方的上次来函，除付款方式外，同意对方其他交易条件。
2. 因本次交易金额较大，资金运转有一定困难，希望对方同意 60 天期的 L/C 付款。
3. 感谢对方的照顾，如同意此付款方式，请速寄合同，以便早日安排开立信用证。

Skills Training for Unit 10 技能训练 10

I. Vocabulary and Grammar Using Skills Training.

Please fill in the following blank with the best answer.

1. We inform you that we have opened an irrevocable credit ______ the London Bank in your favor.
   A. at　　B. in　　C. by　　D. with
2. We advised the bank to amend the clause ______ "partial shipment are permitted."
   A. to reading　　B. to read　　C. to be read　　D. to be reading
3. To amend the L/C would ______ a delay of about two weeks in shipment.
   A. involve　　B. refer　　C. involve in　　D. refer to
4. We have accepted your Order No.321. Please open the relative L/C, ______ here two weeks prior to the date of shipment.
   A. which must reach　　B. when must reach
   C. it reaches　　D. that reaches
5. We think it impossible to have the L/C ______ again.
   A. extended　　B. extending　　C. to extend　　D. extends
6. We have opened an L/C in your favor ______ the amount of $2,222.
   A. for　　B. of　　C. with　　D. in
7. The L/C stipulation should be in ______ accordance with the terms ______ the Contract.
   A. exact, foe　　B. the same, on　　C. exactly, of　　D. exact, of
8. Please ______ that the amendment is cabled without delay.
   A. see it　　B. see to it　　C. see　　D. see to
9. ______ perusal, we find that partial ______ are not allowed.
   A. On, shipment　　B. On, shipments　　C. After, shipping　　D. After, shipment
10. We are cabling you today, ______ you to amend the L/C to read.
    A. ask　　B. asked　　C. asking　　D. to ask

II. English-Chinese Translation Skills Training.

Please translate the following sentences into Chinese.

1. Please extend the shipping date to May 30 and validity to June 15 and let us have your reply ASSP.
2. Please insert the word "about" before the quantity in your L/C No. SW1212.
3. Please instruct your bankers to make the necessary amendments to the L/C and inform us by May 5.
4. Your L/C No. 123 has been found that the price basis CIF has been wrongly given as CFR.
5. Please amend the L/C to be transferable and irrevocable.
6. As the transaction is concluded on CIF basis, please amend the stipulation to read "freight prepaid".
7. There is no word "about" before the amount in the L/C, but it is indicated in the S/C.
8. Please contact your bank to delete this clause on receipt of the fax.
9. As the amount in your L/C is not sufficient, please increase the amount by USD 500.
10. If these terms are agreeable to you, please amend the relative clause to allow transshipment.

III. Chinese-English Translation Skills Training.

Please translate the following sentences into English.

1. 请将第 111 号信用证改为"信用证将于 2008 年 4 月 30 日在中国到期"。
2. 关于第 111 号信用证，我方发现其货币单位与合同规定不一致。
3. 请插入条款"允许分批装运"。
4. 装船期和议付有效期都必须延长 1 个月。
5. 我方保证一收到信用证修改通知书，就按期发货。
6. 要求你方将单价改为"20 美元一件"。
7. 通知你方，信用证规定的货物数量应是 500 台，而不是 50 台。
8. 请参照我方 5 月 5 日电传内容，对下列条款进行修改。
9. 请将信用证上的金额改为"有 5%上下的幅度"。
10. 修改信用证的费用将由你方承担。

IV. Comprehensive Language Using Skills Training.

Supply the missing words in the blanks of the message.

When an exporter receives a letter of c__1__ either by fax or by mail from the i__2__ or from the importer's bankers or through an a__3__ bank, it is always important to e__4__ the details mentioned in the letter of credit. If there is any d__5__, the exporter should immediately contact the importer and request the latter to arrange with the issuing bank of the letter of credit to send an amendment in time.

The following points may be given for reference in the examination of the letter of credit:

1. The L/C should usually be i__6__ without any restrictions, such as "Subject to import

license obtainable", etc.

2. Whether the description, specifications, quantity, number, packing, unit price, shipping time, port of destination, insurance cover, etc. of the goods are in a__7__ with the sales contract.

3. The total amount, v__8__ time and date and place of e__9__.

4. Whether any special clauses or stipulations are mentioned in the L/C regarding shipping d__10__.

V. Business Letters Translation Skills Training.

Please translate the following business letter into Chinese.

Dear Sir or Madam:

We are pleased to inform you that L/C No. BHP-158 issued by the Standard Chartered Bank of Liverpool for our S/C No. 5678 has just been received. However, on examining the clauses contained therein, we regretfully find that certain points are not in conformity with the terms stipulated in the contract. The discrepancies are as follows:

1. Commission is 3%, not 5%;

2. Shipment is to be made during Oct / Nov instead of "on or before 30th October";

3. Goods should be insured for 110% of the invoice value, not 120%.

Therefore you are requested to amend the L/C accordingly. On receipt of your amendment to the L/C, we will arrange for the shipment without any delay.

Yours truly,

VI. Writing Skills Training.

You are asked to write a letter to a foreign company asking for L/C amendment. The letter should cover at least the following points.

1. 金额是 15 000 美元，而非 1 500 美元；
2. 佣金是 5%，而非 3%；
3. 投保金额按发票的 110%，而非 120%；
4. 提单上应标注运费已付，而非运费到付。

Skills Training for Unit 11 技能训练 11

I. Vocabulary and Grammar Using Skills Training.

Please fill in the following blank with the best answer.

1. The goods you delivered are below the standard we expected ________ the sample.

A. from B. to C. on D. in

2. We shall be glad to offer you a sole ________ for the sale of our products in New York.

A. attracting B. agent C. argentine D. agency

3. The machines will be supplied ________ specially designed crates.

A. by B. of C. at D. in

4. When ________, please state your terms of payment and time of shipment.

A. quoting B. being quoted C. quoted D. you're quoted

5. We hope to receive your quotation with details ________ the possible time of shipment.

A. to include B. to be include C. including D. being including

6. We would ask you to do everything possible ________ punctual shipment.

A. ensuring B. to be ensured C. to ensure D. while ensuring

7. Our containers are conformable to the specifications ________ by the International Standardization Organization.

A. lie down B. lied down C. lay down D. laid down

8. We helped them ________ the shipping marks.

A. stenciling B. have stenciled C. stenciled D. stencil

9. This is one set of the shipping documents ________ the consignment.

A. be covered B. be covering C. covering D. covered

10. When the goods ________, you can get the B/L signed by the master of the vessel.

A. have been loaded B. loading

C. being loaded D. have loaded

II. English-Chinese Translation Skills Training.

Please translate the following sentences into Chinese.

1. The shipment has arrived in good condition.
2. I hope you'll be entirely satisfied with this initial shipment.
3. Please exercise better care with future shipments.
4. Can last shipment be duplicated?
5. We regret we can't ship as you desired.
6. We'll send vessels to pick up the cargo at Huangpu.
7. There is an over-shipment of 200 lbs.
8. Can we short-ship 5 tons?
9. Please hold shipment pending our instructions.
10. The goods are all ready for shipment.

III. Chinese-English Translation Skills Training.

Please translate the following sentences into English.

1. 关于上次装运到伦敦的那批货，我不得不抱怨你。
2. 货已装上“东风”号轮船。
3. 我们装运的油多数是散装的。
4. 我们能在货物装运到美国时获得优惠税率。
5. 出口到东南亚的货物的装运条件已大大改善。

6. 他们就礼花的装运期问题进行了谈判。
7. 交货期还没定下来，我怎么会不着急呢？
8. 很抱歉，现在我们还无法告诉您确切的装船日期。
9. 从交货到零售商收到货物总共需要 4 至 5 个星期。
10. 我们最晚在今年 12 月份或明年初交货。

IV. Comprehensive Language Using Skills Training.

Supply the missing words in the blanks of the message.

Dear Sir or Madam:

Thank you for your o__1__. At this time we cannot f__2__your order d__3__ to an u__4__ shipment d__5__ from our overseas s__6__.

We will hold your order for a__7__ of the merchandise, and ship shortly thereafter. U__8__, we cannot p__9__ you with a specific shipping date at this time.

Thank you for you're a__10__ patience in this matter.

V. Business Letters Translation Skills Training.

Please translate the following business letter into Chinese.

Dear Sir or Madam:

Enclosed is an order for which we ask your special attention to time of delivery. It is important that we receive these goods on the exact day mentioned as we have extensively advertised the day of our sale. Please let us know immediately if you have any difficulty in supplying the exact goods ordered. All orders must be delivered complete; no remainders must follow.

Yours truly,

VI. Writing Skills Training.

You are asked to write a letter to a foreign company for shipment. The letter should cover at least the following points.

1. Inform the customer that you can secure the vessel
2. Describe the details of the vessel
3. Ask the clients to confirm

Skills Training for Unit 12 技能训练 12

I. Vocabulary and Grammar Using Skills Training.

Please fill in the following blank with the best answer.

1. Please inform us on what _______ this insurance can be arranged.
   A. terms B. times C. demands D. cases
2. The insurance company is responsible for the_______, as far as it is within the scope of coverage.
   A. case B. claim C. matter D. order

3. We specialize ________all kinds of metals and are always ready to buy in large quantities.
   A. at B. from C. on D. in
4. We will see to it that the L/C ________within the stipulated time.
   A. is opened B. should be opened C. will be opened D. must be opened
5. Your claim for shortage of weight ________USD1,000 in all.
   A. accounts on B. accounts to C. amounts to D. is accounted to
6. Please accept my ________for the delay which has been caused by the unavailability of shipping space from Bombay to London.
   A. forgive B. apologize C. apology D. apologies
7. For the time being, we cannot commit________ any new orders.
   A. ourselves with B. us to C. us with D. ourselves to
8. The wide range of Indian export companies that we ______ insure you of getting just the items that you are looking for.
   A. work to B. work on C. work in D. work with
9. It _______ if you ______the L/C for another 15 days.
   A is appreciated, extend B. will be appreciated, could extend
   C. should be appreciated, could extend D. should be appreciated, can extend
10. We are offering firm ________ on the same terms and conditions as the previous contract.
   A. as follow B. as following C. as follows D. as is followed

II. English-Chinese Translation Skills Training.

Please translate the following sentences into Chinese.

1. What is the insurance premium?
2. Mr. Zhang met Mr. William in the office of the People' Insurance Company of China.
3. This information office provides clients with information on cargo insurance.
4. The underwriters are responsible for the claim as far as it is within the scope of cover.
5. The extent of insurance is stipulated in the basic policy form and in the various risk clauses.
6. Please fill in the application form.
7. What risks is the People's Insurance Company of China able to cover?
8. May I ask what exactly insurance covers according to your usual C.I.F terms?
9. It's important for you to read the "fine print" in any insurance policy so that you know what kind of coverage you are buying.
10. The rates quoted by us are very moderate. Of course, the premium varies with the range of insurance.

III. Chinese-English Translation Skills Training.

Please translate the following sentences into English.

1. 针对这种性质的货物只保水渍险是不够的，请加保偷盗提货不成险。

2. 贵公司能为我的这批货保哪些险呢？
3. 这类险别的保险费率将根据货物种类而定。
4. 保险经纪人会开出承保各类货物的各种险别的费用。
5. 你不仅要研究各种保险所标明的给予保险人的赔偿费用，还要研究它的条件与限制，然后选出最适合你需要的一种。
6. 并不是所有的破碎险都属于单独海损。
7. 投保的险别为水渍险加破碎险。
8. 那么，“一切海洋运输货物险”意味着比“一切险”范围小一些。
9. 在保险业中“average”一词一般是“海损”的意思。
10. 健康保险就是筹集一些钱以预防疾病或受伤而突然发生的经济困难。

IV. Comprehensive Language Using Skills Training.

Supply the missing words in the blanks of the message.

Dear Sir,

Thank you for your email of 9 November, q_____ us for 500 m_____ tons of black tea, your quotation is for C_____ terms. We regret to say that we prefer to have your quotation and offers on C&F terms.

Our position is that we have taken out an open policy with Lloyds of London. Under the policy, when a s_____ is made, all we have to do is to advise them of the particulars. We are on good terms with our u_____ and consequently receive p______ rebates at r_____ intervals.

We would, h_____, be interested to know the scope of c_____ handled by your usual insurance company for our______.

We look forward to hearing from you.

Sincerely yours,

V. Business Letters Translation Skills Training.

Please translate the following business letter into Chinese.

Dear Sirs:

We are glad to inform you that your Order No.799 will be shipped per s/s crystal? Due to leave here at the end of this month.

Unless otherwise instructed, we will arrange to take out an All Risks insurance policy for you on your order. This type of coverage is, in our opinion, necessary for a cargo of this nature.

Yours faithfully,

VI. Writing Skills Training.

You are asked to write a letter to a foreign company for insurance. The letter should cover at least the following points.

1. Re: the customer's letter of Nov 8

2. CIF insurance for 200 sets of bicycles
3. Cover the insurance against all risks

Skills Training for Unit 13 技能训练 13

I. Vocabulary and Grammar Using Skills Training.

Please fill in the following blank with the best answer.

1. We are exporting a wide range of carpets ________many countries.
   A. in B. to C. on D. at
2. Our exports of bikes __________ during the last few years.
   A. have considerably increased B. having considerably increased
   C. have considerable increased D. considerably increase
3. When you shipped the goods last time, many tins ________ because of poor packing.
   A. dent B. have dented C. were dented D. denting
4. You shipped the products in ________ last time.
   A. separate B. dividing C. individually D. bulk
5. I'd like to ____________ the terms and conditions of the contract.
   A. go over B. go under C. go around D. go off
6. As long as they are handled _____ care, there will be no problem. You may ______ it from me.
   A. in get B. in take C. with take D. with get
7. Packing must be strong enough to ________ rough handling.
   A. meet B. stand C. hold D. get
8. Cartons are quite ________.
   A. seaworthy B. seaworth C. worthy shipping D. worth shipping
9. Please ________ that the packing is suitable for long sea voyage.
   A. see B. see through C. see off D. see to
10. We will ________ your valuable proposals to our production department.
    A. transport B. transact C. transfer D. transmit

II. English-Chinese Translation Skills Training.

Please translate the following sentences into Chinese.

1. Packing is included in the term of quantity in the contract.
2. We usually use cardboard cases for packing.
3. Five cases of black tea have been badly contaminated because of poor packing.
4. We are going to ship our products by container this time.
5. To be frank, we've never received any complaints about packing from our clients.
6. The beer will be supplied in tins of 30 kilos net, two tins to a crate.
7. How about the dimensions of the outer packing box?

8. The packing is safe and sound.
9. You'll find the packing beautiful and quite well-done.
10. According to our usual practice, the table lamp should be packed in international standard box.

III. Chinese-English Translation Skills Training.

Please translate the following sentences into English.

1. 至于包装，我们希望你方用木箱包装。
2. 根据报告上的鉴定，破损原因是包装太差。
3. 包装在竞争市场份额时显得越来越重要。
4. 20 盒茶叶装一箱，50 箱装一个集装箱。
5. 你方最好印上例如“小心轻放”和“易碎品”的警告标志。
6. 你打算如何包装这套茶具？
7. 豌豆可以散装，也可以用麻袋装。
8. 我方将用纸板箱进行包装，因为纸板箱相对轻便结实，更容易搬运。
9. 感谢贵方 10 月 7 日来函告知包装详情。
10. 包装是经常引起贸易争端的一个敏感问题。

IV. Comprehensive Language Using Skills Training.

Supply the missing words in the blanks of the message.

Dear Sir or Madam,

Thank you for your letter of May 10 t__1__ with the sample.

For this first t__2__ between us, we would like to make it clear in a__3__ about packing. As tea is m__4__ absorbent e__5__ in hot and rainy season, we hope each i__6__ packing box should be l__7__ with w__8__ polythene sheets. Please s__9__ to it that cartons used are strong enough to protect the goods from any possible damage in transit.

When marking, please s__10__ our initials and order numbers on the outer packing.

We hope the above requirements can be met exactly and await your early shipment.

Yours faithfully,

V. Business Letters Translation Skills Training.

Please translate the following business letter into Chinese.

Dear Sir or Madam:

We thank you for your email of July 19 inquiring about our requirements of packing and shipping marks of the goods under the S / C No. GJ315.

As our buyers are in urgent need of the goods, you'd better ship the goods ASAP. Please pack our goods in boxes of one dozen each, 50 boxes to a carton. Shipping marks to be stenciled on the outer packing should include the warning marks such as “Handle with Care ” and

"Fragile".

We trust that everything will turn out to our entire satisfaction.

Yours truly,

VI. Writing Skills Training.

You are asked to write a letter to a foreign company about the packing of the goods. The letter should cover at least the following points.

1. You are the buyer.
2. The problems with the packing last time.
3. How do you like the goods being packed this time?

Skills Training for Unit 14 技能训练 14

I. Vocabulary and Grammar Using Skills Training.

Please fill in the following blank with the best answer.

1. ________this reason, we cannot accept your claim for a replacement.
   A. By B. For C. With D. As to
2. Your claim for the damage is to be __________ with the insurance company.
   A. met B. field C. satisfied D. compensate
3. All the claim terms were agreed ________ by the two companies.
   A. to B. with C. for D. on
4. We have lodged a claim ________ your company _________ the delay of the goods we ordered.
   A. with, on B. against, for C. against, on D. with, against
5. The buyer made a ________against us for the poor quality of the computers.
   A. claim B. discount
   C. apology D. communication
6. To our regret, the case contains only 4 forks instead of 5 ________ the invoice.
   A. entered on B. entering on
   C. enter on D. which enter on
7. Case No. 77 was found to be three packages ________.
   A. too short B. shortage C. to shorten D. short
8. The goods under Contact No. 890 left here________.
   A. in a good condition B. in good conditions
   C. in good condition D. in the good condition
9. It is most important that the delivery ________ punctual, otherwise our summer sale cannot be carried out.
   A. will be B. would be C. has been D. should be
10. Please inform us ________ the tendency of your market.

A. for　　B. in　　C. of　　D. with

II. English-Chinese Translation Skills Training.

Please translate the following sentences into Chinese.

1. We are lodging a claim for inferior quality.
2. We must lodge a claim against you for the amount of $600,000.
3. The damage is chiefly due to poor packing which is not adequately reinforced.
4. The goods have been so discolored and heavily saturated by rain that they are unsalable.
5. According to the surveyor's report, the damage was due to careless handling during transit.
6. There is a difference of 30 tons between the actual landed weight and the invoiced weight of this consignment.
7. In support of our claim, we are sending you a survey report issued by CCIB.
8. You shipped bulk goods not corresponding in quality with the sample.
9. We have to ask for a compensation of $660.00 to cover the loss incurred.
10. We have examined the contents and found that 16 pieces were missing and the rest were unfit for use.

III. Chinese-English Translation Skills Training.

Please translate the following sentences into English.

1. 鉴于近日原料价格上涨，我们不得不调整部分产品价格。
2. 很遗憾通知你方，3 号箱及 7 号箱破损，箱内货物因包装不良严重损坏。
3. 如果你方退回机器，我们将进行必要的修理，并完好无缺的送还你方。
4. 对于所遭受的损失，我们不得不要求你方负责。
5. 无论如何，我们要求你方采取措施，防止类似事件再次发生。
6. 我们仔细核查了此事，得到的唯一解释是标签弄混了。
7. 发错货物是由于我方包装人员的失误造成的。
8. 我们将在卸货完毕之后检查此货。
9. 我们感到遗憾的是，箱内仅装了 40 台电脑，而不是发票上写明的 45 台。
10. 检验货物时，我们发现部分货物与先前的样品不符。

IV. Comprehensive Language Using Skills Training.

Supply the missing words in the blanks of the message.

Dear Sir or Madam,

Thank you for your letter __1__ March 12, informing us __2__ the wrong shipment of the case containing Model MM89 instead of MM88 __3__ your Order No. 897. When checking the matter __4__ at once with our manufacturer, we found there was a mishandling on the part of their transportation department.

While apologizing __5__ this wrong shipment, our manufacturer suggests you take these machines __6__ a replacement for the wrong ones. Frankly __7__, they are brand-new machines and the price of Model MM88 is about 14% higher than __8__ of Model MM89. In fact, they have been just put on sale in our market and are enjoying a good __9__. The manufacturer would, of course, absorb the price difference to make up __10__ the inconvenience caused to you.

We trust you would accept this as a fair and reasonable solution to the matter.

Yours faithfully,

V. Business Letters Translation Skills Training.

Please translate the following business letter into Chinese.

Dear Sir or Madam:

Thank you for your letter of 3 February. We are extremely sorry to learn that an error made in carton 16 of your Order No. 990.

The missing 100 sets of Apple MP3 were sent this morning by the Southern Airway and the documents have been forwarded to you.

We regret the inconvenience caused by this and the precious two errors and offer our sincere apologies. We will try our best and can assure you that similar errors do not occur again. We wish to be able to serve you in future business.

Yours truly,

VI. Writing Skills Training.

You are asked to write a letter to a foreign company for a low quality claim. The letter should cover at least the following points.

1. What is the problem?
2. What is your loss?
3. What is your evidence?

Skills Training for Unit 15 技能训练 15

I. Vocabulary and Grammar Using Skills Training.

Please fill in the following blank with the best answer.

1. We have accepted your Order No. 313. Please open the relevant L/C, ______ here two weeks prior to the date of shipment.

   A. which must reach　　B. when must reach

   C. it reaches　　D. that reaches

2. We have the pleasure ______ receiving your letter of Nov 3, ______ you inform us that you are satisfied with our goods.

   A. in, which　　B. of, in which

   C. from, from which　　D. on, on which

3. It is ______ that we can get the necessary import license.
   A. out of the question B. out of question
   C. no question D. not question
4. The import and export business in China is ______ by the state trading corporations.
   A. controlled B. handled C. done D. made
5. As arranged, we would ask you to open an irrevocable credit in ______ favor and shall hand over shipping documents ______ acceptance of our draft.
   A. your, against B. your, for C. our, against D. our, for
6. Please amend your L/C No.12344 to read ______.
   A as follows B. as following C. following D. follows
7. We will consider ______ to postpone the discussion.
   A. it B. advisable C. it advisable D. it is advisable
8. We shall ______ insurance against All Risks.
   A. insure B. make C. cover D. have
9. The buyer suggested that the packing of this article ______ improved.
   A. be B. must have been C. would be D. had to be
10. In some cases, we have to ______ the purchase price.
    A. pay B. refund C. reduce D. give

II. English-Chinese Translation Skills Training.

Please translate the following sentences into Chinese.

1. It would be appreciated, if you would send us a price list and two sample books by air immediately.
2. This offer is firm, subject to your immediate reply which should reach us not later than 23rd May.
3. Should your price and shipment date be acceptable, we would place large orders with you.
4. A draft is a written order to a bank or a customer to pay someone on demand or at a fixed time in the future a certain sum of money.
5. Please cover insurance on these goods against All risks and War Risk for 110% of the invoice value.
6. We are glad to note from your letter of the 1st March that you, as exporters of Chinese cotton piece goods, are willing to establish business relations with us.
7. Freight is calculated according to the measurement or weight, or sometimes, on the value.
8. Payment should be made by irrevocable letter of credit in our favor by draft at sight to reach the sellers one month before shipment and remain valid for negotiation in China within the 20th day after shipment.
9. To give you a general idea of the various kinds of cotton piece goods now available for export, we enclose a brochure and a price list.

10. In reply, we very much regret to state that our end users here find your price too high and out of line with the prevailing market level. Information indicates that some parcels of Japanese make have been sold at the level of Stg. 228 per long ton.

III. Chinese-English Translation Skills Training.

Please translate the following sentences into English.

1. 我方在 12 月 1 日信函中告知，欲向你方试订购飞鸽牌自行车 50 辆。
2. 请给我方报 CIF 拉格斯最低价，含 5%佣金，并告知最早的装运日期。
3. 按照合同条款，货物装船后，我方立即邮寄全套的单据。
4. 货物已准备好立即交运，将在明天装船。
5. 在这种情况下，额外保险费将由买方承担。
6. 应该由卖方按发票金额的 110%投保一切险和战争险。
7. 该商品最多只能打八五折。
8. 这种安排对双方都无利可图。
9. 该报盘以我方最后确认为准。
10. 单据已交银行承兑。

IV. Comprehensive Language Using Skills Training.

Supply the missing words in the blanks of the message.

Dear Sir or Madam,

Letter of Credit No. 5634 i__1__ by London Bank has d__2__ arrived. On c__3__ its clauses, we find that transshipment and partial shipments are not allowed.

As d__4__ steamers to your port are few and far between, we usually have to ship v__5__ Hong Kong. As to partial shipments, it would be to our m__6__ benefit if we ship immediately whatever is ready. Therefore we ask you to a__7__ your L/C to r__8__ "Transshipment and partial shipments allowed".

We hope you will s__9__ to it that the amendment is sent without d__10__.

Yours faithfully,

V. Business Letters Translation Skills Training.

Please translate the following business letter into Chinese.

Dear Sir or Madam:

Re: Contract No. 425

We wish to call your attention to the fact that up to now no news has come from you about the shipment under the captioned contract.

As our end-users are in urgent need of the goods contracted, they are pressing us for timely delivery.

It is obviously impossible for us to extend our L/C No. 2046, which expires on March 4.

Therefore we have to remind you of this matter once again.

Your prompt attention to shipment will be much appreciated.

Yours truly,

VI. Writing Skills Training.

You are asked to write four letters about bicycles, including enquiry, offer, counter-offer and acceptance.

附录 I 《外贸英文函电（国际商务函电）》课程能力标准

一、课程性质与地位

随着世界经济的飞速发展，国际交流的广泛化和多样化，为了适应新形势的发展和用人单位对从业人员的要求，为我院的应用英语专业的学生开设本课程。本课程打破传统的外语教学理念，变以语言文学为主要内容的教学活动为以培养具有较强的语言实用能力的专业外语人才为主要目标，以适应我国加入 WTO 后对涉外人才的需求，使学生不仅掌握外贸英文函电的基本知识，并能熟练地加以运用。

本课程是一门实践性很强的外语外贸类职业核心能力课，是其他经济类专业的选开课。课程能力标准紧紧围绕专业的培养目标及相应的人才规格，以就业为导向，以能力为本位，实施系统的课程教学内容。通过本课程的学习，完成专业核心能力培养。

本教材适用人群：国际商务类、商务英语类专业、应用英语专业等高等院校学生。

二、课程能力标准制定背景与论证情况

中国加入 WTO 以后，全球经济一体化的新时代迫切需要外贸英语类复合型人才，大学生人才市场的反馈信息已经突出显现了外贸英语知识和课程的重要性，外贸英文函电课程就是顺应这种需求而产生的。

为了既培养学生的岗位能力，又有助于其以后顺利通过外销员考试，在本课程能力标准设计上采用倒推的办法，完全遵循实用、够用的原则，突出技能、能力培养为主线来设计能力标准。制定依据如下：

1. 专业培养方案（课程在专业中的定位、前后续课程、技能考试的要求等）；
2. 学院制定的《浙江经济职业技术学院课程改革的原则指导》。

本课程标准由课程负责人经过广泛的调研后执笔，经课程所属专业组讨论后，由学院邀请浙江物产集团公司等实际工作部门的专家论证后完成。

三、本课程能力标准构建思路

本课程是应用英语专业一门重要的必修课。通过本课程学习，学生应掌握外贸英语函电的格式、专业词汇、行文方法与文体特点，能完成日常的外贸英文函电的书写、回复。课程内容多与外贸业务紧密相连，用于培养学生对各种常用外贸英文函电的阅读、写作和翻译能力，是应用英语专业的职业核心能力课。

1. 应知目标

外贸英文函电的格式及内容，包括一般的商务信件以及外贸询盘、报盘、还盘、接受、

订单、销售合同、支付方式、信用证、提单、装运、保险、包装、投诉、索赔等知识。

2. 应会目标

基本掌握外贸英文函电的书写、回复。

- 撰写报盘信函的能力——能够撰写询盘、报盘、还盘及复盘的能力；
- 就有关合同条款要求对方修改而进行谈判的能力——如就销售合同、保险、报价、装船、交货等条款要求修改；
- 订立外销合同的能力——能够根据买卖双方谈妥的条件，订立外销合同；
- 审核信用证并要求修改信用证而撰写相关信函的能力；
- 全程函电应对能力——能够读懂外贸业务流程中的往来函电并做出回复。

3. 本课程能力构建的逻辑图

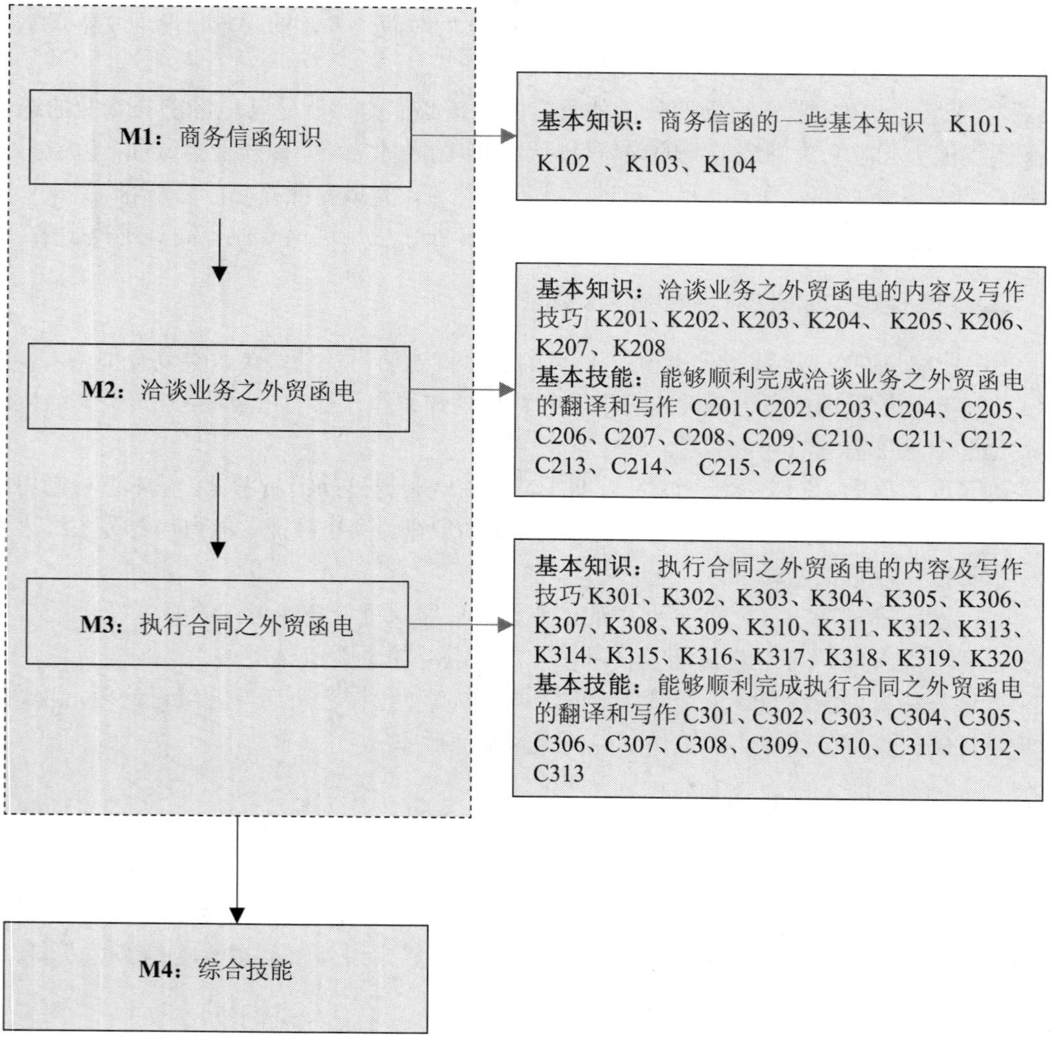

四、课程能力标准分布及其权重

各模块能力标准目标和鉴定标准数量分布表

模块	K（应知目标）	C（应会目标）	KA（应知鉴定）	CA（应会鉴定）	模块权重
一	5	0	5	0	10%
二	11	22	11	22	40%
三	19	18	19	18	40%
四	综合技能				10%

五、课程能力标准及其鉴定要求

模块一、商务信函知识模块

应知目标	应会目标	应知鉴定标准	应会鉴定标准
K101：了解商务信函的写作原则、语言特点。	To understand writing principles and language characteristics.	**KA101:** 能够准确地说出商务信函的写作原则、语言特点。	
K102：熟悉商务信函的组成部分。	Be familiar with parts of business letters.	**KA102:** 能够准确地分析商务信函的主要结构。	
K103：熟悉商务信函的基本格式。	To be familiar with structures of business letters.	**KA103:** 能够准确地说出商务信函的基本格式。	
K104：了解商务信函书写格式的类型。	To know 3 writing formats of business letters.	**KA104:** 能够准确地区分所给商务信函的书写格式的类型。	
K105：了解信封的书写格式。	To know how to write an envelope.	**KA105:** 能够准确地书写信封。	

模块二、洽谈业务之外贸函电模块

应知目标	应会目标	应知鉴定标准	应会鉴定标准
K201：了解要求建立业务关系的函电的写作步骤。 To know the writing steps of a letter of establishing business relations.	**C201**：能够翻译一封要求建立业务关系的函电。 To be able to translate a letter of establishing business relations properly.	**KA201:** 能够分析要求建立业务关系的函电的写作步骤。	**CA201**：能够翻译句子及要求建立业务关系的函电。

续表

应知目标	应会目标	应知鉴定标准	应会鉴定标准
	C202：能够写作一封要求建立业务关系的函电。 To be able to write a letter of establishing business relations properly.		**CA202：**能够根据所提供的信息，写作一封要求建立业务关系的函电。
K202：了解回复建立业务关系的函电的写作步骤。 To know the writing steps of a reply to a letter of establishing business relations.	**C203：**能够翻译一封回复建立业务关系的函电。 To be able to translate a reply to business relations establishment letter.	**KA202：**能够分析回复建立业务关系的函电的写作步骤。	**CA203：**能够翻译句子及回复建立业务关系的函电。
	C204：能够回复一封要求建立业务关系的函电。 To be able to reply a letter of establishing business relations properly.		CA204：能够根据所提供的信息，回复一封要求建立业务关系的函电。
K203：了解询盘的写作步骤。 To know the writing steps of an enquiry.	C205：能够翻译一封询盘。 To be able to translate an enquiry.	KA203：能够分析所给询盘的写作步骤。	CA205：能够翻译句子及询盘。
	C206：能够写作一封询盘。 To be able to make an enquiry.		CA206：能够根据所提供的信息，写作一封询盘。
K204：了解回复询盘的函电的写作步骤。 To know the writing steps of a reply to an enquiry.	C207：能够翻译一封回复询盘的函电。 To be able to translate a reply to an enquiry.	KA204：能够分析回复询盘的函电的写作步骤。	CA207：能够翻译句子及回复询盘的函电。
	C208：能够回复一封询盘。 To be able to reply to an enquiry.		CA208：能够根据所提供的信息，回复一封询盘。
K205：了解实盘的写作步骤。 To know the writing steps of a firm offer.	C209：能够翻译一封实盘。 To be able to translate a firm offer.	KA205：能够分析所给实盘的写作步骤。	CA209：能够翻译句子及实盘。
	C210：能够写作一封实盘。 To be able to make a firm offer.		CA210：能够根据所提供的信息，写作一封实盘。

续表

应知目标	应会目标	应知鉴定标准	应会鉴定标准
K206：了解虚盘的写作步骤。 To know the writing steps of a non-firm offer.	C211：能够翻译一封虚盘。 To be able to translate a non-firm offer.	KA206: 能够分析所给虚盘的写作步骤。	CA211: 能够翻译句子及虚盘。
	C212：能够写作一封虚盘。 To be able to make a non-firm offer.		CA212: 能够根据所提供的信息，写作一封虚盘。
K207：了解还盘的写作步骤。 To know the writing steps of a counter- offer.	C213：能够翻译一封还盘。 To be able to translate a counter-offer.	KA207: 能够分析所给还盘的写作步骤。	CA213: 能够翻译句子及一封还盘。
	C214：能够写作一封还盘。 To be able to make a counter-offer.		CA214: 能够根据所提供的信息，写作一封还盘。
K208: 了解回复还盘的函电的写作步骤。 To know the writing steps of a reply to a counter-offer.	C215：能够翻译一封回复还盘的函电。 To be able to translate a reply to a counter-offer.	KA208: 能够分析回复还盘的函电的写作步骤。	CA215: 能够翻译句子及回复还盘的函电。
	C216：能够回复一封还盘。 To be able to reply to a counter-offer.		CA216: 能够根据所提供的信息，回复一封还盘。
K209：了解订单的写作步骤。 To know the writing steps of a letter of an order.	C217：能够翻译一份订单。 To be able to translate an order.	KA209: 能够分析所给订单的写作步骤。	CA217: 能够翻译句子及订单。
	C218：能够写作一封订单。 To be able to write a letter of an order.		CA218: 能够根据所提供的信息，写作一份订单。
K210：了解接受函的写作步骤。 To know the writing steps of a letter of acceptance.	C219：能够翻译一封接受函。 To be able to translate a letter of acceptance.	KA210: 能够分析所给接受函的写作步骤。	CA219: 能够翻译句子及接受函。
	C220：能够写作一封接受函。 To be able to write a letter of acceptance.		CA220: 能够根据所提供的信息，写作一封接受函。

续表

应知目标	应会目标	应知鉴定标准	应会鉴定标准
K211：了解确认函的写作步骤。 To know the writing steps of a letter of confirmation.	C221：能够翻译一封确认函。 To be able to translate a letter of confirmation.	KA211: 能够分析所给确认函的写作步骤。	CA221: 能够翻译句子及确认函。
	C222：能够写作一封确认函。 To be able to write a letter of confirmation.		CA222: 能够根据所提供的信息，写作一封确认函。

模块三、执行合同之外贸函电模块

应知目标	应会目标	应知鉴定标准	应会鉴定标准
K301：了解售货确认书的内容与格式。 To understand the forms and contents of a Sales Confirmation.	C301：能够翻译一份售货确认书。 To be able to translate a Sales Confirmation.	KA301: 能够分析所给售货确认书的内容。	CA301: 能够翻译句子及售货确认书。
	C302：能够制作一份售货确认书。 To be able to make a Sales Confirmation.		CA302: 能够根据所提供的信息，制作一份售货确认书。
K302：了解售货合同的内容与格式。 To understand the forms and contents of a Sales Contract.	C303：能够翻译一份售货合同。 To be able to translate a Sales Contract.	KA302: 能够分析所给售货合同的内容。	CA303: 能够翻译句子及售货合同。
	C304：能够制作一份售货合同。 To be able to make a Sales Contract.		CA304: 能够根据所提供的信息，制作一份售货合同。
K303：了解国际贸易的三种支付方式及其支付程序。 To know 3 main terms of payment and their procedures.	C305：能够翻译支付方式及支付程序。 To be able to translate these terms payment and procures.	KA303: 能够说出国际贸易的三种支付方式及其支付程序。	CA305: 能够翻译关于支付方式及支付程序的句子和文章。
K304：了解信用证的主要条款。 To understand main clauses of an L/C.	C306：能够分析一份信用证。 To be able to analyse an L/C.	KA304: 能够说出信用证的主要条款。	CA306: 能够根据所给信用证，分析其主要条款。

续表

应知目标	应会目标	应知鉴定标准	应会鉴定标准
	C307：能够翻译一份信用证。 To be able to translate an L/C.		CA307：能够翻译句子及信用证。
K305：了解信用证审核的要点。 To know main points of an L/C examination.	C308：能够审核一份信用证。 To be able to examine an L/C.	KA305：能够说出审核信用证的要点。	CA308：能够根据所给信用证及相关合同，审核信用证。
K306：了解要求修改信用证的信函的写作步骤。 To know the writing steps of a letter of L/C amendment.	C309：能够翻译一封要求修改信用证的信函。 To be able to translate a letter of L/C amendment.	KA306：能够分析要求修改信用证的信函的写作步骤。	CA309:能够翻译句子及要求修改信用证的信函。
	C310：能够写作一封要求修改信用证的信函。 To be able to write a letter of L/C amendment.		CA310：能够根据所给信息，写作一封要求修改信用证的信函。
K307：了解国际贸易中的主要运输方式及其优缺点。 To know main means of transportation in international trade and their advantages and disadvantages.	C311：能够翻译关于运输方式的文章。 To be able to translate articles of shipment.	KA307：能够说出国际贸易中的主要运输方式及其优缺点。	CA311：能够翻译关于运输方式的文章。
K308：了解关于装运信息的信函的写作步骤。 To know the writing steps of a letter of shipment.	C312：能够翻译关于装运信息的信函。 To be able to translate a letter of shipment.	KA308：能够分析关于装运信息的信函的写作步骤。	CA312：能够翻译句子及关于装运信息的信函。
	C313：能够写作一封关于装运信息的信函。 To be able to write a letter of shipment.		CA313：能够根据所给信息，写作一封关于装运信息的信函。
K309：了解提单的功能、种类。 To know functions and types of a B/L.	C314:能够翻译关于提单的文章。 To be able to translate articles of a B/L.	KA309：能够说出提单的功能、种类。	CA314:能够翻译关于提单的文章。
K310：了解提单上的有关信息。 To understand contents of a B/L.	C315：能够分析一份提单。 To be able to analyse articles of a B/L.	KA310：能够说出提单上的有关信息。	CA315：能够根据所给提单，分析其主要信息。

续表

应知目标	应会目标	应知鉴定标准	应会鉴定标准
	C316：能够填写一份提单。 To be able to fill in a B/L.		CA316: 能够根据所给信息，填写一份提单。
K311：了解保险的目的。 To know aims of covering insurance.	C317:能够翻译关于保险的文章。 To be able to translate articles of insurance.	KA311: 能够说出保险的目的。	CA317:能够翻译关于保险的文章。
K312：了解保险费及保险金额的计算方法。 To know premium and its calculation.	C318:能够分析一份保险单。 To be able to analyse an insurance policy.	KA312: 能够说出保险费及保险金额的计算方法。	CA318：能够分析一份保险单。
K313：了解关于保险的信函的写作步骤。 To know the writing steps of a letter of insurance.	C319：能够翻译一封关于保险的信函。 To be able to translate a letter of insurance.	KA313: 能够分析关于保险的信函的写作步骤。	CA319: 能够翻译句子及关于保险的信函。
	C320：能够写作一封关于保险的信函。 To be able to write a letter of insurance.		CA320: 能够根据所给信息，写作一封关于保险的信函。
K314：了解包装的种类及功能。 To know the functions and types of packing.		KA314: 能够说出包装的种类及功能。	
K315：了解国际贸易中对包装的要求。 To know the requirements of packing in international trade.		KA315: 能够说出国际贸易中对包装的要求。	
K316：了解关于包装的信函的写作步骤。 To know the writing steps of a letter of packing.		KA316: 能够分析关于包装的信函的写作步骤。	
K317：了解投诉的种类 To know the types of a claim.		KA317: 能够说出投诉的种类。	
K318：了解如何解决投诉并进行理赔。 To know how to solve a complaint and settle claims.		KA318: 能够说出如何解决投诉并进行理赔。	

续表

应知目标	应会目标	应知鉴定标准	应会鉴定标准
K319：了解关于投诉和理赔的信函的写作步骤。 To know the writing steps of a letter of complaint or claim settlement.		KA319：能够分析关于投诉和理赔的信函的写作步骤。	

模块四、综合技能模块

外贸业务洽谈流程：询盘→报盘→还盘→接受→下订单→签订合同

六、课程能力标准鉴定方法

1. 本课程采用形成性考核方式，总成绩由平时考核和期末考试两部分形成。

总成绩＝平时考核成绩（40%）＋期末考试成绩（60%）。

2. 平时考核成绩（40%）＝平时学习表现考核（考勤，课堂讨论、课堂实训等表现，作业或实践报告上交情况）（20%）+平时实训项目（20%）。

3. 期末采用闭卷考试的方式，时间100分钟。

制定人：方军霞

附录 II　国际商贸常用术语表达

1. 建立业务关系 (establishing business relations)
2. 产品目录 (product list / brochure / catalogue)
3. 价目单 (price list)
4. 具体询价 (specific enquiry)
5. 样品薄 (sample book)
6. 询盘/价 (enquiry / inquiry)
7. 佣金 (commission)
8. 报盘 (offer)
9. 报价 (quotation)
10. 还盘/价 (counter-offer)
11. 递盘/价 (bid)
12. 接受 (acceptance)
13. 拒绝还盘 (declining a counter-offer)
14. 出口目录/单 (export list)
15. 进口目录/单 (import list)
16. 试销、试订货 (trial order)
17. 商务参赞处 (Commercial Counselor's Office)
18. 条件及条款 (terms and conditions)
19. 品名 (description of article / name of article)
20. 支付条款/方式 (terms of payment)
21. 实盘/确盘 (firm offer)
22. 虚盘 (non-firm offer)
23. 标题项下的货物 (the captioned goods / the subject article)
24. 成交 (come to terms / business; conclude a transaction)
25. 行市下跌 (a declining market)
26. 行市上涨 (an advancing market)
27. 确认定单 (confirming an order)
28. 购货确认书 (P/C　Purchase Confirmation)
29. 购货合同 (P/C　Purchase Contract)
30. 销售确认书 (S/C　Sales Confirmation)
31. 销售合同 (S/C　Sales Contract)
32. 会签 (counter-signature)
33. 副本 (duplicate copy)

34. 一式两份 (in duplicate)
35. 一式三份 (in triplicate)
36. 欧洲主要港口 (E. M. P—European Main Ports)
37. 畅销（市场）(a ready market)
38. 另寄 (under separate cover)
39. 议付 (negotiation)
40. 形式发票 (Proforma Invoice)
41. 商业发票 (Commercial Invoice)
42. 领事发票 (Consular Invoice)
43. 海关发票 (Customs Invoice)
44. 汇票 (Draft / Bill of Exchange)
45. 付款交单 (D/P: Documents against Payment)
46. 承兑交单 (D/A: Documents against Acceptance)
47. 信用证 (L/C: Letter of Credit)
48. 跟单信用证 (Documentary L/C)
    光票信用证 (Clean L/C)
    不可撤销信用证 (Irrevocable L/C)
    可撤销信用证 (Revocable L/C)
    保兑信用证 (Confirmed L/C)
    不保兑信用证 (Unconfirmed L/C)
    即期信用证 (Sight L/C)
    远期信用证 (Usance L/C; After-sight L/C)
49. 开立信用证 (establishment of L/C)
50. 信用证改证/修改 (L/C amendment)
51. 信用证延期 (L/C extension)
52. 信用证有效期 (validity of L/C)
53. 装运 (shipment)
54. 转运 (transshipment)
55. 分批装运 (partial shipment)
56. 装货指示 (shipping order)
57. 装运须知 (shipping instructions)
58. 装运通知 (shipping advice)
59. 舱位 (shipping space)
60. 发货人 (consignor)
61. 收货人 (consignee)
62. 交货期 (Date of Delivery)
63. 运输单据 (shipping documents)
64. 装箱单 (packing list)

65. 重量单/磅码单 (weight memo)
66. 尺码单 (measurement memo)
67. 提单 (B/L : Bill of Lading)
    清洁提单 (clean B/L)
    不清洁提单 (unclean B/L)
    已装船提单 (on board B/L)
    记名提单 (straight B/L)
    不记名提单 (open B/L)
    指示提单 (order B/L)
68. 空运单/航空货运单 (Airway bill/ Air waybill)
69. 协会货物条款 (ICC : Institute Cargo Clauses)
70. 发票金额 (Invoice Value)
71. 保险费 (insurance premium)
72. 保险额 (insurance amount)
73. 水渍险 (WA : with average)
74. 平安险 (FPA : free from particular average)
75. 战争险 (WR : War Risk)
76. 一切险 (AR : All Risks)
77. 偷窃及提货不着险 (TPND : risk of theft, pilferage &non-delivery)
78. 罢工、暴力、民变险 (SRCC : strike, riots, civil commotions)
79. 保险单 (Insurance Policy)
80. 保险公司 (insurer)
81. 中国人民保险公司 (PICC : People's Insurance Company of China)
82. 中国保险条款 (CIC : China Insurance Clauses)
83. 海洋运输货物保险条款 (OMCC : ocean marine cargo clauses)
84. 检验证书 (Inspection Certificate)
85. 中国商检局 (CCIB : China Commodity Inspection Bureau)
86. 品质证书 (Certificate of quality)
87. 数量证书 (Certificate of quantity)
88. 产地证书 (C/O : Certificate of Origin)
89. 短重索赔 (a claim for short weight)
90. 加工贸易 (processing trade)
91. 补偿贸易 (compensation trade)
92. 离岸价/ 装运港船上交货 (FOB : free on board)
93. 成本加运费价 (CFR : cost and freight)
94. 到岸价/ 成本、保费、加运费价 (CIF : cost, insurance and freight)
95. 大路货 (FAQ : fair average quality)
96. 财务状况 (financial standing)

97. 咨询 (status inquiry)
98. 提货 (take delivery of the goods)
99. 开证行 (issuing bank)
100. 通知行 (advising bank)

附录 III　世界部分国家或地区货币

国家或地区	首　　都	主 要 货 币
America	Washington D.C.	U. S.　dollar
Australia	Canberra	Australian dollar
Austria	Vienna	Austrian schilling
Belgium	Brussels	Belgian franc (Euro)
Brazil	Brasilia	cruzado
Britain	London	pound sterling
Canada	Ottawa	Canadian dollar
China	Beijing	RMB
China's Hong Kong	/	Hong Kong dollar
Cuba	Havana	Cuban peso
Denmark	Copenhagen	Danish krone(Euro)
Egypt	Cairo	Egyptian pound
Finland	Helsinki	Finnish mark(Euro)
France	Paris	French France(Euro)
Germany	Berlin	Deutsche mark(Euro)
Greece	Athens	drachma(Euro)
Hungary	Budapest	Forint (Euro)
India	New Delhi	Indian rupee
Iran	Tehran	Iran rail
Iraq	Baghdad	Iraqi dinar
Italy	Rome	lira(Euro)
Japan	Tokyo	yen
Republic of Korea	Seoul	won
Malaysia	Kuala Lumpur	Malaysian dollar
Netherlands	Amsterdam	guilder(Euro)
New Zealand	Wellington	New Zealand dollar
Singapore	Singapore City	Singapore dollar
South Africa	Pretoria	South African rand
Thailand	Bangkok	baht

附录 IV　世界各国大银行名称

1. CHINA 中国

People's Bank of China	中国人民银行
Bank of China	中国银行
Agricultural Bank of China	中国农业银行
China Construction Bank	中国建设银行
Industrial and Commercial Bank of China	中国工商银行
China Merchants Bank	招商银行
Communications Bank of China	中国交通银行
Import and Export Bank of China	中国进出口银行
Investment Bank of China	中国投资银行

2. AMERICA 美国

Bank of America	美洲银行
Federal Reserve System	联邦储备系统
First National City Bank of New York	花旗银行

3. JAPAN 日本

Nippon Bank Co.	日本银行
The Fuji Bank Ltd.	富士银行
Daiwa Bank	大和银行

4. ENGLAND 英国

Bank of England	英格兰银行
Barclays Bank	巴克莱银行
Hong Kong and Shanghai Banking Corp.	汇丰银行
Standard Chartered Bank	渣打银行

5. FRANCE 法国

Banque de France	法兰西银行
Credit Lyonnais	里昂信贷银行

6. GERMANY 德国

Deutsche Bundes Bank	德意志联邦银行
Commerzbank	德意志商业银行

7. ITALY 意大利

Banca di Italia	意大利银行
Banca di Roma	罗马银行
Banca Commerciale Italiana	意大利商业银行

8. SWITZERLAND 瑞士

Banque Popular Swisse	瑞士人民银行
Swiss Bank Corp.	瑞士银行公司

9. HOLLAND 荷兰

Algemene Bank Nederland	荷兰通用银行
Amsterdam-Rotterdam Bank	阿姆斯特丹—鹿特丹银行

10. CANADA 加拿大

The Royal Bank of Canada	加拿大皇家银行
Canadian Imperial Bank of Commerce	加拿大帝国商业银行

11. SWEDEN 瑞典

Goteborgs Bank	哥德堡银行
Sveriges Kreditbank	瑞典信贷银行

12. NORWAY 挪威

Den Norske Creditbank	北方信贷银行

附录V　中国主要进出口公司及机构

1. China National Cereals, Oils and Foodstuffs Import & Export Corporation
   中国粮油食品进出口公司
2. China National Native Produce and Animal By-products Import & Export Corporation
   中国土畜产进出口总公司
3. China National Animal Breeding Stock Import & Export Corporation
   中国种畜进出口公司
4. China Tobacco Import & Export Corporation
   中国烟草进出口公司
5. China National Medicines & Health Products Import & Export Corporation
   中国医药保健品进出口公司
6. China National Textiles Import & Export Corporation
   中国纺织品进出口总公司
7. China Silk Corporation
   中国丝绸公司
8. China Arts and Crafts Import & Export Corporation
   中国工艺品进出口总公司
9. China National Light Industrial Products Import & Export Corporation
   中国轻工业品进出口总公司
10. China National Machinery Import & Export Corporation
    中国机械进出口总公司
11. China National Machinery and Equipment Import & Export Corporation
    中国机械设备进出口总公司
12. China National Agricultural Machinery Import & Export Corporation
    中国农业机械进出口联合公司
13. China National Complete Plant Import & Export Corporation
    中国成套设备进出口总公司
14. China National Instrument Import & Export Corporation
    中国仪器进出口总公司
15. China National Technical Import & Export Corporation
    中国技术进出口总公司
16. China Electronics Import & Export Corporation

中国电子技术进出口总公司

17. China National Aero-Technology Import & Export Corporation
中国航空技术进出口公司
18. China National Packaging Import & Export Corporation
中国包装进出口总公司
19. China National Chemicals Import & Export Corporation
中国化工进出口总公司
20. China Metallurgical Import & Export Corporation
中国冶金进出口公司
21. China National Nonferrous Metals Import & Export Company
中国有色金属进出口总公司
22. China National Metals and Minerals Import & Export Corporation
中国五金矿产进出口总公司
23. China National Coal Import & Export Corporation
中国煤炭进出口总公司
24. China National Offshore Oil Corporation
中国海洋石油总公司
25. China Petroleum Engineering Construction Corporation
中国石油工程建设总公司
26. China North Industries Corporation
中国北方工业公司
27. The Oriental Scientific Instruments Import & Export Corporation
东方科学仪器进出口公司
28. China Great Wall Industry Corporation
中国长城工业公司
29. China Resource Co., Ltd.
中国华润有限公司
30. China National Seed Corporation
中国种子公司
31. China Overseas Trading Company Ltd.
中国海外贸易公司
32. China National Foreign Trade Transportation Corporation
中国对外贸易运输公司
33. China Ocean Shipping Company
中国远洋运输公司
34. China Ocean Shipping Agency
中国外轮代理总公司
35. China Export Bases Development Corporation

中国出口商品基础建设公司

36. China National Service Corporation for Chinese Personnel Working Abroad
    中国出国人员服务公司
37. Beijing Foreign Trade Corporation
    北京市对外贸易总公司
38. Tianjin Foreign Trade Corporation
    天津市对外贸易总公司
39. Shanghai Foreign Trade Corporation
    上海市对外贸易公司
40. Guangdong Foreign Trade Corporation
    广东省对外贸易总公司
41. Guangzhou Foreign Trade Centre
    广州对外贸易中心
42. China International Trust & Investment Corporation
    中国国际信托投资公司
43. China Council for Promotion of International Trade
    中国国际贸易促进委员会
44. China National Foreign Trade Advertising Association
    中国对外贸易广告协会
45. The Import and Export Commodities Inspection Bureau of the People's Republic of China
    中国进出口商品检验局
46. China International Exhibition Center
    中国国际展览中心
47. Foreign Economic and Trade Arbitration Commission of CCPIT
    中国国际贸易促进委员会对外经济贸易仲裁委员会
48. Maritime Arbitration Commission of CCPIT
    中国国际贸易促进委员会海事仲裁委员会
49. Patent Agency of CCPIT
    中国国际贸易促进委员会专利代理处
50. Trade Mark Agency of CCPIT
    中国国际贸易促进委员会商标代理处

参 考 文 献

［1］诸葛霖. 外贸英文书信. 北京：对外经济贸易大学出版社，2000.
［2］兰天. 外贸英语函电. 大连：东北财经大学出版社，2004.
［3］葛萍. 外贸英语函电. 上海：上海财经大学出版社，2004.
［4］魏莉霞，周峰. 国际商务函电. 北京：北京大学出版社，2006.
［5］樊红霞，汪奠才. 英文外贸函电. 北京：外语教学与研究出版社，2007.
［6］刘辉玲，王俊. 国际商务函电. 北京：对外经济贸易大学出版社，2002.
［7］秦亚农，李亦. 国际商贸英语函电教程. 长沙：中南大学出版社，2004.
［8］檀文茹，徐静珍. 外贸函电. 北京：中国人民大学出版社，2004.
［9］王万义，李宁. 新编外贸英文函电. 北京：中国商务出版社，2005.
［10］李卫. 外贸函电. 北京：电子工业出版社，2007.
［11］谈芳，朱慧萍. 外经贸英语函电. 上海：学林出版社，2005.
［12］隋思忠. 外贸英语函电. 大连：东北财经大学出版社，2007.
［13］李侨春. 商务函电实训. 北京：对外经济贸易大学出版社，2005.
［14］闫兴伯，黄宪西. 国际商务函电. 北京：高等教育出版社，2006.
［15］广银芳. 进出口单证实训教程. 南京：东南大学出版社，2005.
［16］李宏亮. 商务英语口语实训. 北京：北京大学出版社，2010.
［17］李宏亮. 国际商务函电. 北京：对外经济贸易大学出版社，2008.
［18］尹小莹，杨润辉. 外贸英语函电. 西安：西安交通大学出版社，2011.
［19］刘文广，张晓明. 国际贸易实训. 北京：高等教育出版社，2005.
［20］闫兴伯，黄宪西. 商务英语函电. 北京：高等教育出版社，2001.
［21］郑书燕. 新编商务英语函电. 北京：对外经济贸易大学出版社，2010.